Mountain Echoes

A Collection of Articles by

EDIE HUTCHINS BURNETTE

Jan-Carol
Publishing, Inc
"every story needs a book"

Mountain Echoes
Written and Illustrated by
Edie Hutchins Burnette
Published January 2016

Little Creek Books
Imprint of Jan-Carol Publishing, Inc
Copyright © Edie Hutchins Burnette
Design: Tara Sizemore

ISBN: 978-1-939289-82-7
Library of Congress Control Number: 2016930465

You may contact the publisher:
Jan-Carol Publishing, Inc
PO Box 701
Johnson City, TN 37605
publisher@jancarolpublishing.com
jancarolpublishing.com

for Alison, Amanda, Dale, and John

Letter to the Reader

Mountain Echoes is about my home, my mountains and my people.

My stories chronicle actual events in the history of Haywood County, a mountainous area in Western North Carolina, introduce interesting people and explore many facets of this beautiful place.

The first column was printed March 28, 2004, beginning a journey into the past that consumed, energized and delighted me for more than five years. Researching and composing a story a week, always pressured by deadlines, seemed a daunting task. And it was. But there was always a new idea, a new adventure, if you will, to draw me forward.

Accepting the challenge of this assignment felt as if the doors to my home place had been flung wide open. I was given the opportunity to traverse the entire county in search of its history, to talk to whomever would respond to my endless questions, to find the origins of old traditions. Endless treasures were mine for the searching.

Conversations between my parents and maternal grandparents during long Sunday afternoon drives laid the foundation. Much of what they discussed or pointed out was apparently absorbed subconsciously with faint recollections revived as my memory bank was tweaked. A particular house or building, a season, observations of surroundings, or certain sites were reminders of people, places and events that warranted a closer look. My readers were important sources of information as they commented, questioned, and suggested topics.

Many major sources are no longer living, but I chose to leave words as they were originally written. Indicating subsequent deaths might have diminished original stories.

Presenting columns chronologically as they were randomly written could have made reading difficult, so the stories have been loosely grouped.

I hope you enjoy the reading as much as I enjoyed the writing.

Best Regards,
Edie Hutchins Burnette

Acknowledgments

To all those who graciously shared their stories, assisted in endless research, provided ideas, and encouraged me with their comments, I am grateful beyond words.

Special thanks:

to the *Asheville Citizen-Times* for publishing my columns.

to Quentin Ellison who offered the opportunity to write weekly columns.

to Carroll Jones, double-second cousin, who read and re-read and otherwise assisted me in the unfamiliar world of readying a book for publishing.

to Charles Cathey, distant cousin, the late Joe Worley, and the late Dr. Garrett Smathers who provided significant information.

to Anita Churm, especially, Jenny Morin and other friends who gently harassed me to gather my scribblings into a book.

to my parents, the late Edith and A. J. Hutchins, who assured that I receive an excellent education, and brother, John, for encouragement.

to my late husband Charles "Chili" Burnette who put up with my hours at the computer and didn't complain—well, not too much—about uncooked meals.

Foreword

By Carroll C. Jones

Over more than the last decade Edie Burnette has prowled the hills and coves of western North Carolina in search of Haywood County's history. As readers of her columns, "Mountain Echoes," in the *Asheville Citizen Times* have discovered, very little has escaped Edie's dogged sleuthing and masterful pen. And now compiled in this beautifully-illustrated volume also titled *Mountain Echoes* are many of her favorite Haywood County history columns for us to enjoy again and again.

Much in the vein of John Parris a generation before her, Edie presents to us precise word pictorials of the county's past, highlighting the towns and communities, important and intriguing personages, industries, infrastructure, means of transportation, life styles, cultural activities and more. She even shines daylight through the doors of old barns and grist mills; into rustic outhouses and springhouses; inside houses of God and boarding houses; and onto myriad other tumble-down structures so we can get a glimpse of their past.

No back road was too steep or winding to prevent Edie from finding forthcoming witnesses or other sources to shed truth on the past through her weekly writings. Like a relentless detective on her Haywood beat she interviewed sources, scoured vintage primary materials, and prowled amidst spiders and other slithering and crawling creatures to uncover and disclose one historic case after another. And her devoted readers could never get enough of these chronicles.

Being one such devotee and a lover of history myself, I have relished Edie's illuminating writing over the years. Her columns have sated a voracious appetite for local history on many a frosty winter's night and sultry summer's day. Now, of course, whenever

I experience similar cravings, I can simply reach into my library—right beside a tattered copy of Parris's *Roaming the Mountains*—and pull out a new treasured tome. *Mountain Echoes* is the name of my new book, and thanks to Edie Burnette's uncanny detecting and writing skills it happens to be chock full of haunting echoes from Haywood's past.

Carroll C. Jones has four award-winning books to his credit: *The 25th North Carolina Troops in the Civil War*, *Rooted Deep in the Pigeon Valley*, *Captain Lenoir's Diary*, and *Master of the East Fork*. He has recently completed a sequel to his historical-fiction novel *Master of the East Fork*. Titled *Rebel Rousers*, it is set during the American Civil War and tells the coming-of-age tale of a youthful Rebel soldier who hails from the western North Carolina highlands.

Table of Contents

HAYWOOD COUNTY
IS MY HOME,
MY MOUNTAINS,
MY PEOPLE

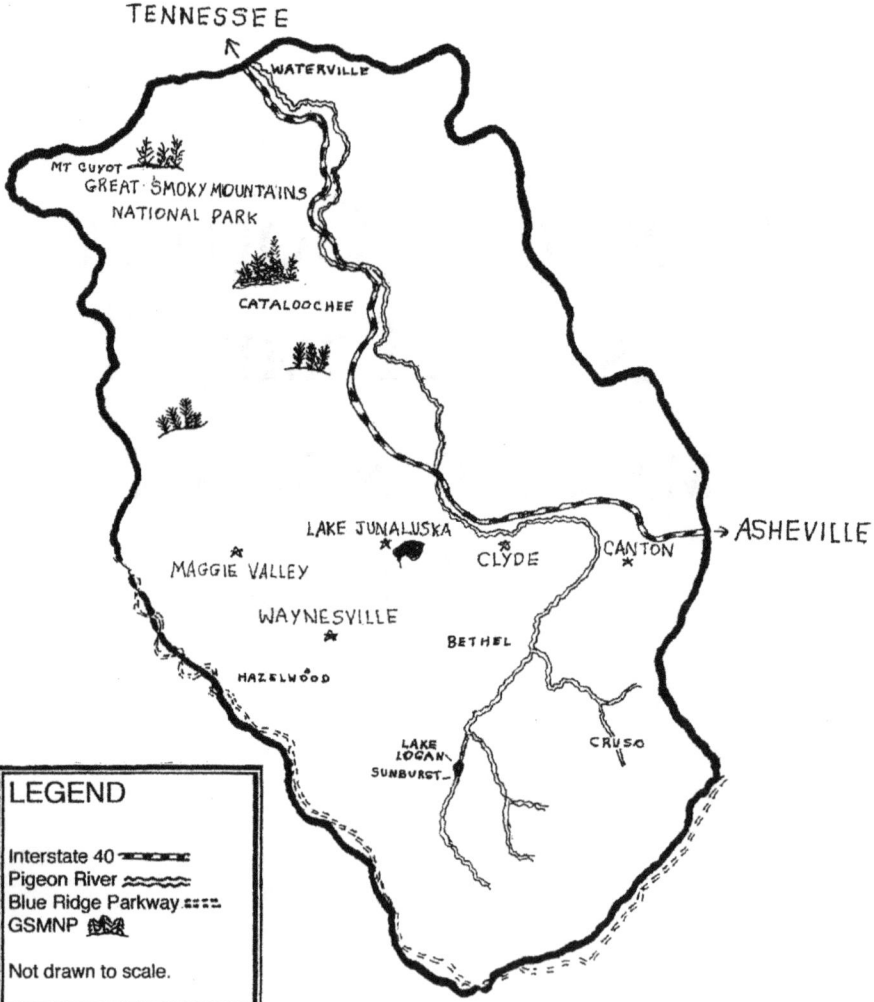

Haywood County's Leaf-like Shape

" H aywood County is shaped somewhat like...a great, rough leaf... with the Pigeon River, flowing northwest...the main stem of this 'big leaf', its tributaries branching out on both sides, being the smaller stems of the leaf."

This description was penned by the late W. Clark Medford, local historian, who added that the stem is inordinately crooked because of the great eastward bend around Canton.

Paraphrasing the words of both Medford and the late George H. Smathers, an attorney specializing in land titles, a bill calling for a new county was introduced in the legislature by General Thomas Love, brother of Colonel Robert Love of Waynesville, and enacted December 23, 1808.

At that time, Buncombe County included all land west to the Tennessee border. Distance from the westernmost parts of Buncombe to Asheville, the only court site, created difficulties for those needing to attend court or transact other official business.

Love's bill, backed by a group of prominent citizens living in and around Canton-Waynesville area, called for the southeastern dividing line to begin "where the southern boundary line of the state crosses the highest part of the ridge dividing waters of French Broad and Tuckaseigee rivers" (South Carolina state line above Rosman), "then along said Blue Ridge dividing waters of Pigeon and French Broad rivers" (north-easterly direction along Pisgah Ridge), "to the top of Mount Pisgah; thence in a direct line to the mouth of the first branch emptying into Hominy

Creek on the side of Jeffe Belieu's" (branch at John C. Smathers place at Turnpike where NC 19-23 leaves Haywood and crosses into Buncombe) "following this branch to its source; then along the top of the ridge" (in a north-westerly direction with the Newfound, Spring Creek, Meadow Fork Mountains and other divides) "to the northern boundary of this State" (with Tennessee, near Max Patch), "and with the Tennessee State line to the line which shall divide this State and the State of Georgia" (near Ducktown, TN) "and with that line to the beginning" (the point at Rosman where NC, SC and GA state lines meet).

A little more than three months passed "until provisions for setting up this county could be fulfilled." The actual separation process occurred March 27–28, 1809.

Natural boundaries, such as mountain ridges, defined many lines.

Haywood County occupied all land west of Buncombe until 1828, when Macon County was created from "the territory of the western part of Haywood," with specified lines drawn. Henderson County, 1838–39, was established with "the Southern portion of Buncombe County, beginning on the top of Pisgah Mountain, on the Haywood line."

Madison was "cut off" from Buncombe and Yancey counties in 1851 and ended at the Haywood line. That same year, Jackson County was carved out, "beginning in the extreme height of Scott's Creek mountains, where the State road crosses; then with the top of that mountain which divides the waters of Pigeon River from the waters of Tuckasege [sic], next to the line that divides the counties of Henderson and Haywood."

A humorous note reports some wag inferred jagged borders were drawn by surveyors under the influence of strong drink. William L. Saunders, who edited a 20 part series *The Colonial Records of North Carolina*, published 1886–1890, scoffed at the idea. He reflected the state was unusually fortunate to have hired men who either abstained or were very capable in the matter of strong drink.

COLD MOUNTAIN

Treasured Lands

" **H**aywood County is one of the fairest and most beautiful sections of North Carolina," wrote the late W. C. Allen in his *Annals of Haywood County*. Others wrote of "vast forests of virgin timber," "cascading waters," and "lovely peaks and valleys."

Preservation and protection of this natural beauty was the aim of events that occurred between the early 1920s and the '30s.

Pisgah National Forest was established in 1916, according to staff at Pisgah Ranger District in Pisgah Forest, encompassing an area of 40,982 square miles. The Pisgah District to the south accounts for 40,968 square miles of the total, and includes both the Shining Rock and Middle Prong Wilderness areas. To the northeast, bounded by I-40 and the Tennessee state line, lies the fourteen square mile Harmon Den section of the forest, according to Michael Hutchins of the Appalachian ranger district in Burnsville.

On June 15, 1934, the Great Smoky Mountains National Park (GSMNP) was established. Cataloochee Valley, in the northwestern corner of the county, was purchased as the eastern portion of the park. One of the largest settlements in the Smokies, the thriving community, with its houses, farms, churches and schools, was home to some 1,200 people who had to leave their beloved valley.

"America's Favorite Drive," the Blue Ridge Parkway, was authorized in the 1930s. Construction, completed in sections, began

September 11, 1939 at the NC-VA line. Haywood's final section was finished in 1958. A Depression-era public works project, the nation's first and longest rural parkway connects Shenandoah National Park in Virginia with the Great Smokies Park, and took half a century to build. Curving along the Haywood County/Transylvania border, fifty-two miles of the parkway are in Haywood County, according to David Anderson, resident landscape architect for the parkway. The scenic highway can be accessed at Wagon Road Gap, Beech Gap, Balsam Gap and Wolf Laurel Gap.

The first Appalachian Trail Conference, a gathering of hikers, foresters, and public officials who supported the goal of a scenic footpath from Maine to Georgia, was organized in 1925 in Washington, D.C. Seventy miles of the 2,160-mile trail run along the North Carolina-Tennessee state border with its northern terminus at Baxter Peak, Katahdin, in the central Maine wilderness. Its southern terminus lies at Springer Mountain, a designated wilderness area in North Georgia.

The trail was completed in 1937, with much of the construction done by hiking clubs and other volunteers. The federally protected greenway became a national scenic trail when the National Trails System Act became law in 1968. Eighty years after its inception, in 2005, it became the Appalachian Trail Conservancy, a name that better reflects the goal of "preserving the trail experience for generations to come."

Impassioned individuals initiated the push for the Great Smokies and the Appalachian Trail. Author Horace Kephart came to Bryson City from St. Louis, hoping to restore his health. He became so enamored with the area that he never left. Disturbed by what he saw as decimation of the land and disruption of people's lives by large-scale logging, he promoted the idea of a national park in the east, catching the attention of prominent Knoxville, Tennessee residents, who took up the cause. Benton MacKaye of Massachusetts was convinced that fast-paced lifestyles in urban and industrial areas on the East Coast were harmful to people, who needed a planned wilderness area to which they could escape and renew themselves. He called his vision the Appalachian Trail.

The big picture here is that we and those who follow can enjoy unspoiled beauty of Haywood County in these protected areas.

Highest Peak in Haywood County

Jutting into the sky, on the North Carolina-Tennessee border, is Mount Guyot, Haywood County's highest peak.

At 6,621 feet above sea level, this mountain is 900 feet higher than Mount Pisgah, on the border of Haywood and Buncombe counties, and lies within the Great Smoky Mountains National Park. Mount Guyot is among twelve peaks in Haywood County topping out at 6,000 feet or more.

The mountain's existence and geographical status was learned when writing a story several years ago for The Asheville Citizen but mentioning the fact elicited blank stares and much skepticism. Lynwood McElroy of Waynesville, an inveterate hiker at eighty-four, is not among the skeptics.

"Yes, I have climbed Mount Guyot," he said, "about fifteen years ago. It is a rough hike and the trail is bad, poorly marked," he said. "It is hikable but extremely difficult. I don't recommend it for the average hiker."

During the nineteenth century, geographical and geological expeditions in the Smokies were conducted. Among the people involved were two familiar names, Thomas Lanier Clingman and Dr. Elisha Mitchell. Rivals in a scholarly sense, both were trying to determine the highest peak in the Southeast. Mount Mitchell in Yancey County (6,684 feet), and Clingman's Dome in Swain (6,643 feet) bear their names. Unfortunately, Mitchell was killed in a fall on the slopes of the mountain named for him.

Arnold Henry Guyot (pronounced Gee-ot, with the g as in get), a distinguished Swiss-born physical geographer who held an endowed chair at Princeton University, was reportedly invited by Clingman to join him in his study of the mountains.

Information gathered by Guyot was incorporated into a map published during the Civil War. During three years, 1856 and 1859-60, Guyot made the first detailed surveys of an area now included within the GSMNP. Mount Guyot was named in his honor for his efforts in providing information about geology and topography of the Smokies. "I am pretty sure Guyot climbed the mountain," McElroy said.

The oldest USGS maps of areas eventually included in the GSMNP were of Cowee in 1885, Knoxville, Nantahala in 1895 and Mount Guyot in 1893. They were updated in 1912 and, combined, were the basis for later mapping of the park and its surrounding areas.

Funds were raised to buy areas including Greenbrier, Mt. LeConte, Mt. Guyot, the Chimneys and a portion of Clingman's Dome owned by Champion Fibre Company., Despite the efforts of both North Carolina and Tennessee, the funds weren't sufficient. John D. Rockefeller Jr. made up the shortfall with a donation in memory of his mother, through the Laura Spelman Rockefeller Memorial Fund. A marker commemorating his gift was erected at Newfound Gap, on the boundary of North Carolina and Tennessee.

When the Cherokee were forced to relocate to Oklahoma on the infamous Trail of Tears, around 1,000 Cherokee refused to submit to the government's edict and managed to survive by hiding in the hills. A chief is believed to have hidden somewhere between Clingman's Dome and Mt. Guyot.

An Internet account by a hiker who had bushwhacked his way to the summit, said, "I suspect Mount Guyot is the most remote county highpoint in the southeastern US." McElroy suspects so, too.

Elevation: Hallmark of Haywood

" **H**aywood County has the highest mean elevation in North Carolina," James Ferguson of Fines Creek told me, as we paced on adjoining treadmills at Haywood County's Health and Fitness Center

Interesting fact, but what, exactly, does that mean?

It means that elevation creates a unique situation for this county.

Ferguson explained that while no town in Haywood approaches the highest elevation in the state, our county, viewed as a whole, is the highest. Other towns, Boone in Watauga County for one, are loftier.

To clarify, the word "mean" is used in mathematical computations. The mean of a collection of numbers is their arithmetic average, derived by adding them up and dividing by their number. A mean is a simple average, or the mid-point between two extremes.

Researchers who deal with such facts have added a given number of highest elevations with a given number of the lowest elevations in each county, divided the total by the given number and found that, on the average, Haywood is the highest county. Haywood's mean elevation is listed by one source as 3,600 feet. San Juan County in Colorado is the highest, at 11,240 feet, followed by Taos County, New Mexico, at 8,510 feet. In Tennessee, Johnson County is at 2,927 feet.

This mean elevation explains why all the water in Haywood County is its own. Haywood is the only county in North Carolina in which all water flows out while none flows in from outside. Every stream, creek, and the Pigeon River originate here. The only water route out of the county is the Pigeon River that flows into Tennessee, with one small exception. Hominy Creek drains into Buncombe County.

Elevation also explains Haywood County's relatively cooler temperature, one factor that has always drawn tourists, Ferguson said. As early as the late 1800s and early 1900s, travelers escaping the heat of the lowlands discovered a summer refuge in the lush green coolness of the mountains. The result is what I like to think of as the era of grand hotels within our bounds, lavish places like White Sulphur Springs Hotel, Eagle's Nest Hotel, and the Piedmont Inn. Sadly, none of these remain.

Haywood, in its entirety, is also believed to be the highest county by mean elevation east of the Rocky Mountains. Avery County argues this point, but since Haywood, with 546 square miles, is nearly twice the size of the smaller county, it contains much more high elevation land area.

Haywood has thirteen mountain peaks over 6,000 feet elevation, according to Haywood's Tourist Development Association. Mount Guyot is the highest point at 6,621 feet, and also claims the distinction of being the fourth highest mountain east of the Mississippi River.

Black Balsam Knob, in the Great Balsam Mountains in the southeastern section of the county, is the highest grassy bald in the entire Appalachian range.

Haywood Tourist Development Association lists the following mountains with elevations exceeding 6,000 feet: Shining Rock, 6,010 feet; Cold Mountain, 6,030 feet; Tennent Mountain, 6,040 feet; Grassy Cove Top, 6,055 feet; Sam's Knob, 6,055 feet; Plott Balsam, 6,088 feet; Reinhart Knob, 6,095 feet; Big Cataloochee, 6,180 feet; Black Balsam Knob, 6,214 feet; Mount Lyn Lowery, 6,291 feet; Waterrock Knob, 6,292 feet; Richland Balsam, 6,410 feet; and Mount Guyot, 6,621 feet. Mount Sterling, at 5,835 feet, almost reaches the list. Mount Guyot hovers on the Tennessee state line and its peak is all but inaccessible except for the fittest, heartiest hikers.

Early Settlers' Influence

Our mountain culture echoes those of the first settlers, immigrants all, who moved into our mountains and called them home. These people, our ancestors, may have arrived with few material possessions. However, their intangibles, their skills and personal characteristics packed snugly in minds and memories, continue to influence who we are and how we live.

Those called "Scotch-Irish" or, as some prefer, "Scots-Irish" left indelible impressions and worthy characteristics that we should take care to preserve, even emulate. They played a large role in shaping our homeland and people.

David Matthewes and wife Maggie of Beaverdam trace their roots back many generations into Scotland. He explains that the Scotch-Irish are generally people whose ancestors migrated from Scotland to Ireland and then to America.

Matthewes describes the Scotch-Irish as "fiercely independent, individualistic, honest, and honorable people who had the ability to sustain themselves. They were very self-sufficient." Survival of our ancestors surely depended upon these traits.

"The first thing they did (when establishing a settlement) was build a church and a school. Only then would they concentrate on building homes," Matthewes said.

Religion and the freedom to worship as they saw fit was a primary reason for their emigration. Presbyterian churches, their denomination of choice, were among the first churches in this area.

Other influences on our culture are numerous and diverse. One doesn't have to look far to find them.

Our speech, music, and dance: watching Irish dancers and others at some of the first Folkmoot USA performances left me in awe. Recognition of footwork and movements seen in mountain square dancing was immediate and intriguing.

Our crafts: these settlers knew how to spin and weave and fashion baskets of native materials. Mountain crafts shops are filled with prime examples of these skills, and schools to teach, to perpetuate, these arts are numerous.

Our buildings: the Scotch-Irish used rock to build foundations, chimneys, and fences, even entire structures, the remnants of which are still evident today. Driving along a back road with Ernestine Upchurch, we passed a large barn and several small outbuildings with still-sturdy rock foundations. "You are looking at the Scotch-Irish influence," she said. She should know, since those are her roots and research into the past is her passion. Others can be seen in places like Fines Creek and Jonathan Creek.

Stacked stone walls or fences, some quite old, dot this county.

Log construction was perfected in Scotland and Ireland, long before log cabins were erected in Western North Carolina (WNC).

Gravestones, some crudely chiseled, in cemeteries from one end of the county to the other, bear a preponderance of names and variations of those of Scotch-Irish descent. They include McCrae, Mingus, Palmer, Ferguson, McCracken, and Campbell, to name a few.

Whiskey: stills and home-brewed whiskey are not confined to this area, but we can thank the ingenuity of the Scotch-Irish for the mountain reputation as "moonshine" territory.

We don't hold the patent on people who are committed to educational excellence, or the freedom of the human mind to question and make its own decisions. Nor are we the only independent-minded folks who are suspicious of authority and accustomed to fighting to hold on to what we consider rightfully ours. But these characteristics, and more, echo those of the Scotch-Irish.

Garden Creek

Farmers who first plowed fields along Garden Creek and beyond had to have known with certainty that American Indians once lived alongside the Pigeon River, on land now divided by highways US 276, NC 110, and NC 215.

Plow blades, jerked along by a plodding mule, sliced furrows through untilled land. Fertile soil was exposed in their wake, as the first settlers plowed the valley floor in anticipation of a bountiful crop to feed families in their new home.

It may not have happened with the first plowing, but eventually plow blades and hoes began uncovering more than soil, rocks, and rabbit burrows. Imagine their surprise when they first found evidence the land had been occupied before their arrival.

Arrowheads were surely easily identified, but there was more, much more. Pottery shards imprinted with designs, clay pipes, and tomahawk heads (primitive axes). Wherever soil was scraped and dug, the ground gave up more and more artifacts.

Children followed the plows even years later, retrieving objects, much to their delight. The fruits of their gatherings were separated, washed and picked over, then displayed or packed away for safekeeping. Some became so enthralled with their findings they would proudly claim that Indian blood coursed through their veins.

Archaeologists became interested in the Garden Creek area two miles from Canton, land belonging to James and Richard Plott and George Smathers, as early as 1880. After a series of six excavations, beginning with crude digging and progressing with more scientifically conducted explorations, the historical significance of Pigeon Valley emerged.

The people who first lived here were called a prehistoric culture, predecessors to the Cherokee who came later.

A climate that became increasingly attractive to human habitation resulted when glaciers covering this area finally retreated. Food abounded, water was plentiful, and wide, flat valleys along the Pigeon River were ideal for settlements.

Garden Creek is believed to have been a centralized town, a place of importance; probably headquarters, in a place some called Kanuga

A mythological name for Haywood County sites inhabited by early Cherokee, Kanuga would have encompassed a large area including valleys and mountains. One source says "Kanuga" in Cherokee language means "the meeting place of many peoples," underscoring archaeological findings.

Cherokee Predecessor's Mounds

Three mounds that were made by the people who would become Cherokee were excavated at Garden Creek near Canton, and provided insight into the lives and customs of early dwellers. Charcoal, animal bones, mussel shells, charred acorns and nuts and other residue in fire pits gave clues to their foods. Since Cherokee were good farmers, they likely grew maize (corn), squash, pumpkins, and beans.

Popular perception, of villages dotted with teepees or conical tents, is not compatible with evidence of palisades or wooden supports seen in opened mounds.

Houses in surrounding village areas, defined by post mold patterns, were apparently square or rectangular in shape, and built around raised clay or stone fire pits. Charred remains suggest walls were of close-ly-spaced upright poles covered with woven cane matting, bark, and some mud daubing. A peaked roof, centered with a fire hole, was likely covered with bark or straw thatching. Dwellings were arranged around a central plaza and there may have been smaller structures for sweat baths, storage bins, pottery kilns, and skinning racks.

Bead and shell necklaces and other adornments buried with skeletons indicate the grave contained a person of leadership.

Multilayered mounds were built over partially subterranean cere-monial earth lodges. The lodges included burial chambers, entrance wall trenches, fire pits, drainage ditches, earthen benches, and platform areas. One was conical in shape and measured eighty feet in diameter and eighteen feet in height. Two buildings surrounded by a vertical wall fence had topped it. Three skeletons were encased in three-inch thick clay envelopes.

Earth lodges existed before the mounds were formed. Carefully placed boulders formed clay-capped mounds, some covering collapsed wooden posts, topped with layers of soil over deteriorating lodges. Mounds seem to have had religious or ceremonial significance. Flat-topped mounds may have supported temples or houses for officials. Mound building in this area began around A.D. 200 or 300.

At least two unexcavated mounds still exist here, although farming activities have reduced their size. And artifacts still turn up, especially after plowing followed by hard rain.

One family has in its possession a braided, solid silver ring, cold ham-mered from a Spanish doubloon, believed to have originated in South Florida around 1550 to 1560 when Spanish explorer Hernando de Soto arrived to search for gold. A solid granite ear spool also appeared. Per-fectly round, centered with a circular opening, the outer rim is smoothly grooved so skin would grow around it securely after its insertion in an earlobe. Trinkets would have been hung through the opening. Both have been examined and carbon dated at the Smithsonian Institute. Their collection includes a fearsome-looking tomahawk head, patterned bits of pottery, arrowheads, and primitive tools.

Garden Creek is now a patchwork of housing developments and pro-ductive farmland. Wonder what else lies buried beneath it all?

Trains Forever Changed Haywood County, Western North Carolina

When the first train rolled into Ford of Pigeon, the locomotive trailed black smoke, spewed cinders, and carried the odor of change, drastic change, to Haywood County and the rest of Western North Carolina. The date was January 28, 1882, according to late historian John P. Arthur.

This area's relative isolation came to an end, gradually but definitively. The tracks were, symbolically, a closed door flung wide open. Primarily an agricultural county at the time, industries would soon follow the tracks.

"The railroad that had been creeping (from the east) for years over the Blue Ridge reached the place, a depot was built and it became the terminus of the road for nearly two years," wrote the late W. C. Allen in *The Annals of Haywood County*. Allen named engineer S. S. Aldridge as the man who ran the first train into town; engineer W. P. Terrell, the first to run the train across the Pigeon River and Captain W. H. Hargrove, the first depot agent. "For some years after the railroad reached the village, there was considerable activity. The name Pigeon River was changed to Buford in honor of the president of the railroad company," Allen said. Buford was later renamed Canton. The railroad was an asset when Peter G. Thomson decided to build a pulp mill in the town.

Over the next sixteen months, the Western North Carolina Railroad was sold and became the Danville and Richmond Railroad.

As tracks slowly advanced westward, the town of Clyde became the site of a large stockyard operation and the small hamlet grew and prospered. "J. M. Shook gave the lot upon which the depot was built," Allen wrote.

More lines were laid, and a depot was built at Lake Junaluska to serve guests and personnel at the Methodist Assembly.

When the railroad was completed to Waynesville, "it was a great occasion. It called many of the old residents to see the sight," Allen wrote. Already a popular destination for tourists coming to the county to escape summer's heat elsewhere, more hotels were built to accommodate them. The depot was located in the Frog Level area of town. The last passenger train arrived at that depot in 1949.

Hazelwood became heavily industrialized in the area around the railroad.

As the railroad continued its journey west, one more depot was built, at Balsam, below the popular Balsam Mountain Inn.

Pigeon River Valley

Massive boulders define the bed of Pigeon River's West Fork, seen from Triple Arch Bridge on NC 215. As the river twists and turns down the mountain, ducks under rock overhangs, falls over worn granite, and spews foamy spray within its rocky confines, one wonders at the powerful forces that carved this river's path down the mountain.

Other areas induce visions of cataclysmic events that shaped Haywood County's terrain with its rivers, streams, convoluted mountains, jagged rock cliffs, deep valleys, and level bottomlands.

Garrett Smathers of Waynesville has some answers regarding the shaping of our environment, based on extensive research and his experiences as a scientist dealing with ecology, geology, and other related areas.

In layman's terms, it began with the Ice Age, although glaciers didn't reach as far south as North Carolina. "Some geologists believe glacial advances, with furthermost locations in southern Pennsylvania, Illinois and Missouri, affected the climate in high mountains of Western North Carolina, causing periglacial conditions that affected some of the geology we see today, called boulder fields," Garrett said.

I like to think of it as nature's use of an ancient and extreme cooling and heating system that left soil and rock immobilized by frigid temperatures for long periods of time. Then nature created havoc by warming the earth's surface, allowing it to move with melting ice flows rampaging through the mountains.

"Scientists believe that three world-wide glacial periods have occurred on the earth, with each followed by a warming period," Garrett wrote in a report prepared for the town of Canton. "Advances changed the Western North Carolina mountains from cool to cold, with severe arctic conditions that included permafrost," he said. Permafrost is soil or rock that remains below 0°C throughout the year, and forms when the ground cools sufficiently in winter to produce a frozen layer that persists throughout the following summer.

"The present Pigeon River watershed area, when glacial advance was most intense, would have been in an arctic alpine climatic condition...the river would have been frozen over during fall and winter but during short spring and summer seasons, its headwaters and main stem would have thawed and flowed swiftly through the valley below, carrying heavy loads of gravel and dislodged boulders," he said.

"Some geologists believe," he wrote, "that freezing and thawing (heaving) of permafrost soils and rock fracturing above the 3,200-foot elevation in Western North Carolina caused great flooding, landslides, and creation of boulder fields and alluvial fans (fan-shaped rock and gravel deposits) on some mountain sides. These erosional features can be found along headwaters of the East and West Forks of Pigeon River and elsewhere in Western North Carolina."

These glacial advances and retreats are recorded by time periods and have names, such as the Wisconsin Stage, which Garrett says had a profound effect on the climate of what is now the southern United States. "The Wisconsin, which ended about 10,000 years ago, helped create a variety of habitats in Western North Carolina that gave rise to one of the most biologically diversified areas on the North American continent," he said.

"Pigeon River Valley must have been a wild and beautiful wilderness, having developed after an ice age engendered climate that had broken its tens of thousands of years grip on the Western North Carolina mountain environment," Garrett said.

Post Office Sites

Early post office sites can be an indication of initial settlements and areas of growth within a county. Information garnered from the Branson North Carolina Business Directory names Haywood County's mail centers during the late 1860s, along with a wealth of other information.

In 1866–67, North Carolina's governor was Jonathan Worth of Randolph County. Andrew Johnson of Tennessee was US president. The 8th Circuit Court convened in Haywood in April and September, F. M. Davis was the sheriff, and the county had nineteen churches. Two hotels and two schools were in operation, all in Waynesville. County population numbered 5,801.

Six post offices were listed that year. Forks of Pigeon was one, located in Colonel Joseph Cathey's general store in the Bethel area. Richland Valley was another, apparently located in W. B. C. Garrett's general store. The other four were Waynesville, Jonathan's Creek, Pigeon River, and Mill's River. Garrett was Haywood's representative in the State Convention of 1865 and J. R. Love, Jr., was a member of the state senate.

In 1867–1868, Mill's River post office was no longer included but Crabtree was added. This edition described Haywood County: "Out edges mountainous, finely watered by the Big Pigeon River and branch running down through the county and forming a beautiful and rich valley. Scenery enchanting."

The next year showed no change, but in 1872, Ivy Hill, Jonathan's Creek, Pigeon River, and Pigeon Valley joined the roster. Population had increased by some 2,000 individuals, to a total of 7,921. Additions in 1877–78 were Crab Tree, Fines Creek, and Cataloochee, making a total of nine.

The Directory doubled in size in 1884. North Carolina's population was increasing, and more businesses were necessary to meet the needs of more people and a changing society.

Haywood had more post offices and this time their locations were pinpointed. Cove Creek was 6 miles north of Jonathan's Creek; Crab Tree, 6 miles north of Iron Duff; Fines Creek, 6.5 miles northeast of Crab Tree; Forks of Pigeon, 2.5 miles south of Garden Creek; Garden Creek, 3.5 miles southwest of Pigeon River; Jonathan's Creek, 9.5 miles north of Waynesville; Mount Sterling, 19 miles northwest of Cove Creek; Peru, 4 miles east of Crab Tree; Pigeon River, 6 miles east of Pigeon Valley; Pigeon Valley, 2.5 miles north of Tuscola; Sonoma, 1 mile northwest of Forks of Pigeon; Springdale, 6 miles east of Sonoma; Tuscola, 4 miles northeast of Waynesville; Waynesville, 202 miles west of Raleigh, on the projected line of Western North Carolina Railroad.

Haywood had fourteen manufacturers: three tanneries, two wool-carding businesses, four blacksmiths, three coopers, a millwright, and a harness and saddle maker. Two mica mines and one copper mine were listed, as well.

By 1890, the population had grown to 13,331 and post offices totaled thirty. New to the list were Canton (replacing Pigeon River), Clyde, Cruso, Dellwood, Dutch Cove, Ella, Fannie, Ferguson, Hurricane, Iron Duff, Lavinia, Palm, Pant, Plott, Retreat, Rush Fork, Split Mountain, Teague, Tito, and Western.

Eight volumes of the directory were published at irregular intervals from 1865 to 1896. Each includes varied information on each county in the state with lists of county officials, merchants, farmers, livestock, mines, schools, and churches, to name a few. Levi Branson of Raleigh collected the data and published the books. According to his biography, Branson was a teacher, minister and publisher who had a vast network of contacts from every county. His books are preserved in the archives at University of North Carolina, Chapel Hill.

PALMER'S CHAPEL, CATALOOCHEE

Cataloochee Valley

Cataloochee Valley was a large and prosperous settlement in Haywood County when the National Park Service began acquiring land for the Great Smoky Mountains National Park, land that included the valley.

In the early 1800s, the first settlers began populating the lush valley. In this wilderness, pioneers saw the potential in an area rich with forest growth and plentiful water. They saw tall trees for harvesting, fast running streams for fishing, game for hunting, and fields for farming. Ringed by layers of mountains, the valley in its natural state has been described as an exceptionally beautiful place.

Old photographs and written descriptions indicate that, eventually, Cataloochee became home to numerous families who built both log cabins and large frame houses as well as barns, cleared fields for planting and for pastures, erected grist mills, a school, and a church, and thrived. Although isolated, those who dwelled there worked together and were rewarded by a community that was largely self-sufficient.

Palmers, Woodys, Caldwells, Nolands, McCrackens, Suttons, Halls, Hannahs, Messers, Burgesses, Boyds, Campbells, Moodys, Partins, McGahas, and Sloans are among the surnames of those who lived there.

More than a hundred years passed before the devastating news spread that the residents would lose their homes, their land, and their valley and have to move elsewhere to make way for the Great Smoky Mountains National Park.

Although the idea for the park was conceived in 1923, a bill authorizing protection of the area as a park was passed three years later, in 1926. Fundraising for purchase of the land had begun in both North Carolina and Tennessee, but a contribution of $5 million by philanthropist John D. Rockefeller Jr. sealed the deal.

Homeowners were approached with offers to buy their land, as were large companies who were cutting timber in the area. More than 6,000 people owned small tracts of land that were home to them and had been for years. They did not want to leave, nor did they see the proposed payments as ample compensation for their property. Condemnation suits, especially against the large businesses, were begun in 1930.

As the park became reality, some experienced feelings of ambivalence. Knowing that the land would be forever protected was a cause for celebration, but sad times prevailed as people packed as many of their belongings as possible and left their homes, many in tears.

Stories of Cataloochee Valley and the people who called it home abound as descendants of the original settlers have recorded what they remember or were told, preserving a good bit of its history.

Many of us have romanticized life in Cataloochee. Reading the accounts of men and women who made the valley what it was is a reminder that these were actual people, strong people, who worked very hard to achieve a good life.

Cataloochee Turnpike

T he Cataloochee Turnpike, no superhighway by today's standards, was completed in the early 1860s, giving residents of isolated Cataloochee Valley improved access to the rest of the county and beyond.

Noted historians John Preston Arthur and W. Clark Medford write of the Turnpike in their historical accounts, calling it the first wagon road in the Great Smokies.

Cherokee who used the Cataloochee Valley primarily as a hunting ground laid the route, creating a track or path as they traveled in and out. The Turnpike closely followed this trail. As early as 1821, "the Cataloochee track" was one of only two roads crossing from North Carolina into Tennessee. The other was a "wagon road" on the Hiawassee River.

The Cataloochee Trail, stretching from the Cove Creek area in Haywood County to what is now Cosby, Tennessee, connected area Cherokee villages with those in Overhills country. Later travelers are said to have found the trail worn a foot deep in some places, including Bishop Francis Asbury who used the trail in 1810.

The path was sufficient for the first settlers in Cataloochee but as the valley became more populated, a road that would accommodate wagons or sleds was needed. By the late 1850s, a road had been built from Jonathan Creek up Cove Creek.

The county authorized the building of a toll road from Cove Creek to Cataloochee in 1825 with fees charged for different categories, such as a man and a horse, an extra pack horse, hogs, and cattle. This road apparently offered little improvement.

Work began on the Cataloochee Turnpike in 1856. Beginning from Palmer's Chapel, it went across the mountain to Ball Gap, down to Little Cataloochee, then toward Mt. Sterling. Completed in the early 1860s, it closely followed the old Cherokee Trail.

The Turnpike was not modernized until the 1920s. Although dynamite was available by then, the improved road was wide enough only for a wagon in most places. It was a vast improvement, though.

The steep, winding, mostly graveled road into today's Cove Creek Community and eventually Cataloochee is a true mountain road experience. The sharp turns accompanied by an elevation increase to approximately more than 4,000 feet cross both the Cataloochee Divide and Sterling Ridge before descending into the valley.

When the National Park Service announced plans to develop Cataloochee as a tourist area inside the Great Smoky Mountains National Park, calling for paving Cove Creek Road, opposition was widespread and emphatic. Threatened by lawsuits and eventually budget cuts, the proposed development was dropped.

Arthur wrote of the difficulties of building roads in earlier times. "Powder was scarce and tools were wanting for construction of roads in the early days. Dynamite and blasting powder were then unknown. Ridges offered the least resistance to the construction of roads because the timber on their crests was light and scattered and because, principal consideration, they were level enough on top to allow wagon wheels to pass up or down on them. But they were frequently too steep for the overtaxed oxen and horses of that time. Level places along creeks and rivers were the next places where a road could be built with least labor, but these were always subject to overflow. When there was no other escape from it, "side-cutting" was resorted to but as it took a longer road to go by a gentle grade than by a steep climb, the steeper road was invariably built," he penned.

"These roads or trails, rude and rough, narrow and steep as they were, constituted the only means of communication between the scattered settlers...and were matters of first importance. They (roads) were located by unlettered hunters and farmers who knew nothing of civil engineering and were opened by their labor...(men) who could ill afford spare time from the support and protection of their families...whenever rock ledges and cliffs were encountered; the road builders usually 'took to the woods.' They went as far around them as was necessary to avoid them."

Choosing Home Sites

A rich and beautiful wilderness lay before the first settlers who came to this area. Drawn by the beauty and the potential, these men and women were immediately challenged by the necessity of taming a bit of this wilderness in order to survive and establish a place to live.

Some had received land grants for services rendered, some had passed this way as troops waging war against the Native Americans and returned to stay, others had heard of a fertile and lovely place where one could forge a new life by living off the land.

The first settlers in our area had, by all accounts I have read, a priority list for property they deemed suitable for establishing a home in what was then a wilderness: a reliable source of water, level ground with rich soil for growing their food, and a ready source of timber to harvest for building a dwelling. Concern for safety from various elements had to have been another consideration.

In these mountains, however, rich bottom land was limited. Late-comers had to utilize mountain slopes for home sites, bound by the same priorities. Establishing their farms and homes was more difficult, in most cases. They had no motorized equipment for gouging roads into hillsides or for shearing off the top of a mountain.

Ed Kelley, who has hiked extensively through this area, has seen evidence of old hillside home places, foundations and rock walls. He noted that houses seemed to have been built in areas where the terrain provided a natural platform for houses. None that he has seen were built in a steep-sided cove, especially one with a creek, since that topography provides a natural route for flowing water during heavy rains.

The first, settler, Jonathan McPeters, it is said, chose the valley through which Jonathan Creek flows. Others were drawn by similar valleys such as Pigeon, Beaverdam, Maggie, Cataloochee, and Clyde.

These various locales were relatively accessible, characterized by flat land near a river or a healthy stream that could be cleared for farming. Trees felled during the clearing could become building timbers, firewood for warmth, crude but serviceable furniture, tools, and fences.

They were wisely satisfied to live in places surrounded by, but not atop, mountains. The steeper slopes were utilized for hunting wild game for food, and maybe clearing a gentle slope for higher summer pasture land. The rare buildings on mountainsides were huts or lean-tos for those tending livestock or a hunter's temporary shelter.

Geologists describe how these mountains were formed. Upheavals beneath the earth's crust formed the peaks and valleys, helped along by rushing waters powerful enough to move boulders and carve pathways where there were none. Topsoil, along with trees and underbrush, was washed down some of the same paths cut by boulders. A mountainside collapsed and rearranged the topography. Fractured rocks submitted to the forces of freezing and thawing and split apart, tumbling down, down, as the force of gravity demands.

These first residents wouldn't have known these facts, precisely, but common sense likely guided them to avoid dangerous terrain.

When I Was Young, So Was the Blue Ridge Parkway

S unday afternoon road trips and the Blue Ridge Parkway, seventy-five years old in 2011, were synonymous when I was young. I realize now the serendipity of having grown up with the parkway as a frequent playground.

Attempting to retrace those drives in my mind is difficult because old roads and newer routes have become too mingled. Bridges, landscape, and even the river have changed, altered by both fierce floods and modern technology.

Since my grandparents were welcome and regular passengers on the weekly drives, we left Canton driving the "back side of the river" (NC 215) to their house so they could board the "bus", an ugly, hulking, extremely reliable Nash known as Old Huldy. Journeying on, we crossed over the Pigeon River on old iron bridges, eventually gaining access to Lake Logan Road.

Familiar landmarks indicated where we were going: The three-story white house on Dr. A. P. Cline Sr.'s farm, black bear hides stretched on a weathered shed, the Friendly House with a neat log cabin beside it, Reuben B. Robertson's cabin "Sit and Whittle" across the tranquil waters of Lake Logan, the former site of a logging community named Spruce, and a beautiful stone structure known as Triple Arch Bridge.

Upon reaching Beech Gap, we usually turned eastward onto that part of Haywood County's approximately fifty-mile stretch of the Blue Ridge Parkway, undulating along mountain ridges. Scenery changed abruptly from deep forest views to that of endless sky and layer upon layer of mountain tops, sometimes etched sharply against the horizon with sun rays and sometimes brooding among heavy deposits of fog but always breathtaking.

First stop was the parking lot, facing the massive rock face of Devil's Courthouse. A sacred site for the Cherokee who once claimed this land as theirs, Cherokee lore tells us that within this mountain is a deep cave where the devil holds court; the dwelling place and private dancing place of the slant-eyed giant, Judaculla. The oft-repeated legend can lead to sinister meanderings in a young mind. A short walk along the highway and a steep climb ended with a bountiful view of treetops, deep valleys, mountain peaks, and a breathless sensation from looking down the vertical rock. The yearning to creep carefully to the edge was powerful, but quickly squelched by parental warnings and a rock wall.

The Black Balsam area, rife with trails, views, and interesting names, was never bypassed. Black Balsam parking area, reached by a forest service road, is situated at the base of Sam Knob, a two-summit mountain known as Big Sam and Little Sam. Trails from that point lead to Shining Rock Wilderness and the summit of Cold Mountain, to the picturesque balds of Tennent Mountain, Sam Knob, and Silvermine Bald, to the descending pathway along Flat Laurel Creek. The ridges and hollows of Fork Mountain are part of the view. My grandfather talked of locales he called Turnpike, Fodder Stack, Sixteen Canyon, Big Rock House, and Little Rock House, all Fork Mountain hollows where he hunted bear.

Graveyard Fields would likely be the last stop of the day. Dead tree stumps, imitating gravestones in a graveyard, tell the stories of a mighty wind that toppled trees hundreds of years ago and a 1925 fire that burned the recently logged area. We slipped and slid down the bank to choose flat rocks in the shallow waters of Yellowstone Prong, on which to sit for some refreshment and dangle our feet in the water. Downstream the placid stream evolves into a multi-tiered, frothing waterfall. Upstream, a relatively easy hike reaches the upper falls. Lofty peaks above include Shining Rock Wilderness and Cold Mountain, reached from that vantage point only by an arduous scramble through heavy brush on the steep slopes.

Looking Glass Rock heaves up its mound of granite in the distance, over in Transylvania County. Eons ago, the mass was likely a wannabe volcano that cooled too fast. It would be many years before I ate a picnic lunch from atop its relatively smooth, rock summit.

To return home, we could retrace our route or continue on toward Buncombe County, leaving the parkway at Pigeon Gap and descending through Cruso on US 276. Given a choice, this was my preference, as I liked to hear again about Wagon Road Gap, Frying Pan Gap, and those who manned the fire tower.

Wagon Road was originally a footpath. Later it was widened to accommodate wagons traveling between Brevard and Waynesville. Pioneers gave Frying Pan Gap its name, but the inspiration behind the name has been lost in the mountain mists. Some say an odd-shaped spring in the gap prompted the name, while others claim that a frying pan always hung from a tree in the gap. Nearby Frying Pan Mountain is topped by a 70-foot tall steel tower built in 1941, which is now on the National Register of Historic Places. Constructed by the US Forest Service, the tower was used to look for fires until the early 1990s.

Along the way, conversations became history and biology lessons from two men who had hiked, hunted and explored much of the terrain through which we passed. The story of Sunburst and Champion Fibre Company, the contributions of the CCC (Civilian Conservation Corps) as the nation recovered from the Great Depression, the challenges of building the parkway, the paths of old railroad grades from the days of heavy logging, and the sad story of the demise of mighty chestnut trees were recounted over and over. Biology lessons never ended as leaf shapes and bark texture named various trees, wildflowers were identified, and the life cycle of the forest was discussed. Characteristics of various outcroppings of rock were not ignored. Sightings of trillium, Jack in the pulpit, lady's slippers, or whatever was in season were exclamation points.

Great Smoky Mountains National Park, a Magnificent Gift

I magine a gift of immeasurable value, one so precious, so unique, that it can never be replaced, so immense that no amount of gift paper can wrap it.

We are all the recipients and should consider ourselves custodians of this gift known as the Great Smoky Mountains National Park (GSMNP), which celebrated its 75th anniversary in 2009.

Over 5 million acres of public land was preserved in perpetuity as our heritage, shielded forever from development and logging. The GSMNP contains layer upon layer of ancient mountains, believed to be the oldest on earth; indescribable beauty in the shapes of towering peaks, waterfalls, rivers and creeks, trees, plants, wildlife; ecosystems so diverse that there may be none other like it elsewhere on this planet; a rich cultural history. The most visited national park in the nation is ours to enjoy, study, and protect.

The GSMNP includes five forest types with more than 130 species of trees and 4,000 other plant species, some of which live only in the Smokies, according to figures published by the National Park Service. Mammals living there number sixty-five species, including bear, deer, elk, red wolves, and bobcats. More than 230 species of birds can be found, as well.

Artifacts were left behind by the Cherokee, the area's first inhabitants, and by early settlers—all who were here before the park was created. Gathered and studied, these artifacts reveal historical facts and pictures. Seventy-eight historic structures—grist mills, schools, homes, churches, and barns—are preserved within the park.

The birth of the GSMNP was prolonged and difficult. Initially, many of its would-be recipients were not appreciative. The cost was too dear, they cried, in terms of uprooted families, lost timber revenue, and deprivation of personal hunting grounds. Proponents of a national park in the east wrangled over its location.

Unlike older national parks in the relatively unsettled west, individuals and large companies privately owned land designated for the park. These owners had to be persuaded to sell or forced to move at great monetary cost, a price that the Federal Government could not pay for land acquisition. Determined citizens, and the states of North Carolina and Tennessee as major contributors, gathered donations large and small. In the end, the philanthropic Rockefeller family was persuaded to donate $5 million dollars, enabling supporters of the park to acquire the last parcels of needed property.

Labor pains in the birthing of the park were excruciating for many. Families lost their hard-won farms on land that their ancestors had grubbed out of the wilderness. Two notable examples are the former settlements in Haywood County's Cataloochee Valley and Tennessee's Cade's Cove.

Horace Kephart's words, written in his book *Our Southern Highlanders*, point out that we would be living in a vastly different environment had the park not been established. He came here in 1904 and marveled at the richness he found; the trees, the beauty, and all the resources. He was devastated some years later when he saw bare, eroded mountainsides left behind by loggers. In the beginning, cutting timber to sell was a matter of subsistence for individuals and small operations. Word spread, though, and timber seekers came with their massive machinery and work crews. They denuded almost 70 percent of the area's trees, leaving behind only debris and pocked, pitted earth. Without creation of the park and its ensuing protection, we could be living in a treeless land resembling the urban sprawl of Atlanta or Chicago, with widespread development rather than the sanctuary of the park.

GSMNP has been recognized with two international titles. As an International Biosphere Reserve, it is part of the United Nations' program designed to help protect and preserve the great cultural and biological areas in the world. GSMNP is a World Heritage Site, a voluntary program aimed at preserving the earth's resources and history, because of its collection of Appalachian cultural artifacts from both the 19th and 20th centuries. The park and its resources are of world-wide importance; hence, the two international titles.

Pigeon Valley History

" They named this Pigeon Valley. The river and gap were named that, too, because of the awesome view of the pigeons, as each autumn they migrated through.

"From earliest colonial times they came with thousands darkening the sky. It looked like a big black thunderhead cloud when these passenger pigeons flew by.

"And when they roosted on the mountains some say it looked black as night. In fact they named one Dark Mountain, and to the old folks the name fit just right.

"The river still winds its leisurely path. The mountains still majestically stand. And in our minds' eye, if we look through the gap, we might still see them covering the land."

With these words, *Walking in the Footsteps of Those Who Came Before Us*, an oral history of Bethel, begins.

Charles Cathey, narrator, was born in Pigeon Valley in 1938. He speaks further of the origin of the Valley's name. "Back when I was just a boy, my grandfather told me stories that his father had told him, about when the pigeons migrated through this valley they would stretch from one mountain top to the other mountain top, blocking out the sun." Cathey learned through research that at one time passenger pigeons, now extinct, were the most populous bird in the world. "There were billions of them and when they came through this part of the country, they blocked out the sun." He learned from one source that the birds migrated down through the Shenandoah Valley in such vast numbers they were in a formation a mile wide and 300 miles long. "They were like a large cloud in the sky," he said.

Walking in the Footsteps of Those Who Came Before Us is a collection of oral accounts touching on various aspects of the history of Bethel. The Bethel Rural Community Organization (BRCO) is responsible for gathering the stories and storytellers featured on the video, produced by Douglas Chambers. Beautifully told and illustrated by fine photography, the video is an invaluable tool, preserving the area's history in the words of those who know it best.

Charles Miller, Dr. Mary Michal, Riley Covin, Bill Terrell, Doris Cathey, and the late Ted Darryl Inman are recorded as they discuss the Rutherford Trace and the vast Cherokee settlements in Haywood County, the intriguing history behind Lenoir Devon Acres, the three churches, the schools that served the community through time, local ghosts, the roles of the Catheys, Terrells, Inmans and others in the growth of this county, and much more, far too much to list.

"Bethel, a small quiet rural community is located in the heart of Pigeon Valley in southern Haywood County...to the northwest stands Big Stomp Mountain, also known as Rice Mountain...the remnants of an old wagon road cross the ridge at this point. This road was part of the route used by mail carriers in the latter part of the nineteenth century, as they usually brought the mail on foot from Waynesville, fifteen miles to Lavinia station near Bethel," Cathey relates.

"The people of Bethel hold their heritage and history as dear as their land. The stories and history that these lands evoke provide nourishment for the soul. In days gone by, most of Pigeon Valley's oral history was kept alive as it was told and retold, while people visited each other on a Sunday afternoon," he said.

The video and a series of four books, written by Evelyn Coltman and published by BRCO, are carefully researched and record innumerable facts about Bethel's history. The entire collection is a treasure trove for both amateur and professional historians.

Area Names

Determining the origin of unusual names for areas in Haywood can be difficult.

Towns are easier, often well documented. Colonel Robert Love, considered to be founder of Waynesville, was a great admirer of General Anthony Wayne who gained fame as a Revolutionary War leader. Love chose to honor the man by naming the town, then called Mount Prospect, for him.

After a series of names (Ford of the Pigeon, Pigeon River and Buford), Canton town fathers were contemplating a name change for their village. C. L. Mingus spied the name Canton, Ohio on a nameplate attached to a truss bridge crossing the river, and suggested that Canton would be a fitting name.

Clyde is said to have been named for an official of the newly-arrived railroad in 1883.

Maggie Valley is named after former resident Maggie Mae Setzer. Her father, John "Jack" Setzer, petitioned for a new post office to simplify mail delivery in a remote location and submitted the names of his three daughters, Maggie, Cora, and Mettie. The US Postmaster chose Maggie.

Some of these communities had distinctive characteristics. Early settlers in Beaverdam near Canton found numerous beavers and their dams in the creek flowing through their community. Crab apple trees were supposedly plentiful near the head of a stream in Crabtree. A Scotsman named Aaron McDuff lived in what we know as Iron Duff. When a petition to name a post office there was submitted in the 1880s, his name was requested. Misread, the petition was approved and Aaron Duff was dubbed Iron Duff.

Fines Creek, once called Twelve Mile Creek, became known by that designation because of a skirmish in the dead of winter between a posse and some Cherokee who had stolen horses. A white man named Fine was killed. Unable to transport his body, his comrades broke the ice covering the creek and placed him in the ice cold water, planning to return in the spring to retrieve him. True to their word, they returned later for the body, but it was not to be found.

In early days, the area along the Pigeon River was heavily populated by flocks of pigeons; hence, we have the river of that name as well as Pigeon Township. Utah Mountain off Jonathan Creek was home to some Mormon elders who gained a small following. After encountering ill feelings against them, they returned to Utah but left the name. Plott Balsam is the namesake for John Plott, whose land extended onto this mountain. Early hunters built pens or traps in Wolfpen Gap to catch wolves. Jonathan McPeters, thought to be the first man to live in the area, built a cabin on a creek and lived there a short while, so Jonathan Creek got its name.

Richland Creek in the western part of the county, according to tradition, ran through rich bottom lands. Those who first lived there saw this as rich (fertile) land and combined the words into one.

Appropriately, some locales bear Cherokee names. Cherokee Chief Junaluska and some of his warriors saved General Andrew Jackson's life during the Revolutionary war. The Methodist Assembly grounds' lake was named for him, as was the mountain peak, now known as Eagle's Nest. *Junaluska* means "by the water." Cataloochee is from *gad-a-lu-tsi* meaning "waves of mountains." Soco Gap is from the Cherokee *Sagwa'hi* which means "one place."

Stamey Cove was called "tite-run" because the old road ran through a place so narrow that during cattle-driving days the closed-in section of the road caused problems. Dutch Cove was settled by German immigrants who spelled their new home Deutsche Cove. Garden Creek was called "Flowery Gardens."

Cruso was named by James Riley Trull, a postmaster who was reading *Robinson Crusoe* when he was pressed for a name for the community. Spelling was heard as Cruso, the community along US 276.

Origins of other names are not readily found, such as the place called Rabbit Skin. One source told me it was a section with poor, thin soil, but another said that a young boy, asked where he lived, pulled the name from his imagination.

Hangin' Dog, Hurricane Creek, Bear Wallow, Buzzard Roost, and White Oak! Intriguing names with unfound origins.

Indian Pipes

Soul-touching Views, Experiences

Our mountains wear myriad faces and colors, appealing to different people in different ways:

A clump of bluets nestled beside a tiny stream that whispers its way over a bed of smooth rocks.

Rushing waterfalls pounding over a mass of huge boulders, thrown and tumbled by years of surging water.

Ranges of mountains in blue monotones, marching unceasingly into the horizon.

A turk's cap lily raising its stately head from amidst a clump of waist high ferns.

The sun peeking its head over the majestic Smokies, piercing the early morning fog with sharp rays.

A backpacker's tent by his own personal waterfall.

A half-buried railroad spike, testifying to the presence of a long ago railroad bed.

Dinner in a window-walled restaurant near Mount Pisgah that serves the sunset along with fresh trout.

A yellow-fringed orchid atop Cold Mountain on a cool, windy July day.

Peaks lifting their heads above a sea of mist.

Quiet pools of water, perfect for daydreaming and watching the crawdads flirt with the tadpoles.

Bears huffing their way, lumbering through their mountainous territory.

A rock garden thick with ferns, planted by nature.

A breakfast of hard-boiled eggs and ham biscuits in a sun-dappled thicket near Shining Rock.

A toothbrush marring the scenery by a spring on Green Mountain Trail.

Squirrels leaping and chattering among tree branches at a picnic area.

A poncho ripped away by water's force in a foolish attempt to ford a rain-swollen, fast-running stream turned river on Little East Fork.

Nature's annual spring flower show that carpets the forest floor with trillium and may apples on Balsam Gap.

Jack in the pulpit clad in spring suits of green, brown and purple. Elusive pink and yellow lady's slippers and translucent Indian Pipes.

Lunch on the mound of granite called Looking Glass on a bright sunny day.

The high-pitched shriek of a child plunging into an icy pool after a pant-shredding trip down Sliding Rock.

Hiking ridge tops that offer spectacular views of sky and mountaintops before plunging into the forest, shaded by a thick canopy of trees.

Skirting the wall at Devil's Courthouse to carefully inch down to a rock ledge jutting over the valley far below.

A leaf-strewn path that gives way to a narrow, rock ledge that must be traversed with care.

Outcroppings of quartzite in the Shining Rock Wilderness area, aged by moss in muted shades of gray and green.

Watching a full-grown doe in Pisgah National Forest daintily tiptoe past a camper, who sits still and quiet beside his tent.

Skunks sniffing their way around a campfire in the Smokies as campers freeze in their places, afraid to breathe.

Awakening around midnight to sit up and experience a face-to-face encounter with a bear through a flimsy, mesh camper window.

Exploring old buildings, walking old trails and watching the elk in Cataloochee Valley.

Melting marshmallows over a crackling campfire while sounds of the night punctuate the surrounding darkness.

A sense of awe pervading the spirit, inspired by the handiwork of a master craftsman.

Turk's Cap Lily   Bluets

You People Sure Talk Funny

Appalachian Speech

Our mountain talk is distinctive, making us unique. Our colorful and oft misunderstood dialect is an integral part of our heritage, and deserves appreciation and preservation.

This native speech isn't necessarily bad grammar, not always indicative of a lack of education, or something to be ridiculed. Agreement with this point of view is demonstrated in a scholarly book entitled *Dictionary of Smoky Mountain English,* compiled by Michael Montgomery and the late Joseph Sargent Hall. Words are defined, and quotes and their sources are named.

Some of these examples, all familiar to me, are in the book or in my brain. Each is fun to explore and understand. The dictionary quotes some very familiar names: authors Horace Kephart, John Parris, Wilma Dykeman, John Arthur, former ranger Mark Hannah, even Popcorn Sutton of Maggie Valley.

"That was the *awfullest* (good, excellent) mess of beans I ever saw." "There were so many to pick from and I was too *choicy* (particular, choosy) and ended up getting none."

"I ain't got nothin' *agin'* (against) you." He will be here *dreckly* (directly, meaning soon, right away, or later)."

"*Holp* is a pronunciation of help." "*Feller* is a pronunciation of fellow."

"That bear and my dog had an awful *fit* (fight)."

"Mama, he *jobbed* me with a stick. *Whup* him." (*Job* means to jab or strike, and *whup* is whip.)

"I'm *fixin* (getting ready to) to go to town. You want anything?"

"It *tuck* (took) us a whole day to go from Canton to Tampa. That's a *fur piece* (long distance) to travel."

"That field *growed* (grew) a right *fair* (good) crop *atter* (after) we got the *bresh* (brush) cleared."

"That church you're a-lookin' for is just over *yonder* (a direction, usually accompanied by a pointing finger)."

"We hear tell that they are *a-fixin* (going to) to get *hitched* (married)."

"*Listen at* (listen to) that *racket* (noise) they're making. *Whur* (where) are their parents?"

"Their son is going to *make* (become) a doctor."

"It is *nigh* (near) time for this preaching to get started."

"*Ever* (every) once in a while I *git to* (start) thinking about that funeral."

"*Hit* (it) *wuz* (was) a hard hike, but we finally *topped out* (reached the top of a mountain) at Cold Mountain."

"He *recollects* (remembers) a time when that area was full of chestnut trees."

"They were *teetotally* (entirely, completely) worn out."

Pa says that he wants some *sweet milk* (whole milk, not buttermilk) with his cornbread.

And the all-inclusive "they." *They* (there) used to be a big orchard on that hill over there.

Phrases or words sometimes flit through my mind or fall from my mouth and I wonder, "Where did that come from?" Words from the past tend to echo through our recollections.

Our speech defines, identifies us. Proud of my mountain heritage, I confess to feeling a bit smug to know that I can talk and understand "mountain speak" and grieve when I observe its dilution.

Mountain Talk

M ountain talk. Our colorful dialect. Our heritage.

Often a target of ridicule, seen as something to poke fun at, the speech of Western North Carolina, the Southern Appalachians, especially that of the old-timers, has its roots in Scotland, Ireland, and archaic England.

As a matter of fact, the brogues of other areas within and without North Carolina share some of the same origins.

After all, we are descendants of immigrants. Searching for speech patterns, unique words and pronunciations, and terminology, and recording it for safekeeping is now a mission for a number of scholars, researchers, and preservationists.

They should be applauded.

Gary Carden of Sylva, Neal Hutcheson and Professor Walt Wolfram of Raleigh made a video entitled *Mountain Talk*. It was filmed in Western North Carolina and aired periodically on PBS. They visited people on their home turf and recorded much invaluable information on mountain talk.

Wolfram and Hutcheson ventured even further, traveling the length of North Carolina to capture dialects from the Outer Banks to Murphy, in *Voices of North Carolina*, another video documentary.

Si-gogglin. Poke. Plumb. Yonder. Airish. Feisty. Clabber. You'uns. I swan. Sound familiar to anyone? The words mean, respectively, crooked, bag or sack, an intensifying adjective like completely, an indeterminate distance or locale, cool and windy, energetic and full of life, sour milk, other people (singular and plural), and an expression of amazement.

"I am plumb tard out frum totin' this poke a fur piece frum over yonder. B'lieve I'll pull up a cheer and set a spell with you'uns."

Understand?

Makes perfect sense to me and delights my ears. The example may be extreme for this day and time. It may not be, either.

These are the distinctive sounds of pure mountain dialect, without corruption from television or any other outside source. It's dialect passed down through generations, from countries beyond the boundaries of the United States.

Such speech would have been attributed, unequivocally, to uneducated hillbillies at one time. As more people see the value of tracing and understanding our heritage, uneducated is no longer accepted by all as synonymous with unintelligent.

Our ancestors could not have survived without intelligence and ingeniousness. And many of us like to be known as hillbillies. The label emphasizes our uniqueness.

Some scholars are convinced that mountain talk can be found in the words of Shakespeare and Chaucer. Others question this premise, believing the ultimate sources are found in Scotland and Ireland.

I plead ignorance. Echoing Carden, "I am not a scholar." I just like "the way it used to be."

Jency Messer of Canton, an educated woman, English teacher, and wife of the late N.C. Rep. Ernest Messer, never entirely abandoned her colorful mountain speak, even in Raleigh among state officials.

Still yet, she was an excellent teacher and writer. *Still yet* means continuing.

The truth is, we are gradually losing our traditions, including language, as the outside world creeps further into the hollers and coves, ending the cultural isolation that protected the old ways. We are also losing, too fast, those who have kept alive the uniqueness of our mountain culture.

The flow of cultural change cannot be stopped. All any of us can do now is record old songs that often relate actual events, interview true mountain folks, write about what we see and hear, and hope it will be enough.

Will this suffice? I *recken* (guess, believe, suppose) it will have to.

Mountain Dialect

"To outsiders it sounds strange, even uncultured. But what many North Carolinians do to the King's English was done centuries ago by the Queen."

The quote is from a booklet entitled A *Dictionary of the Queen's English*, published by the North Carolina Department of Transportation (NCDOT) and loaned to me by Charles Cathey of the Colonel Joe Cathey clan. He had picked it up years ago and saved it. Undated, its appearance indicates that it is not a recent publication.

"The correspondence and writings of Queen Elizabeth I and such men as Sir Walter Raleigh, Marlowe, Dryden, Bacon and even Shakespeare are sprinkled with words and expressions which today are commonplace in remote regions of North Carolina...in the coves and hollows of the Blue Ridge and Great Smoky Mountains..."

"However, the characteristics of North Carolina speech are not all holdovers from the Elizabethan era. Like most southerners, we speak not prose but metaphor and our dialect and idioms are devised for function, not beauty." An interesting and descriptive reference to mountain dialect.

Divided into three sections, the pamphlet lists definitions of old English words and phrases, then some examples of North Carolina dialect, and some of the more colorful expressions we have heard.

A very soft object, one that has lost its rigidity, or even the condition of a frightened or sickly person is said to be "limp as a dishrag." Extreme poverty is described as "poor as Job's turkey" although use of that particular name is not explained. Rural people were well acquainted with shelling corn by hand and the roughness of a corncob; hence, the expression "rough as a cob." "Mad as fire" indicates a show of fiery temper.

"Bless (her, his, its, your) heart" is an expression of affection, sympathy or condolence. "'Eh law" is an interjection signifying agreement, puzzlement, or resignation. "Right smart" indicates a considerable amount. "Tuckered out" means exhaustion.

Some of the more colorful words include *quietus*—a calm period, or putting a stop to rowdy behavior; *picayunish*—nit picking or being particular to an extreme degree; *nuss*—to hold, especially a child; *kiver*—a bed covering; *mess*—enough for a meal. Others are *haint*—a ghost; *hope* or *holp*—past tense of help; *hist* (pronounced heist)—to raise; *holler*—to shout, or an area in the woods; even *hern* for hers and *hisn* for his.

Smidgen, a bit, is a word in the section designated as definitions. A *cowcumber* is a cucumber and *pizen* is poison. *Slue* is many while *nary* is not any. To get rid of something is to *git shet uv* and one *jines* or joins. A *drap* is a drop and a coat might be *flang*, or flung, on a chair. To be

45

obleeged is to be obliged or thankful. Children are *learned* to read, as opposed to taught. I *recken* (believe) he is gone.

If a fight occurred, participants were said to have a *fit*. An abundant amount was called *lavish*. A *salet* was a mess of greens, and a bag was a *poke*. *Bile* is boil while *blowed* is blown or blew. One would *ast* or ask for something. That dog is *arter*, or after, a rabbit.

The conclusion quotes the late Dr. Frank C. Brown of Duke University, who wrote a collection of books on North Carolina folklore that remains as the most extensive collection of a state's folklore. "So many expressions now on the lips of living North Carolinians, though sometimes held in contempt by the half-educated, have been employed over the centuries by some of the greatest writers: Alfred, Chaucer, Shakespeare and the translators of the Bible."

EARLY
LEADERS

Colonel Robert Love

C olonel Robert Love is credited with founding the town of Waynes-ville, and his brother Thomas with setting boundary lines for the formation of Haywood County.

This family played a big role in Haywood County, according to local historians W. C. Allen and W. Clark Medford, whose books are generously sprinkled with references to one Love or another, listing their accomplishments and other facts.

Allen writes, "The people in this territory west of Buncombe were fortunate in having General Thomas Love in the legislature in 1808." It was Thomas Love's bill, passed December 23, 1808, that carved Haywood County out of Buncombe, thus shortening the travel distance for folks in Western North Carolina who had business to transact in court or other official matters.

Thomas was elected as one of Haywood's representatives in state government consistently until 1820, according to Medford. In 1814, he was appointed by the state as one of a group to run the line between North and South Carolina, a rough job through heavy wilderness, according to Medford. However, Allen names his brother Robert as the one selected for this undertaking. Thomas moved to Macon County in 1830, then later to Tennessee.

Thomas Love's bill called for a levy or land tax to be paid to the sheriff to provide money to erect public buildings. Court met in private residences until a courthouse, jail and whipping post were built, according to Allen. Thomas Love was one of twelve men who held the first court session in the new county.

This all took place in Mt. Prospect (Waynesville). When court officials were named, Robert Love vied with Felix Walker for the position of Clerk of the Court and won. Haywood became an actuality March 28, 1809. Two locations were considered as the site for the county seat, Mt. Prospect and Tuscola (near Lake Junaluska), with some heavily favoring the latter location. Robert Love donated sites for a courthouse, a jail, a public square, and for Green Hill cemetery in Mt. Prospect, apparently settling the debate.

Love suggested naming the new county seat in honor of Revolutionary war General Anthony Wayne. His proposal was adopted and Mt. Prospect became Waynesville, Allen wrote.

Among the names of those taking the earliest state grants as land speculators was that of Robert Love. He had inherited a large fortune from his mother, which he invested in vast areas of land in Haywood and Jackson counties. It was, at one time, one of North Carolina's largest estates.

Medford called Robert Love "one of the prime movers in this county's early organization and development." He died in Waynesville in 1845, and is buried in Green Hill Cemetery.

Colonel Joseph Cathey

Various historians have chronicled the history of Haywood County, and from their words emerge strong evidence of the firm foundation on which this county was laid. This foundation, however, is not one of stone and mortar or bricks and steel. This enduring foundation is a human one, mixed with the wisdom and foresight of a group of extraordinary men.

Colonel Joseph Cathey was one of those men, one of the key ingredients in this foundation.

During his lifetime, 1803–1874, he donned many hats and wore them all effectively. He was a farmer, a storekeeper, a miller, and a reluctant politician. He was a leader in his community, and is said to have had some knowledge of medicine.

His father, William, was one of Pigeon Valley's first settlers. Cathey had no siblings, but when he and Nancy Hyatt married, they had nine children.

His contemporaries regarded him as a highly intelligent and knowledgeable man. His eulogy credited him with being "of sound practical judgment, well versed in all subjects...He was an excellent farmer, merchant, miller, trader, a good family physician, and a most excellent legislator. He was well versed in the general principles of law, theology, medicine, physics, and almost every department of knowledge."

High accolades for a man with, apparently, no formal education. His neatly-written and carefully-preserved ledgers and correspondence are those of an educated person, although no schools were established here during his childhood. He could read, write and do mathematical calculations.

Cathey's decision to locate at the fork of the Pigeon River contributed to his entrepreneurial success. Fertile land for farming, his property was accessible to many areas and ideal for locating a large store. Water to power his grist mill was readily available in the Pigeon River.

His focus was on developing his community. He built a large store, described by descendants as a long building with huge fireplaces at both ends and four rooms, where travelers could sleep. He stocked it with a wide variety of items that people living in Pigeon Valley might need, from saddles and tools to food. Since it was a popular gathering place, the store was the perfect spot for the location of a post office. It was called the Forks of Pigeon Post Office.

Content with his family and his enterprises, he had no interest in politics. But as a man respected for sound judgment, his contemporaries saw him as an excellent choice for office, dealing with political matters affecting the county. Strong urging forced him into agreeing to serve as Haywood County's representative in the Constitutional Convention of 1835 where his leadership qualities were recognized statewide. Seven years later he served a term in the State Senate, again an unsought position. He could surely have advanced up the political ladder, but he refused and returned to his Pigeon Valley home to stay. Too old to fight in the Civil War, he was given the honorary title of colonel as an indication of respect.

Colonel Joseph Cathey was, indeed, one of the strong pillars underlying the structure of this county.

CIVIL WAR
EXCERPTS

Civil War Letters

"**A** New Year's gift, my deare; what shall it be. I would love to give you a new year's kiss this bright morning."

So wrote Rezia Stradley Osborne on January 1, 1862, to her husband Roland C. Osborne in Fort Lee, South Carolina, where he was stationed during the Civil War. Roland Osborne of Canton has eight letters written by his great-great-grandmother to his great-great-grandfather during the war.

"So may its closing day (the new year) find you in your own quiet home surrounded by your dearest friends...and an honorable Citizen of an <u>Independent Southern Confederacy</u>," she wrote. Home was Haywood County.

The scenario is that of a woman twenty-four years old, with a four-month-old baby. She's ill and unable to walk, and despairing the absence of her husband and life in general. She lived with her parents in Beaverdam, north of Asheville, in a fine-looking log cabin. Missing her home in Pigeon Valley, she wrote long letters in a flowing script, surely with pen nib dipped repeatedly in ink.

Questioned about getting crops started, she answered she considered it "very important" and if she was "like I used to be and was back in our house," and had tools to work with and a "clever girl" to stay with her, she would try to have things ready for him.

Her reports of events at home are revealing. "Jo is at home, yet his health is very delicate. I am afraid he can't stand the winter; his Col don't take one bit of care of his men...they have been ordered to Kentucky but the men have been starved and dragged about until they are unable to go."

She hears of battles in Port Royall, SC, Roanoke, NC, and of troops sent to Cumberland Gap. "I would send you the Asheville News but it is only half a sheet now; hardly worth the trouble," she wrote.

Two volunteers from Reem Creek Campground stopped by. They had been ordered to march to Tennessee. "It looks like Western North Carolina men will have to come back for their own home... Asheville ought to be fortified immediately; the Tories of East Tennessee are threatening to burn it down."

"Jo returned to camp...they are stationed on the Rail Road to guard it; from Greenville to Chattanooga."

On April 1, she wrote from Pigeon River, having returned home in better health. "Your wheat looks splendid and clover crop is growing well. Your oats are sown. It would do your heart good to ride up Pigeon Valley and see how pretty the mountains and wheat are."

Then, "I want to quit writing to you and talk awhile. I feel like I would soon see you. I pray that I may."

That was not to be. Her husband died August 5, 1862 of typhoid in a Williamsburg, Virginia hospital. He never saw his son. She remarried two years later, to an attorney in Asheville.

Other excerpts tell bits of stories, reveal her feelings, and indicate deteriorating conditions at home.

"May be the warm wather [sic] will kill all the Yankeys [sic] at the South. It is said that there is 20,000 of them sick at Louisville, Kentucky."

"...a great revival going on at Hominy Church...I wish it would reach as far as Locust Fields."

"We hear the militia has been called out of Buncombe to fight the Tories in Madison."

"We have all forgot about coffy [sic]; we like rye better."

"The (Pigeon) river is up. I think we should build a bridge across that river."

Confederate Soldier Letters

R oland C. Osborne was a man weary of war, longing for home and family, hungry for good food.

Osborne was the Confederate "solger" from Pigeon Valley, recipient of letters from wife Rezia, quoted above. He was assigned to Company F, 25th regiment, a Confederate infantry of soldiers from nine western counties and one company from Georgia. They assembled in Asheville in August of 1861, and were sent to Grahamville, SC. The infantry soldiers remained there until March of 1862, according to a website on Confederate North Carolina Troops.

"I wanted to be home preparing to make a crop and enjoying the sweet comforts of being with my dear wife and boy and friends," he wrote on March 1, 1862, to his sister Haseltine "Tine" Osborne Plott, who lived in Pigeon Valley.

He was in North Carolina on November 3, 1861 when he wrote from Camp Davis near Wilmington (quoted as written).

"I had just come to the conclusion that you all had forgot that you have Brother in Army of Confederate States. But I will hier remind you that you have one & would like to do his country some service," he wrote. "I am still mending and...may continue so doing for I asshure you I have sufered....if a boy ever did. I do not believe we are gowing to get into a fight down hier. There is some talk of moving us to Virginia now. I can't tell whether or not we will gow or not."

Osborne was a distant relative of Jimmie Henson of Lake Logan Road, who called to say she had Osborne's letters among other correspondence saved by family members. She and husband Richard found them in a crawl space, after they bought the house built in 1867 by Pingree Priestley and Charity Haseltine Osborne Plott, in 1970. "Tine" was Jimmie's great-great-aunt, and Pingree's sister Adeline Lucretia was her great-great-grandmother.

One letter is written on blue stationery, with a flag and Confederate States of America imprinted on it (quoted as written).

"We are camped in an old long leaf pine thicket on a sound (probably Mitchell's Sound on the NC coast). I think we are going to go to Charleston, SC, in a few days since thier is not much danger hier. I think I would rather stay hier this winter as I am inclined to think it will be healthy." He wished his sister could send him a sack of flour and a box of big apples, butter, and a glass of sweet milk or cream. He hoped his father had set out a big watermelon patch.

"I will look upon the day I am released as the greatest day of my life," he wrote.

He wrote to his friend Hack (from Pigeon Valley) that he did not think they should write too often, or include many details. He seemed to fear that specific information would get into the wrong hands.

Osborne died in 1826 of disease in Williamsburg, Virginia.

His regiment was among those in the Army of Northern Virginia that surrendered with Robert E. Lee at Appomattox. In Virginia, they had fought in the Seven Day's Battle near Mechanicsville, as well as at Fredericksburg, Plymouth, Drewery's Bluff, and then the nine-month Petersburg siege in the spring of 1864.

Union's Kirk Wreaked Havoc

C olonel George Washington Kirk is described by Civil War historians as cruel, ruthless, and a scoundrel. In today's world he could be called a guerrilla, possibly even a terrorist. According to history buff James Howell of Canton, some compare him to General George Sherman, burning his way through Georgia.

Haywood County was the scene of many of his savage raids.

Kirk's Raiders crossed the Tennessee line in the vicinity of Mount Sterling in the spring of 1865, burning, pillaging, and killing along the way.

"He just about wiped out Jonathan Creek," Howell said. "He had 600 men, 400 cavalry, and 200 infantry."

"He was a scoundrel," said Earl Lanning of Waynesville. "Every war has someone like him."

On Jonathan Creek, two former Confederate soldiers, Absolum Carver and Francis James Ervin Rice, were killed. "They were riding to patrol the community when they were both shot from their horses on the mountain above Dellwood. They were crossing the mountain on their way to Waynesville," said Charles Miller, another local historian. "Lanning, Howell, and I found their marked graves in the Rice and Carver cemeteries in the Beantown area off Jonathan Creek last week." Rice was the great-grandfather of Jack Rice of Canton.

Kirk sent a detachment into Crabtree while he and the rest of his men rode into Waynesville where they burned the residence of Confederate Col. Robert Love as well as the old jail, after releasing the prisoners. Several citizens were killed, some were captured; stores were pillaged and numerous horses stolen, according to the late W. C. Allen, local historian.

Louise Ross of Crabtree tells that her grandfather White Parton, who lived in Beantown, took his horses, other livestock, hams, and other provisions into the Sugar Cove area as a precaution because he did not think they would travel that high. "And they didn't," she said. "My mother told me he had gotten word that Kirk was coming and getting closer, looking for anything he could find."

"When they left, they went to Balsam and camped for the night. A bunch of Haywood County farmers surrounded them and fired into the group. They came back through Waynesville and headed to Soco Gap. A small group of home guard stationed there attacked them, so they came back through Waynesville and went across Balsam. They must have been here three or four days" Howell sad.

Born in Tennessee's Green County, Kirk enlisted in the Confederate army, but soon deserted, switching loyalty. His assignments along the Western North Carolina and Tennessee border included guiding Unionist mountaineers and escaped prisoners of war to Union-held territories, securing safe houses for refugees, recruiting men to be part-time guerrillas and guides, gathering intelligence, and stealing horses.

The Union considered him bold and efficient, but in Western North Carolina he was feared as a ruthless guerrilla commander. He wasn't content to stay within his guidelines and committed many atrocities, terrorizing people, burning buildings, using prisoners as human shields, and looting. Silver spoons are said to have jangled from his cavalry's bridle reins. At one house, spigots on molasses barrels were opened, flooding the cellar; feathers from beds and pillows were stirred into the mess, and bucketsful of the mixture were flung onto furniture, walls, and ceilings.

Sulphur Springs' Last Civil War Skirmish

"Near this site the last shot of the War Between the States was fired" reads, in part, a plaque placed by the Daughters of the Confederacy near the former location of White Sulfur Springs Hotel.

The 1865 skirmish is said to have been one of the most unusual of numerous encounters between Confederate and Union troops during four years of bloodshed that left lingering traces of bitterness and territorialism, even today.

Union Colonel William C. Bartlett's 2nd North Carolina Mounted Infantry had been raiding, pillaging, and burning homes in Haywood County. He was probably unaware that General Robert E. Lee had surrendered to General Ulysses S. Grant on April 2, 1865 at Appomattox, Virginia. He and his 2,000 troops marched into Waynesville, where he established headquarters while his men made camp on Sulfur Springs property west of Waynesville on May 6, 1865, according to local historians.

Unbeknownst to the soldiers in blue, they had settled in the proverbial briar patch. Local volunteers, already devastated by losses of menfolk, crops, and homes, were struggling to exist and supplementing Confederate troops to rid themselves of Union raiders. The Thomas Legion, comprised of Confederate General James Green Martin and Colonel William Holland Thomas (for whom the Legion was named), marched from Jackson County and camped near Dellwood with their white and Cherokee soldiers on May 6, 1865. Colonel James R. Love stationed his command of 250 soldiers on Balsam Road above Bartlett, leaving him almost surrounded.

The detachment of Confederates from the Thomas Legion had served in the Shenandoah Valley Campaigns of 1864, before being sent to their native North Carolina mountains to deal with troops like Bartlett's as well as "bushwhackers," who were also creating havoc.

Not expecting any organized opposition, the Union soldiers were surprised when attacked by Thomas' men. One Union soldier was killed, and the remainder are said to have retreated to Waynesville. Bartlett requested a two-day armistice, hoping in vain that reinforcements would show up.

The evening before the armistice ended, bonfires were lit by the Cherokee on ridges surrounding Waynesville, creating the illusion that Waynesville was completely surrounded by superior forces. The next morning Thomas' Cherokee troops, whooping war chants in feathers and war paint, further intimidated the Union soldiers. Thomas declared, loudly and sternly, "If your men don't surrender I will unleash the Indians to scalp your Yankee regiment...Legion will not surrender their arms and equipment." Martin intervened and he and Holland, both aware of Lee's capitulation and knowing that further hostilities were pointless, met with Bartlett at the old Battle House and negotiated a surrender. Bartlett is thought to have taken a few guns to appease Union commanders and left with his troops.

Local historians, the late W. C. Medford and the late W. C. Allen, wrote similar accounts of the event, citing notes by Confederate Colonel W. W. Stringfield of Waynesville as their source.

OLD-TIMEY MEDICINE: A MIXED BAG

Old-time Remedies

Memories of old-time remedies linger, often leaving a bad taste in the mouth. Some were homemade. Traveling salesmen, called snake oil doctors by some, peddled salves, tonics, and elixirs.

The Cherokee, said to have used herbs and other plants growing in the wild, were very successful in treating different maladies. Hopefully, their concoctions were more palatable than some used in the not-too-distant past by our parents, grandparents, and their parents before them.

Croup could be a frightening experience with its barking cough and labored breathing, even fatal. Barbara Carswell Bolden was dosed with groundhog oil when she was so afflicted. "We were really sick before we complained. It was worse than awful, but we dang sure got better," she said. Her dad killed the groundhogs and her mom rendered oil from their fat, strained it, and stored it in jars.

Sale of Cloverine and Rosebud salves, actually still available, earned spending money for Mary Shook Hargrove, my grandmother. "We used it for scratches, scrapes, cuts, insect bites, everything. It was all we had," said my aunt, Cora Lee Devlin.

Then there was cod liver oil. It was supposed to be good for whatever ailed you. Actually, cod liver oil is said to contain more vitamin A and vitamin D per unit weight than any other common food. A teaspoonful went down more easily if you held your nose.

Fletcher's Castoria and castor oil were laxatives, although a tiny dose might ease colic. They were vile-tasting, nauseating liquids that also induced vomiting. Castor oil was useful for meting out discipline. "If you don't stop that, I am going to give you a dose of castor oil," was a very effective threat.

Turpentine has been used medically since ancient times to treat lice infestations, rid the body of worms (parasites), and as a chest rub for sore throats and nasal congestion. When a cousin mangled some fingers in a cider press, my grandfather, laughing heartily, wrapped the hand in turpentine-soaked cloth and his wounds healed.

Thankfully, Vick's Salve replaced mustard plasters for chest congestion. Ground black mustard mixed with other ingredients soaked a scratchy, woolen, heated cloth that was placed on the patient's chest. Unless used carefully, a plaster or poultice could cause severe burns. Vick's was used in the same manner, dabbed below nostrils already rubbed raw, or heated in a spoon with a match so the sick could breathe the vapors.

Old-time drugstores carried a compound called "camphorated oil," extolled in a song: "John Brown's baby had a cold upon his chest so they rubbed it with camphorated oil." Yuck! The oil gave relief from cold symptoms, inflamed sinuses, and clogged nasal passages when applied externally. Camphor, used improperly, can be poisonous.

Mildred Pharr was "dosed up with a mix of molasses and sulfur every fall." "It purifies the blood," she said, and "heals fall sores or boils. It didn't taste very good. You had to hold your nose to get it down."

Tiger Balm was used for arthritis, various teas like chamomile and valerian were soothing, and goldenseal was used to stop bleeding. The list seems endless.

Patent Medicines

The yellow tin once held eight capsules, headache remedies composed of acetophenetidin, aspirin and caffeine. "Martin's Capsules" is written above a drawing of a mother bird dropping a capsule into a nest occupied by four baby birds. The medicine was mixed and packaged in Canton by Dr. and Mrs. W. S. Martin, according to Brainerd Burris, co-owner of Martin's Drugstore. "The tablets were used broadly in the 1920's to 1925," Burris said. "We were still using them in the late '20s."

Before the days of modern medicine, with its medicine cabinet of sophisticated drugs regulated by the federal Food and Drug Administration, people relied on elixirs and compounds called "patent medicines," although few, if any, were actually patented. Some were effective, some were completely useless (unless the patient craved the alcoholic content), and some were dangerous.

Carter's Little Liver Pills, Doan's Pills, Fletcher's Castoria, Lydia E. Pinkham's Vegetable Compound, Geritol, Hadacol, Cloverine Salve, Vicks VapoRub. Bromo Seltzer, and Scalf's Indian River Medicine were familiar names among the hundreds touted by salesmen.

Wayne Carson remembers Scalf's Indian River Medicine and Black Draught on the shelves at the old Cut Rate Drugstore in Canton.

Kickapoo Indian Medicine inspired Al Capp's "Kickapoo Joy Juice," featured in the comic strip *Li'l Abner*. The manufacturer was located in Connecticut, far from any Kickapoo Indian tribes.

Hadacol, with its outrageous claims as a tonic, took the country by storm, primarily because of the equally-outrageous marketing techniques used by its creator, a Louisiana state senator named Dudley J. LeBlanc and endorsement by well-known country singers. Twelve percent alcohol, Hadacol is said to have been potent and vile tasting. Jerry Lee Lewis recorded "The Hadacol Boogie," a song written by Bill Nettles.

Early drug reps traveled from home to home extolling their potions, which were claimed to cure everything (from venereal diseases, tuberculosis, cholera, neuralgia, epilepsy, scarlet fever, and paralysis to so-called female complaints), or hawked their wares at circus-like traveling medicine shows.

The Great American Fraud, written by Samuel Hopkins Adams and published in 1905, led to the passage of the first Pure Food and Drug Act in 1906. The statute did not ban the alcohol, narcotics, and stimulants in the medicines but it required them to be labeled as such, curbing some of the more misleading, overstated or fraudulent claims that appeared on the labels. In 1936, the statute was revised to ban them.

Cloverine Salve is still on the market as a skin care product, which is basically all it ever claimed to be. Early advertisement claimed it was "highly recommended for sores, burns, cuts, ulcers, chapped hands, face and lips, common sore throat, chafes, galls, nasal catarrh, itching piles, sunburns, tired, sore, and aching feet; discovered by a physician, used by people of refinement, and sold everywhere. The Wilson family of Tyrone, Pennsylvania manufactured the salve.

Crying from a scrape, a bee sting, even when an old hen flogged me on the top of the head, I was often told by my grandmother to come in the house and she would "doctor me" with Cloverine Salve. No panacea, sometimes it took the sting away. Popular as a fundraiser, Cloverine rewarded its sales people, my grandmother included, with posters, Depression glass, decorative boxes and such. Its sale was regarded as a respectable way to earn a little spending money.

Folksy Sayings

One spoonful of cookie dough for the baking sheet, and one spoonful for me. "Eating raw cookie dough will give you worms," I was told long ago. One of many homespun warnings, the adage aimed at putting a stop to fingers dipping into the tasty mixture and the clamor to "sop the bowl." Probably not one bit of truth in it.

"Don't play in the fire or you will wet the bed," was undoubtedly meant to prevent one's stirring glowing embers with a stick or poker. Probably a fire safety measure.

Milking the cow in the morning was a chore that usually incited fights among Barbara Carswell Bolden and her sisters, with the milker squirting milk on her sisters and any cats that might pass by. Their mother admonished them, "If you waste milk, the cow will go dry."

"And for goodness sakes, don't play with frogs or you will get warts," Bolden remembers.

Appendicitis must have been especially feared. If you bit your fingernails, ate raw apples or unpopped kernels of corn, or swallowed chewing gum, an attack of appendicitis might ensue.

Depriving Susie Curtis of the pleasure of petting her dog was irritating at any time. However, when thunder and lightning raged in the sky, she was told that dogs or other animals attracted lightning and to leave the dog alone. Water was said to have the same attraction for lightning bolts.

Curtis was also warned not to drink milk when eating fish. Why? Does it cause a stomach ache? Along that same line, neither was she to drink milk while eating watermelon.

When Nancy Garrett developed a small patch of ringworm on her arm, she heard "You have been kissing a cat."

"A whistling woman and a crowing hen always come to a bad end," according to Linda Nye's grandmother, Laura Moore.

Years later Pauline Thompson, who kept house, cooked, and helped raise three children for Nye's parents, Dr. and Mrs. Roy Moore of Canton, came to Nye's house to help with a new baby. She was horrified when Nye began clipping the baby's nails. "You will make a thief of that child," she said. "You are supposed to bite a baby's fingernails off, not clip them."

These folksy sayings were undoubtedly meant to end specific behaviors. Proof of truth in predicted outcomes has never been evident to me, although there may be some basis in lightning warnings. They are both amusing and heartwarming to many of us.

Spring: A Time of Renewal

Mountainsides herald the arrival of spring as pastel shades of green contrasting with chartreuse creep up the slopes and fill the valleys. Brown-edged summits are poised to assume the colors of spring as new leaves continue unfolding, displacing the old.

White bonnets donned by dogwood trees mingle among the greens, circles of lace that Mother Nature has dropped here and there.

A faint perfume accompanies the cascading blossoms of locust trees, resembling strands of leis tightly woven of miniature white orchids.

Mountain Laurel

Trillium

Bloodroot

Rhododendron, heavy with blooms this year, mass together in colonies so intertwined that individual plants are indiscernible. Their bursts of vivid shades of pink seem to headline spring's flower show.

Spots of orange and yellow signal the occasional presence of flame azaleas, a shrub seen less frequently, with an airy configuration that showcases their delicate blooms.

Mountain laurel's display of tiny, star-shaped, ten-ribbed white blossoms edged in pink and touches of red is more delicate than those of its rhododendron and azalea cousins. Glossy, deep green leaves enhance tight clusters of blooms.

Other trees contributing to the seasonal show include joyous redbuds, tulip poplars, and Carolina silver bells, which create the impression of light snow as white or pink petals fall from bell-shaped flowers when their blooming is completed.

The show goes on underneath the trees as fern and wildflowers brush aside dead, brown leaves to greet spring in carpets of varying patterns and colors.

May apples spread their canopies to protect the delicate white blooms and eventual fruit that grow from their stems.

A hillside of trillium is profuse in white. Pink-petalled variety is more difficult to find.

Jack in the pulpits stand proudly erect with hoods capping the trumpet-shaped pulpit, veined in purple. Trickles of water dampen the earth, providing the preferred habitat of this unique species. Discovery of delicate but showy lady's slippers is exciting.

Bluets, dwarf crested iris, and violets add touches of blue. Bloodroot and trout lilies are other samples of the botanical bounty carpeting the hardwood-forest floor.

Ferns, one of the first plants on earth, are intriguing. Tightly-spiraled fiddleheads unfurl to expand into fronds, the leaf of a fern. Some grow close to home, the soil that supports its growth, while others seek loftier heights.

As the axis of Earth tilts toward the sun, warmth plays chase with winter's chill and daylight hours rapidly increase, awakening both plants and people and encouraging them to "spring forth." Spring is often seen as a time of growth, of both tangible and intangible renewal, of new life being born.

THE WAY IT WAS

Springhouses

Remnants of early life in Haywood County are plentiful in our mountain landscapes, sketching a way of life that has all but disappeared.

Buildings, or what is left of them, define the manner in which people lived long before our time. "Out buildings," they are sometimes called. Most were put together for a specific purpose.

Apple houses, corn cribs, wood sheds, meat houses, the ubiquitous outhouses, barns, and springhouses were the most common.

Springhouses are a favorite of mine.

When people made their way to our area to establish homes, a spring with a good supply of water was of primary importance. Once found, it would have been cleaned of leaves and other debris and defined in some manner, probably surrounded by rocks like two I have seen on Hemphill.

Busy tilling the soil, building houses, barns, and new lives, a family might leave the spring unprotected indefinitely, as those on Hemphill. Others covered their precious water supply with sheds of one kind or another, many fitted with shelves or ledges for storing milk, butter, eggs, and other perishables to keep them unspoiled in their primitive refrigerator.

My grandparents had a well house, an attached addition to their house, dug into a bank and built of rock. Water trickled constantly in a shallow trough in the area where food was stored. Insulation of earth and rock combined with water evaporation kept it cool. As a child, I gravitated to the well house for its feel and smell, and to use a hand pump that dispersed clear, sweet water. It tasted far better than our city water, to me.

A springhouse I've visited often must have been a deluxe model. Essentially intact, the wooden building nestles in a thick grove of rhododendron beside a fast-running creek. The spring itself is in the floor of a fair-sized porch with ledges, with plenty of room in which to work. A wide trough still carries water through the enclosed area, where shelves stand to hold food.

Another room with chimney is reached by a separate entrance. Clothing and linens were washed and rinsed there, in iron pots over a fire. One can almost feel the presence of women washing in lye-soaped water, stirring with a paddle that would also have been used to lift clothing from the boiling cauldron.

A bridge over the creek allows access to the springhouse, several yards from the house. The building and its spring are intact, although needing a thorough cleaning.

A nice place to visit when sun heats the air, its coolness and that of the creek is refreshing even as you approach.

For us, springhouses are a novelty, even picturesque, but to those who came before us, they were a valuable necessity to sustain life.

Area Outhouses

The ubiquitous outhouse, privy, outdoor john—whatever you chose to call it—wasn't exactly a topic for polite conversation, but it was a necessity before indoor plumbing.

These crude septic systems were nothing more than shacks with a roof, a door, and usually a floor that were built over a pit in the ground. The seat was like a wooden box with a hole cut into the top, extending from wall to wall. Some had several holes of varying sizes. Fancier structures might have lids for the holes.

Surviving buildings demand big dollars now; for ornamental use, of course.

OUT HOUSE

Old-timers tell of mad dashes to the outhouse in winter to sit in the freezing cold, an ordeal—particularly at night. Summer was little better, with heat accentuating the odor. A bucket of lime or lye helped alleviate that problem. Since tissue paper wasn't readily available, or pennies for buying it were too precious, catalogs, newspapers, or whatever was at hand had to suffice. And truly, corncobs were also used.

Spiders were a special horror, since webs were always draped around the walls. Visions of crawling spiders on my skin inspired trips to the woods or behind the boxwood hedge.

Jim Coward, eighty-two, said one set of his grandparents had a four-holer. It had two large holes, a medium sized opening, and one small one for children. He and his siblings fought over who got the small one. His other grandparents had a privy built over a creek. So much for water quality. His wife Ruth remembers a trip out of state, stopping at a rest area that had outhouses. And that was only thirty years ago!

Chamber pots, sometimes called "thunder jugs," could be used indoors, but the user was responsible for sanitation duty.

Outhouses are still around, in rural areas. One across the road from the old Hemphill school building lists badly, while a couple on US 276 are erect and well-kept. Undoubtedly, some folks still rely on them.

Pranksters found them irresistible. My brother, John Hutchins, and some cousins learned the hard way that you didn't throw rocks at the privy when it was occupied by Granny.

Bonfires fueled by oft-stolen outhouses were a ritual at Pisgah High before the annual football tussle with Tuscola, resulting in the area's depletion of readily available privies. Senior football players, including a teacher's son, were the culprits one year. Since the outhouse was still in use, the boys paid the school woodworking shop to build another and put it back in the field from where it came.

During the Depression in the '30s, among the many buildings erected by the Works Progress Administration (WPA) were a couple million new and improved privies.

Lye Soap

R uth Trantham, mother of a high school classmate, was the result of a search for someone who had actually made old-time household provisions and dietary staples: things like lye soap, hominy, and cured hams.

Ruth Trantham is a book with many pages. When this multi-talented lady with a still-keen mind spoke with relish of all she has seen and done during her ninety-three years, I became so caught up in the adventures of her life I couldn't wait until she turned the next page.

A young wife with one son during the early 1930s, the Depression years, she became closely acquainted with hard work. A few years later with an ailing husband and two more children, both girls, living on a farm in Buckeye Cove near Canton, she combined ingenuity with more hard work and her husband Art's true calling as a nurseryman to guide her family on a secure path.

"I have to tell you the first little story in how I learned to make lye soap," she said. "We were living in Swannanoa with my sister and her husband and my sister made a big batch of soap and stored it in an outdoor toilet over a creek. They had a dog, a big old dog, that began to have fits and we would watch it running around and around all over the place. Well, she went out there one day and saw she was missing soap, a lot of soap. That dog had been eating the soap. She moved it somewheres else and the dog got better."

"When we killed a pig," she said, "we would have all this grease from frying (the meat) and saved it to make our soap out of. We put it in a big black pot with three legs, lit a fire under it, poured in some water, and when it began to boil we poured the lye in. Then we poured it in a pan and when it began to set up, we would cut it into pieces. A lot of people made soap." The mixture had to be stirred most of the day until it was ready.

On wash day, they carried water up from the creek, put it in a black pot over the fire to get warm, then used the soap and a washboard to wash the clothes, Trantham recalled. "My mother always used bluing. She would get a stick of bluing and put it in the wash water and if she didn't think the clothes were white enough, she would put them back in and scrub some more. My mother was spotless. If a shirt wasn't snow white, it wouldn't go on a body. She wore me out. I'm not that particular."

And the lye? "We saved the ashes from the (wood) stove, poured water through the ashes and caught the lye in a container," she said. Lye can cause severe burns, so using enough water to get the proper concentration is important. She was usually able to get a can of lye and didn't have to rely on ashes and water too much.

"My mother boiled her clothes in lye water before she washed them," Trantham said. "All my black pots are in my basement. I saved them."

Christmases Past

C hristmases past bore little resemblance to the glitter and bustle of today's holiday. An orange was a special treat for children, along with peppermint candy, according to those who described their long-ago Christmases to me.

The average age of those who talked about their annual observance hovers around 90.

"We didn't have any lights for our Christmas tree," said Ruby Rogers of Little East Fork, "but we did have some tinsel. And I mixed up some Ivory Flakes with water and spread it on the tree branches. It looked just like snow."

"We cut a tree off the mountain until someone gave my husband a pretty spruce tree," she said. Her husband Vaughn pointed out a spruce tree in the front yard that he estimates must be 70 feet tall. "I dug it up and we used it for Christmas, then replanted it for years until it got too big for me to handle," he said.

"One year, I got a little doll with eyes that opened and closed," said Ruth Trantham of Beaverdam. "My mother would string garland from corner to corner. It was a red chenille-like rope. We used crepe paper to decorate with, too. And Christmas cards if we had any. We played and sang and always had fun." A once-a-year trip to Asheville was a Christmas treat. "We walked to town and caught a Trailways bus," she said.

Phoebe Huffman of Canton said, "It wasn't much. I guess we done as good as most people back then. We were happy to get anything. An orange was great, or an apple." One of eight children, Huffman continued, "We didn't have a tree. On Christmas Eve, we each set out a chair—they were cane-bottomed chairs—but we didn't know how Santa Claus got there." One gift, actually an essential, arrived early because they couldn't go with bare feet in the snow. "When we was little our daddy, a carpenter, would go off to work. He would be gone a week or so. Before he left he measured our feet with a stick and he came home carrying a tow sack with a pair of shoes for all of us. My granddaughter doesn't like to hear this, but we liked hog killing time the best because Daddy would boil a pig's bladder and clean it out to make a ball. That was the only ball we had," she said.

One of Huffman's friends Ruby Kilpatrick, one of five children, grew up on a farm in Thickety. "Our daddy cut a pine tree off the farm. We cut strips out of newspapers or any paper we had, and mixed water and flour to stick them together in links. We put a sock on the mantel. We got candy and a little present. I remember one doll with a head that would break if you dropped it," she said. On Christmas day, a tenant farmer brought his family to their house. "We ate and then sang and played games," Kilpatrick said. "The only light we had was oil lamps and candles."

Christmas in Cataloochee Valley was much the same as elsewhere according to Raymond Caldwell, who lived there for 15 years in the old Jessie Palmer house on what was known then as Indian Creek. "We got the same as most everyone else for Christmas; an orange, peppermint candy, and a small gift of some kind," he said. "We hung stockings our mother had knit on the mantel. We made sure they were clean socks. It was all pretty primitive stuff. I enjoyed going into the fields to cut a Christmas tree that we decorated with strings of popcorn. We probably ate more than we strung." They did have some electricity, enough for a light bulb in each room and to run a small radio. "My cousin was taking an electrical class and rigged up a dynamo to run a corn grist mill near our house. They ran a line to the house, but we didn't have a refrigerator or anything like that," he said. There were eight children in his family.

"We had a celebration at the school, a program of some sort, just before Christmas. Some of the parents would come," Caldwell said. "Christmas was very quiet except sometimes the young men would run off some moonshine and have a party."

Hominy

Hominy, a close relative of grits, was a staple in the limited diets of early settlers, along with pork. Native Americans, who introduced them to growing corn and showed them how to use it for food, probably saved many from starvation.

Ruth Trantham,ninety-three, wasn't a settler and was certainly in no danger of starving, but she can tell you how to make hominy the way her mother taught her. She needed only three ingredients: dried corn, water, and lye.

"After harvest, we pulled dried corn that was left in the field. My mother always used Hickory Cane corn because it was solid white, flaky and made good hominy. The kernels were small and flat. That corn didn't round out, wasn't too thick," she said. "That was the kind of corn that people used," she said.

"I took my big old black iron pot and hung it by its handle over the charcoal and filled it with corn, water, and lye," she said. "Then you spent all day cooking it."

This was an outdoor process. The fire had to be tended closely to keep water constantly simmering and water had to be added from time to time so the pot didn't boil dry. "The lye was needed to soften that hard hull on the corn. Way back, I made lye by running water through ashes and used just a little bit. Later I could buy lye and didn't have to go to all that trouble," Trantham said. "The hulls came loose and floated on top of the water, like skim, and I just cleared those off."

"Then you washed it and washed it and washed it in clean water," she said. "When all that husk comes off the corn, you've got hominy."

"I put a little salt on it and snacked on it. I've washed many a handful to eat. I had to go to the pot and taste it to see when it was done. I cooked it until it was tender but not mushy. That night I would cook it with butter and make some cornbread. We liked to eat it with cracklin' bread, too."

It didn't take much corn to make a batch of hominy. When the outer covering softened and split, the kernels swelled, or "plumped up."

Various recipes or "receipts" call for salt and pork or such things as cream, butter and sugar, or molasses. Mixed with some meal, it was fried and eaten as bread. Making a batter for pancakes required some milk and eggs. Hominy was eaten for breakfast, at lunch, and with the evening meal. And there were times when hominy was the entire meal.

Some of our ancestors had highly valued "samp" mills and ash hoppers in their yards. The hopper was a V-shaped wooden funnel that held wood ashes. Water was run through the ashes to make lye. Samp was a name used for processed corn. The samp mill was a giant mortar and pestle constructed with a tree stump and a block of wood suspended from a tree limb that acted like a spring. The block pounded dried corn and cracked the hulls. Kernels could be used to make hominy, or pounded over and over to produce coarse meal or even a finer flour.

Trantham still has her black iron pot. "We broke the handle and my husband made another one out of wire," she said. "You had to have a black pot to boil your clothes and to make hominy."

"All-purpose" Aprons

G randma wasn't completely dressed in the morning until she donned her apron, an essential part of her wardrobe. Dresses were few, washing them was a chore, and the apron shielded her clothing.

Those ever-present aprons were an essential part of her wardrobe, not as a fashion statement, but as useful, all-purpose garments.

"An apron was more than protection for clothing," said Bonnie Hibbs of Springdale. "It was a utensil." She remembers her grandmother grabbing hot pans from the oven with her apron. She had no pads or insulated gloves.

Some were made like a pinafore, with a strap encircling the neck. When the strap wore away, the bib was pinned to the dress with two safety pins. Others simply tied around the waist. Many had pockets, like a cobbler's apron.

Cloth for aprons was often hard to come by, but feed sacks worked just fine in lieu of nicer fabric. These cover-ups were rarely bought. Like other clothing, they were sewn by hand. My grandmother, a skilled quilter, used pieced together remnants of fabric for some of her aprons. They are faded and fragile, but they are among my treasures.

"My grandmother Crawford who lived in Clay County always wore one," Nancie Mehaffey said. "The bib had a pocket for a key, and no one messed with her key." It was the cellar key, and food was stored in the cellar. "There were two other pockets," Mehaffey said. "She kept a 'wiping rag' in one to wipe perspiration from her face. Her Birch wood 'snuffing stick' went in the other. She would dip into her snuff with that stick, put snuff in her mouth and then the stick always went back in that pocket."

"Nunny was always cooking," Marilyn McDowell said, "and she always wore an apron. We talk about her often, and someone always mentions that she wiped flour from her hands on the back of the apron and it sifted all over the floor." Nunny also used an apron pocket to hold her false teeth, her grandchildren remember. When she needed them, she turned her back, grabbed her teeth and put them in her mouth.

Those aprons were used for innumerable chores. They carried chicken feed to the chicken house, eggs from the chicken house, vegetables from the garden, apples for a pie, and kindling wood for the stove. If unexpected company arrived, an apron tail could dust a lot of furniture.

They were great for wiping away a baby's tears or scrubbing a grubby face, as a hiding place for bashful children, and a cover-up for bare arms in the cold.

In my mind, I can still see my granny step out the kitchen door and flap that apron, shooing away chickens. She flapped it at flies or other winged annoyances, as well as those with two legs. "You children go on off and play and get out from under my feet," she would say.

I don't know why or when the use of aprons diminished, but that Cleaver woman on TV in the '50's always wore one. Contemplating their many uses, I could use one; one with lots of pockets, to simplify my life. One pocket could hold the phone, always off its base and buzzing from another room or another level of the house. Another could carry pad and pencil and I would cease making notes on envelopes, napkins, or whatever else is handy—and then losing them.

Grandma had good reasons for wearing her aprons from daylight to dark, most everywhere she went.

Washboards

Washboards are scarce now. Those with faded letters and other signs of wear occasionally show up in an antique store; new ones, brightly painted and useless except for decoration, are novelties. Actually, the biggest current market for this tool designed for washing clothes may be for use as a musical instrument.

The washtub, its dented sides testifying to hours of use, and the washboard once hung side by side on the springhouse wall, in my recollections. Household essentials they were, and a similar duo could be found at most any home.

Washboards appeared during the 19th century as an alternative to the old method of beating clothes on rocks and were traditionally made with a series of wooden ridges mounted in a rectangular frame, the right size to brace in a slanted position in a washtub and scrub dirty clothing. Scrub boards were no major invention, but rubbing a shirt along the corrugated surface or ridges was a vast improvement to draping it on a rock in a cold stream and beating it with a paddle. Less wear and tear on fabric, too. Children clamored for a turn to use the new contraption until, a few bruised knuckles later, each one realized that scrubbing clothes was work, not a game.

As washboards became more common and production continued into the 1900s, later versions used galvanized steel, or even glass, for the ridges. More than 15 million were produced and sold by the Columbus Washboard Company of Columbus, Ohio, from 1926–1955. After World War II ended, methods of washing clothing became more mechanized but washboards continue to be useful for various groups of people—residents of Amish communities, for one.

A list of directions eventually included with Columbus' products were humorous: "It is okay to wash laundry in cold water. Put water in the tub until 3/4 full. Put underwear into the water to soak. Rest the soap bar at the top of the board. Rub underwear (garment), over soap and then rub item vigorously on the metal (glass) rub surface (step five). Repeat step 5 until item is clean. Put shirts in water and use step 4 to clean. Wash pants the same way. Last item to wash would be your socks. Allow them to soak and then use step 5 many times. Do not discard water. Soak your feet for 20 minutes; it will feel sooo good! Dry your feet; apply foot powder, clean socks and boots. Discard dirty water, refill bucket and rinse until no soap remains. Wring out clothing items and pin on clothesline to dry. We hope your laundry days are warm and breezy."

The music-making potential of the washboard was recognized early on by a people hungry for musical instruments. Its surface was strummed, sometimes with thimble-capped fingers or with spoons, by old-time musicians or jug bands. A whisk broom brushed on the board also produces interesting sounds.

If "Panhandle Pete," also known as Eddie Nash, was still alive, Canton's Labor Day audiences would be tapping their toes to the rhythm of his washboard and other paraphernalia carefully rigged together to form his one-man band. And a youthful Joe Sam Queen would probably still be shadowing every booming, clanging step taken by this local phenomenon.

Musical washboards, some with bells, whistles, or even small cymbals attached, have gone big-time now. There are concerts, conventions, and other events devoted to bands that rely on the unusual instrument.

Wood Stoves

Wood-fired cook stoves drew families to old-time kitchens with their warmth and the aromas of cooking food. Burning wood crackled every now and then in the firebox and perfumed the air with a hint of wood smoke. For many, memories of those kitchens evoke an accompanying sense of security, a sense of home, a step back into a simpler world.

Versatile, the stoves went beyond cooking food. Reservoirs on one side were the only source of hot water, and steaming kettles on the cooking surface added moisture to dry air. Warming bins across the top often yielded a snack.

"I grew up with one," said Wayne Griffith. "I chopped wood for the fire. It may be all in my head, but food cooked on a wood stove seems to taste better. Food cooks slower. People would cook a big pot of beans almost all day long. And that's how Mama heated her water."

"My mother and grandmother set their bread and leftover bacon in warming drawers. It was always warm," he said.

"My grandmother, Claudette Huskey, had a big family to feed. Watching her cook on that big wood stove was amazing to me. My grandparents never had electricity."

Griffith and his wife Jane have a small wood stove in their kitchen, "mostly for looks."

"That stove saved us during the blizzard in 1993. The power was off for days and we cooked on it and stayed warm," he said.

Throughout the early 1900s, the wood stove was an essential for every home. Actually, it was a simple piece of equipment. The firebox was on one side, and opened from the front and the top. Wood and kindling placed there was ignited and the fire heated the stove top, the oven, and water in the reservoir. "Eyes" were round openings in the top with covers that could be lifted by using a special tool that did not get hot and burn hands. Ovens had a temperature gauge on the front. A stovepipe carried smoke outside the house. Some were very basic, while others were ornate.

Learning to cook on a wood stove requires practice. With no knobs to turn, no temperature regulators, moving pots away from or closer to the fire and a watchful eye on the oven's contents are necessary. Canning fruit and vegetables during the summer is hot work.

My grandmother's stove was green enamel, with two warming compartments on top. A blue and white percolator, possibly graniteware, bubbled and burped on one eye. A thermometer was centered on the oven door, and the firebox was on the left.

My brother John, an engineer, was more interested than I in how it worked. "It was a Warm Morning brand," he remembers. "Granny would open a door beneath the firebox, and shake the grates to make the ashes fall into a pan below to be emptied outside. There were bars below the warmer and on the oven door to hang towels to dry. She saved the ashes to make soap." Someone had connected a large copper water tank to the stove to heat larger quantities of water. Stove wood was always stacked in the adjoining well house. Her pots may have been enamel, but her skillets were always black.

"I watched her in the morning, open the door to the firebox and lay a fire. She took the top off the firebox to stir the fire. She always had an apron tied around her waist and she used it to wipe her hands." John remembers. Our grandfather cooked, too, but only thin cakes of cornbread to feed his bear dogs.

"Today's younger generation wouldn't know how to lay a fire," Griffith said. "That might be useful knowledge some day. I am teaching my grandchildren to fire up the wood stove."

Wood-burning cook stoves are available for purchase now, and some cooks prefer them to electric or gas ranges.

Food from Hard Work, Not the Supermarket

Supermarkets are swamped with shoppers these days if a weather forecaster mentions even the slightest possibility of snow. We leave our warm houses and drive to a warm grocery store in a warm car, returning laden with bags of food for freezers, refrigerators, and shelves. We are spoiled.

There was a time in these mountains when supermarkets didn't exist. Roads were little more than muddy, rutted paths and transportation was by foot or for a fortunate few, horse and sled or wagon, even if a store was available. There were no labels to read, no coupons to clip, and no ads for comparing prices.

After talking with old-timers for almost two years now and recording their words, I have learned a lot about hard work, ingenuity, and survival.

"We made do," has been an oft-heard statement.

Their primitive supermarkets were close to home: smokehouses, corn cribs, spring houses, pits in the ground, root cellars, rafters, crocks, and sacks.

Produce was heaped in pits, resting on layers of straw and protected by an upper layer of more straw, soil, or brush. Some were topped by a haystack. Potatoes, turnips, onions, and upside-down cabbages are said to have kept well in their underground storage space. Beans labeled orally as "leather britches," or "shuckies" were strung on thread to hang from rafters and walls. How many beans do you have to dry to last a winter?

Apples were piled in apple houses and root cellars. Apples, peaches, pears, whatever was available, were dried and many recall eating "some mighty good pies" filled with dried fruit.

Hog-killing time was one of the year's most important events, and very little of the slaughtered animal was wasted. Lard was rendered from fat, hams were cured by several methods, and meat was ground into sausage. Skin, head, brains, and intestines were scraped, cleaned, boiled, and seasoned to emerge as cracklings, chitlins, pickled pigs' feet, livermush, and souse meat. A smokehouse for storing meat, no matter how crude, was an essential building.

Pork might be supplemented with fresh meat from bear, deer, squirrels, and rabbits.

Crowing Hens and Other Superstitions

"A whistling girl and a crowing hen are sure to come to some bad end." Or, "A whistling woman and a crowing hen will frighten the Devil out of his den."

Folklore records this adage or superstition as an old proverb originating in Ireland or England. A crowing hen was believed by some to forebode evil or disaster and bring bad luck.

A Crowing Hen....

Laura Singleton Moore of Bethel took it seriously, creating a vivid memory for grandchild Linda Moore Nye.

Nye's father, the late Dr. Roy Moore, took his wife and their three young children to his mother's home in Bethel every week for Sunday dinner. Linda remembers one Sunday in the early '40s in particular. Not finding her grandmother in the house, Nye ran outside.

Laura Moore, a large woman who was always clad in long dress and equally long apron, was holding a chicken by the neck on the chopping stump by the coop, hatchet in hand. "I asked her why she was killing the chicken when she already had fried chicken ready," Nye said.

Whap! Nye fled as the body of the beheaded chicken flopped around, as they do.

"She explained to me later that the hen was crowing instead of cackling and that meant it was a bad chicken, bad luck, and had to be killed," Nye said. "I have never forgotten it," she said. "I may have thrown up, but I can't remember."

Coincidentally, Nye's sister Barbara Pless of Wilkesboro, who did not witness the beheading, has recently seen a program on chickens reporting that a tumor can cause a hen to crow,. Apparently, the phenomenon isn't all that rare and results from hormonal changes, infections, or tumors in domestic fowls.

Harper's New Monthly Magazine wrote about superstitions in an April 1882 edition. Upon hearing a hen crowing, a farmer reminded his wife that it "betokened misfortune", according to the account. She laughed that morning, but in the afternoon her sister, four children, servant, and poodle arrived with two large trunks to spend the summer. She became a believer of the crowing hen omen, her farmer husband said. "They nearly ate us out o' house and home."

The two-legged egg producers, justifiably maligned or not, have inspired many old sayings that endure. "Running around like a chicken with its head cut off is one." Another, "money (or whatever) is as scarce as hen's teeth."

Our ancestors packed more than clothing when they crossed the ocean bound for America. They brought along their old customs, adages and superstitions, sharing them with others when they got here.

I can't vouch for the idea that a crowing hen with out-of-control hormones is a portentous omen, but I developed a strong aversion to chickens at an early age when one flogged me quite thoroughly on top of my head. Like Nye, I have never forgotten it.

Other widely observed superstitions target New Year's Day.

New Year's Day

"Pass the black-eyed peas. Don't forget the collard greens and hog jowls. And that cornbread looks mighty good." Ham might be substituted for hog jowls.

Supper table conversations throughout the Southern Appalachians have echoed these requests for many years. The long-held belief is that these foods assure good luck and prosperity for the coming New Year.

Black-eyed peas are the essential part of the meal. Greens alone won't do the trick. Eating peas for luck is thought to date from the Civil War. Originally planted to feed livestock and later as a staple for southern slaves, few supplies were available in the unsettled South and the peas kept both people and animals alive.

Some add a shiny penny or dime to the pot of peas. The person receiving a serving that includes the coin gets the best luck. Joe Bob Fish, sixty-eight, of Canton remembers his mother, Clara Lou Fish, and her mother, Hester Welch, always stirred a coin in the peas. "That goes as far back as I can remember," he said. "My grandmother died about twenty years ago. I don't know if they did that to make everyone eat their peas or if they believed it brought good luck, but they always did it. We ate creasy greens and cracklin' cornbread, too, and the whole family got together. My grandmother really believed in the old customs."

Traditionally, it was thought that what you did and ate on New Year's Day affected your luck for an entire year. Making your way through the day could be compared to maneuvering through a mine-field, if you honor all the timeworn traditions.

Our roots are showing in most all our holiday traditions.

Drovers' Travel

The Buncombe Turnpike bore little resemblance to today's interstate system, but it enabled our ancestors in the mountains of Western North Carolina to sell surplus crops and livestock for much-needed cash.

Captain Hack Hargrove of Pigeon Valley was among those who made difficult treks to distant lowland markets and left scribbled notes of his experiences. Carroll Jones, my cousin, has written an account of our great-grandfather's journeys down the turnpike based on those scrib-blings, from which we get a glimpse into the drovers' world and gain insight into the importance of the Turnpike.

"In 1827 the Buncombe Turnpike was completed, linking Greeneville, TN with Greenvlle, SC...served for more than fifty years as the primary artery of transportation...opened up the mountains to outsiders wishing to engage in commerce in a region hitherto inaccessible," Jones wrote. "Of more importance to the local mountaineer farmers, this road provided the means by which their surplus farm crops and livestock could be transported and sold or bartered at distant lowland markets."

Hargrove's life changed in 1861 with onset of the Civil War. After four long years of fighting, he returned to Pigeon Valley and recommenced his annual market journeys down the Buncombe Turnpike. The road was in deplorable condition from use by troops and neglect compared to its pre-war state. Thick timber planks that once covered or "corduroyed" the road were rotted and washed out, but it was still serviceable and useful to the mountain farmers and merchants—and to Hack Hargrove, Jones said.

Hack became a teacher and farmer, living with his wife Nannie Cathey in Pigeon Valley of Haywood County, where they raised corn and wheat crops. Currency was scarce, causing the farmers to use a portion of their surplus corn and wheat yields to barter for goods and services locally. But the returns for these valuable crops were much higher in Greenville or Augusta—high enough that Hack and his neighbors could justify the long arduous trip there each fall.

On November 17, 1870 Hack set out on a trip to the market in Augusta, Georgia with an entourage of helpers, a covered wagon loaded with grain products and apples, and a collection of livestock including swine, cattle, and turkeys, returning a month later on December 17.

From the Pigeon Valley Hack would have led his procession down an existing county roadway, which generally followed the route of today's NC 110, to the village of Pigeon River (Canton) near where they would have encountered the Western Turnpike, the primary east–west route through the Western North Carolina mountains. Completed around 1850, this vital thoroughfare connected Asheville with Waynesville and points further to the west.

This turnpike snaked eastward through Newfound Gap and followed the course of Hominy Creek into today's Candler and Enka areas, continuing east by the fashionable health resort hub of Sulfur Springs and across the French Broad River at Sandy Bottom into Asheville. From Asheville he would have rolled onto the Buncombe Turnpike and headed due south, passing through the villages of Hendersonville and Flat Rock, and travelling across the Green River. A treacherous descent of the mountains through Butt Gap and Saluda

Gap followed in order to reach Traveler's Rest and the Greenville areas, according to Jones.

The Poinsett Bridge, recognized as an historic site in mountains above Travelers Rest, South Carolina is constructed of rock, and is a picturesque reminder of drovers' travels.

GRIST MILLS

Indispensable
Grist Mills

Water rushing through the confines of the raceway splashed and sloshed, rotating the waterwheel on the gristmill; a mesmerizing sight and sound if you watched it awhile. In contrast, the interior of the mill vibrated and groaned as corn was crushed into meal by the heavy, circling millstone. Chaff from the corn floated in the air, coating surfaces and people with its distinctive odor and dust.

Visions of cornbread hot cakes smeared with butter or crumbled into a glass of milk (a frequent supper menu item), coupled with relief that they were free of the tedious job of grinding corn into meal by hand, may have filtered through the minds of those waiting for their meal. Besides, the wait provided a chance to visit, tell tales, and swap knives, since mills were often gathering places.

As Haywood's population increased, enterprising farmers with property near a fast-flowing source of water realized that water-powered grist-mills could grind their corn more easily and bring in some extra money.

During the late 1700s and early 1800s several mills were built in Haywood, eventually dotting the various communities of the county.

Historian Clark Medford named many of the mills, opining that Thomas Hemphill's mill on Hemphill Creek was probably one of the first, built in the late 1700s. His listing, with my additions, includes others built around the turn of the century: Welch's above Waynesville, Love's at Waynesville, Bradshaw's (later Davy McCracken's) on lower Crabtree Creek, Cook's in Dutch Cove, Blaylock's at Bethel, Noland's and Joseph Lusk's on Fines Creek, Howell's below Waynesville, Jacob

Owen's at Cove Creek, Joe Cathey's at Forks of Pigeon, Worley's on Beaverdam, Clyde Roller Mill owned by J. L. Morgan, and an unnamed one on upper Jonathan Creek.

Tanna Timbes inherited her family's Francis Mill on US 276, outside Waynesville. The deteriorating building, still standing and with water-wheel attached, was built in 1887. It is being renovated by the Francis Mill Preservation Society.

Jean Trantham Littlejohn remembers her embarrassment on Saturday mornings when she drove an open jeep carrying corn to Rhodarm-er's Mill, a motor-driven operation known earlier as Garden Creek Mill, outside Canton, waiting there during the grinding. She also remembers Thompson's Mill on the Pigeon River near Thickety with its stenciled sacks for meal and flour.

Those indispensable old mills were sturdily built of wood, often with a rock foundation. The building had to withstand heavy vibrations as well as occasional floods.

Wooden raceways carried water from dammed-up creeks or rivers, dumping their load into waterwheels. The turning wheel activated the millstones, some of which were fashioned of local stone. Pulleys and belts necessary to the operation were made of hand-tanned leather. Gates on the raceways closed off the flow of water when the mill wasn't operating.

"Pounding mills" preceded grist mills. Built on the principle of pounding or grinding corn or grain by hand with mortar and pestle, the water-powered mill, eliminated the laborious, time-consuming task of pounding by manual labor.

The builder made do with what he had, only timber and an axe, to erect the crude pounding or "tub" mill on a creek. The hand-wrought assemblage of the rustic mill, seen in an old photo among my father's memorabilia, defies an accurate description. The weary-looking man standing alongside his handiwork could be an engineer in today's world.

A primitive process, to be sure, but it worked. The ingeniousness of the builder is apparent.

A small mill powered by hand came later, a slight improvement but still a very slow process. A larger mill operated by horsepower would be a bigger improvement later on.

The Francis Grist Mill

The millstones at the Francis Grist Mill have languished for the past thirty-three years while the building that houses them has slowly deteriorated, seemingly destined for oblivion.

During the summer of 2004, evidence that the mill was receiving an infusion of new life became apparent. The building was stabilized and beams, posts, and siding were replaced, the flume was rebuilt, and a missing porch was restored. Inside, original equipment that runs the mill was also receiving attention. Major repairs required in the building's restoration took six weeks (two weeks each summer for three years) with the help of many volunteers.

On April 26, 2008 the mill marked its 121 years of existence and its renovation with the production of 150 pounds of corn meal. For Tanna Timbes, owner of the mill and its surrounding property, seeing the result of the volunteers' determination to restore the mill was an emotional experience.

"Living next door, I would stand in my living room window looking at the mill and wondering how we could restore it," she said. "My job, as a child, was to sweep out the mill. Chaff covered everything so I swept it down through the many holes in the floor and watched it float into the machinery room below wondering if my grandfather, Pappy, was going to fuss at me!"

William Francis, Timbes' ancestor, built the 19th century mill, completing it in 1887. An accomplished carpenter, he used yellow poplar, oak, and hemlock thought to have been harvested from his property to construct the building and its original waterwheel. The millstones were shipped from Richmond, Indiana. A diversion dam of logs caught the flow of a creek rushing down the mountain, creating a pond from which water could be released to power the mill before being returned into the creek to travel on for other farms.

By adding decorative touches above the doors and windows and underneath the eaves, William Francis succeeded in making his building unique. Another unusual feature is his inclusion of a "water table," a board that juts out above the "water apron" to protect it from excessive water damage. "It is what we would call a drip cap," Tanna said.

Her memories include making mud pies from residue in the flume, further underscoring the importance of the mill to a young girl growing up.

For eighty-nine years, folks living in the Francis Cove community carried corn and wheat to Francis Mill to be ground into meal and flour, until the millstones were stilled in 1976. Translating that time span into numbers of cakes of cornbread, loaves of bread, cakes and pies is incalculable.

A gathering place for those who lived in the community, news was exchanged while corn and wheat were ground. One might say that the mill provided food for the soul as well as for the body.

William Francis' son Monteville Pinkney Francis inherited the mill from his father, and in 1914, replaced the wooden wheel with one made of steel. Upon the death of M. P. Francis, his son Dewey V. Francis assumed responsibility for operation of the mill until he died in 1976. Ownership then passed to Dewey's daughter, Hester Ann Francis Boone, whose dream of restoring the mill was unattainable due to the untimely death of her husband and personal health problems, Timbes relates.

Today, Hester's daughter, Tanna Timbes, owns the mill. In 2003, she founded the Francis Mill Preservation Society (FMPS), and sent out the word that help was needed. The response she received astounded her. "Without the help of volunteers and business owners who donated materials, this (renovation) would not have happened, she said." She also gives credit to Heritage Conservation Network in Boulder, Colorado (HCN), which specializes in restorations all over the world. The group agreed to help with the restoration and was instrumental in the (FMPS) receiving several grants that made the restoration possible.

FRANCIS GRIST MILL

The Francis Grist Mill Diary

This diary belongs to Francis Grist Mill, on US 276, just outside Waynesville, North Carolina.

1976-2004: Getting old is not for sissies. My joints creak, the waterwheel won't turn, and part of a wall has fallen down. My gears are probably frozen in place. I long for the days when I was useful, grinding corn and wheat to keep my people fed.

2004: Who are these people, looking at me, making notes? One fellow said he was with the Heritage Conservation Network in Boulder, Colorado. New beam and posts? Siding? Unstable? I could have told them that and more.

July, 2004: They are back with more people and some of them look familiar. One man lives just up the road and little Tanna (Timbes), who swept my floor, is all grown up. Why do they have all those tools and equipment? I hope they aren't here to pull my gear teeth!

July, 2004: It has been a busy two weeks since HCN began this workshop. I am stable again! A new sill beam rests where the old one was rotting away, and five new posts have replaced the old ones. These people have spent hours cutting and chiseling mortises and tenons. That huge machine called a crane had to lift the 26-foot sill beam and get it in place! Nineteen volunteers from nine states and Sweden spent 1,800 hours beginning my restoration, not including some forty others who brought food, drinks, and manpower.

July 2005: They are back for another two-week workshop! Some of them are earning college credit for putting me back together. I wonder if they know that some of the folks around here, volunteers with Francis Mill Preservation Society, have been spending hours working on my facelift.

These good people repaired the support beams under my heavy millstones, put more new posts on my east wall, repaired joist ends, installed new floor joists and new floor planks for the machine room floor, and were so careful that the new was like the old. The siding and battens on my south side were reinstalled and I have new siding on the east wall. Before they left, they restored some of my fascia and eave moulding. This year the sixteen volunteers included four returnees from Ohio, Michigan, Florida, and Texas, along with other students from Michigan, Georgia, and North Carolina. Add to that an additional thirty-five who came with food and power equipment.

July 2006: Repairs to my structure are finished and I am now stable, completely enclosed, and watertight. Bridge timber that supports my heavy millstones has been repaired, the siding on my front wall has been replaced, and they are beginning to reconstruct the flume that collapsed in 1980 under a heavy snow. Flume tower foundations have been excavated and poured and five are completed. Volunteers will finish the flume. Eighteen mill volunteers were here, three returning for the third year. Others were from Florida, Michigan, Texas, and North Carolina.

Again, thirty-five other volunteers ran errands, fed everyone, and brought needed materials.

June 22–24, 2007: My new steel waterwheel has been installed by nine FMPS volunteers and a crew from the Water Wheel Factory in Franklin, North Carolina.

Luckily, I still have much of my original equipment, such as stones, overhead belts and pulleys, wooden gears, and a variety of grinders. With new belts, it all still works with the help of John Lovett, a millwright hired to get everything in working order.

July 2007: The flume box has been installed and it is handsome. Volunteers from FMPS, Raven Road Builders and Plemmons Plumbing have refurbished the milldam and connected the wooden flume to the pond with an underground pipe.

September 22, 2007: The waterwheel turned during the 2nd Annual Music at the Mill!

April 26, 2008: I ground 150 pounds of corn meal!

I feel like my old self again—ready to work! I surely have a long list of thank you notes to write, including those who financed my return to good health; the Steele Reese Foundation, Society for Preservation of Old Mills, Terrence Mills Preservation Fund, James McClure Clark Foundation, Janirve Foundation, MAST General Store, Society for Industrial Archaeology, and the Haywood County Community Foundation. This has truly been a community project!

A STITCH IN TIME...

Feed-sacks Clothing

More than fifty years have gone by since women shopped in farm supply stores or at gristmills for fabric from which to sew clothing and other household needs. Even then, they did not browse through neatly stacked bolts of cloth, but through stacks of filled feed sacks. Garments fashioned from this cotton fabric had to do with thrift, availability, and choice.

"There were four girls in my family. When it was your turn to get a new dress, you got to go to the mill with Dad and pick out the color for your dress. I always picked red," said Doris Powell. After corn was ground into meal at the grist meal, it was poured into feed sacks.

More than a few wore clothing sewn from flour or feed sacks— dresses, shirts, undergarments, and nightgowns—especially during the Great Depression in the 1930s, although evidence indicates that the practice began well before the Depression and continued after World War II. During the '40s the economy began to improve, but the need for war supplies discouraged the manufacture of many items destined for civilian consumption. Using feed sacks for sewing was one way to show patriotism.

Barrels, wooden boxes, and some tin and pottery containers were initially used for shipping and storing foodstuffs, but in the 1800s these containers were gradually replaced by cotton sacks. Companies that made the sacks eventually realized that material in solid colors, then later in patterns, was a marketing tool.

Ninety-one year old Mary Collins of Clyde liked to sew, unlike her mother. She demonstrated her talent early on when she began making her mother's dresses, and then those for herself and her three sisters. Admiring her work, others began requesting that she sew for them.

"Using feed sacks was popular at that time. We thought it was fun to select our own patterns. It was interesting back in those days when you didn't waste anything," Collins said. "At least two matching (100-pound) sacks were needed for a dress, more if you had a pattern to match up or a large size."

"We washed the sacks until all the stiffening was gone before cutting out the pattern. The cloth wore good and did up nice, and the dresses lasted quite awhile. Using a light starch, they ironed very well," she said. "Some were nice enough to wear to church or as party dresses."

Sack patterns were mostly flowers, she said, but there were a few checks or prints of different objects in various colors. Her attitude explains the demand for her sewing skills. "People were doing the best they could do. When it was the best they could do, you wanted it to look good," Collins said. "Things were hard to come by and they were always proud of their dresses and enjoyed wearing them."

In the absence of plastic, cellophane, foil, and the variety of fabrics used today, feed and flour sacks were used for anything and everything: pillow cases, sheets, aprons, dish towels, dusting cloths, bibs, diapers, woven rugs, and quilts. The durable, adaptable sacks strained milk or juice, covered a cooling pie, stuffed a crack, lifted hot objects, carried a lunch, polished furniture, cleaned the stove or table, and scoured and scrubbed.

Labels printed on some sacks created humorous situations. The story is told of an otherwise dignified lady seen bent over pulling weeds in her garden along NC 110. Unbeknownst to her, her position revealed her underwear—stamped with Yukon's Best. Before the advent of patterned sacks, attempts to completely remove the labels printed on sacks weren't always successful.

Powell remembers her first red dress fashioned with a gathered skirt. She favored a boy in her grammar school class and wanted to catch his attention by twirling around so the full skirt would flare into an unrevealing but eye-catching circle of fabric. " It worked," she said.

Functional Quilts

Quilts, one of the most visible and colorful symbols of our heritage, are prized possessions.

The stories they could tell if we could trace the origins of individual pieces!! Fabric scraps may have been a favorite dress, a feed sack, a necktie, a curtain, a worn jacket. Perhaps one was stitched as a wedding gift; another might have covered the bed of a grandchild.

Quilting in today's world is often considered an art form, but, early on, they were a necessity. Simple and functional, they provided warmth.

With fireplaces the only source of heat in a house, bedrooms could be quite cold. My cousin remembers slipping into bedclothes in front of the fire, then grabbing his discarded clothing and dashing up the steps to a cold bed. Sleepers huddled under layers of quilts, if they had them.

And in days filled from sunrise to sunset with toil, piecing a quilt could have been a welcome diversion, a method of self-expression, Perhaps they provided some decoration for otherwise drab and sparsely-furnished houses.

Folding one of my grandmother's quilts, I see her tiny stitches and a multitude of fabric bits, some solid colors, some patterned. The origin of each piece of cloth, gathered together, could surely tell many stories. She designed and made it in 1949 to be auctioned as a fundraiser for her church, Piney Grove United Methodist.

Quilting was more a matter of saving money than art. Women were making something necessary for their household and needed to make them as efficiently as possible. They were painstakingly sewn together in bits of time sandwiched among the demands of mothering, cooking, gardening, and other chores.

Romanticized views of making quilts have women quilting by the fire at night as well as gathering for quilting bees that alternated collective stitching with huge meals and square dancing. Truth is, quilting by the light of a fire or the dim glow of an oil lamp would have been very difficult. Few families had houses large enough to accommodate a quilt frame and large groups of people. I suspect that quilting gatherings happened in later years, in larger houses with more adequate lighting.

The shadowy memory of a young child recalls my grandmother with sisters and friends sitting around a quilt frame suspended in the dining room, stitching and visiting. I always wondered what they had done with the long dining room table.

Lou Anne Cogburn of Cruso was putting some finishing touches on a quilt sewn by Cruso Friendship Club for this year's Hospice raffle quilt. "We just finished the Hospice quilt," she said. "They asked us to make it this year." The group is also crafting a quilt for the raffle at Cruso Community Center's annual Quilt Show, held the fourth weekend in August.

Her mother-in-law, the late Nina Cogburn, taught her to quilt. Nina had a quilting frame, a rectangular wooden one. It initially hung from the ceiling, but later it was tied to ladder-back chairs. She quilted during wintertime, passing her creations on to family members.

Lou Anne named a few of the old quilt patterns that have passed down through the years: Double Wedding Ring, Grandmother's Fan, Dutch Girl, Dutch Boy, Nine Patch, Ohio Star, Log Cabin, Dresden Plate, Lone Star, Dahlia, Butterfly, Sunbonnet Sue, Flower Basket, Bow Tie, and Sampler.

"Flower Garden is an old pattern that is still popular. Jacob's Ladder is another old one," she said. "String Quilts are made of narrow, left over pieces, whatever size you've got. People had to use whatever they had and never wasted anything. They used to make quilts from feed sacks. Small scraps were often used to make Crazy Quilts, too." Cogburn explained that many quilts feature decorative stitches, embroidery, and appliqués.

Mildred Pharr of Cruso is another talented, prolific quilter. One afternoon she showed me dozens of quilts she had made, most of which she would give away, a virtual rainbow of quilts. Much of our time was spent looking at her Underground Railroad quilt, with her explaining what each block was supposed to indicate to fleeing slaves. The story is that ten different quilts, hung one at a time on a fence, directed slaves to take different actions. The Monkey Wrench indicated they should prepare the tools, including actual, mental, and spiritual, for their long journey. Bear's Paw meant they should take a mountain trail, out of sight, and to follow bear tracks to find food and water. Flying Geese pointed in a direction to follow, while Drunkard's Path directed them to create a zig-zag path, not walk in a straight line. Bow Tie advised them to change clothing, use a disguise. Log Cabin meant seek shelter. Although historians differ on whether such a system existed, the quilts are interesting.

QUILT PATTERNS   EHB

Versatile
Feed Sacks

The versatile feed sack was indispensable from its inception during the early 1900s and provided some colorful variety in an otherwise drab-looking existence.

Clothing and other household necessities made of feed sacks have historically been considered a byproduct of the dark days of the Great Depression. While the two marched hand in hand during that era, an altered image emerged when Louella Stringfellow of Clyde shared feed sack memorabilia from her extensive collection as well as the fruits of her research on this icon of Americana. Their use predated the Depression and continued long afterwards. Other fabric was expensive and often not easily available.

Delicate pastels in a multitude of tiny pieces, stitched into a bay leaf pattern quilt, adorned the wide, time-worn boards of the 215-year-old Shook House in Clyde as she verbally traced the evolution of feed sacks. She illustrated her words with frequent references to the displays of items sewn years ago from the fabric. Curtains hung in the windows and cloth was stacked on a table. An old-timey sunbonnet sported a cheerful flower pattern. The little girl who wore the meticulously fashioned dress with a contrasting, tucked inset on the bodice was surely well-dressed.

The feed sack story began in the early 1800s when grain, seed, and food were packed for shipping and storage in tins or heavy boxes and barrels. Tin rusted; wooden containers were easily damaged, difficult to transport and certainly not waterproof. Hand-sewn sacks were not strong enough to carry heavy loads. Invention of stitching machines in the 1830s brought change when chain-stitched seams became strong enough to hold contents in a canvas bag during transport. Mills began weaving inexpensive cotton feedbags, Stringfellow related. The sturdier sacks were easier to handle and could be draped over a horse's back.

Realizing the popularity of the plain, unbleached cotton bags with thrifty housewives undeterred by the fact that they couldn't effectively eliminate logos printed on the cloth, manufacturers introduced solid color and later colorful print sacks minus the printed labels. The design business became competitive, resulting in more than 40,000 different patterns, Stringfellow said.

Feed sack fabrics became colorful with pretty patterns, thanks to savvy suppliers looking for more profits. Border prints for pillowcases, curtains, and skirts were created, along with pre-printed patterns for dolls, stuffed animals, appliqués, and quilt blocks.

"Whatever was going on in America at the time was reflected in fabric patterns," she said, "World War II, the popularity of Margaret Mitchell's novel *Gone with the Wind*, the characters newly created by Walt Disney."

Theme prints echoed not only Walt Disney but also Davy Crockett, Cinderella, the Old West, story books, nursery rhymes, comic books, and eventually, movies. Seasonal prints were well-liked, especially at Christmas. So were scenic or travel prints.

"I begged my mother to empty flour from the sack imprinted with the doll pattern, so she could make that doll for me," Stringfellow said. "When I went to the first grade, I wanted to play on the monkey bars during recess but wouldn't until I saw another child with underwear like mine, underwear stamped with the name of a milling company. She became my best friend."

Coarse thread or string used to stitch the sacks was also useful. "We always had some wound in a big ball," Stringfellow said. "It was useful for quilting, tatting, crocheting, and knitting. We used it for anything that needed to be tied up."

John Burress of Bethel remembers using the thread to make toys. "We tied rubber strips to forked sticks with that string to make slingshots," he said.

Four sacks were required to make a sheet. Sleeping on the sheets was fine, Stringfellow said, unless there were three people in the bed. "I had to sleep in the middle many times," she said. "The heavy (commercially made) stitches were always in the middle and those seams hurt."

Feed sacks were being produced and used for home sewing as late as the 1960s, but sanitation became an issue and their use as containers for flour, sugar and other foodstuffs was discontinued, according to Stringfellow.

Bed Turning

An old-fashioned "bed turning" was once a social event, offering ladies an opportunity to invite a few friends into their homes for some much-needed companionship in a less mobile society than the one in which we live.

A bed turning also provided women an opportunity to show off handmade quilts to their friends, to display their handiwork.

Lacking large spaces in which to showcase the quilts, spaces such as the former school auditorium used by the Cruso Quilters or the Shelton House's clean barn in Waynesville, women used the most logical place available–a bed.

Correspondence with avid quilter Katrina Blankenship of Powhatan, Virginia clarified the meaning of the term bed turning. I had imagined it to be a spring-cleaning ritual during which feather beds were taken outside for airing and dusting after a long, cold winter in a small, smoky cabin.

"This term and event is spreading quickly," she said. "(It) is great for guilds of people who want to show off their quilts. Years ago, women would get together and bring all their quilts to show their friends and neighbors...they would lay them out on a bed, have refreshments and a time of fellowship and turn the quilts (fold them over) and talk about the pattern, fabrics, the quilting of each."

"Quilts on a wall seem like 'art' and quilts lying on a bed seem more utilitarian, warm and cozy," she said.

Conversation would surely have centered on the various quilt patterns, the fabrics used, and the length of time taken to assemble each quilt. You can be certain that stitches would be closely examined to see if they were evenly spaced and neatly done.

Patterns could have included Log Cabin, Dresden Plate, Double Wedding Ring, Grandmother's Fan, Bread Basket, or even a Crazy Quilt.

PAPER MILL GROWS, NURTURES A TOWN

The Roots of a Paper Mill and the Town of Canton Are Entwined

C anton and the paper mill known as the Champion Fibre Company grew together. Peter G. Thomson chose the location for his new mill for its natural resources—timber and water. He chose exceptionally wisely when he sent his son-in-law to oversee the building and operation of the plant and to interact with a third natural resource—the potential workforce.

Future employees of the mill were primarily farmers who set their own working hours and were unaccustomed to regular paychecks. Proud, hardworking people lacking formal education, as a rule, they were capable, often ingenious.

Robertson demonstrated sincere affection, appreciation and respect for these mountain men and women who would eventually work in the mill and they, in turn, appreciated and respected him. He took large steps, as seen in the following accounts, to assure their successful transition to a different way of life. He had good business sense, of course, but he sincerely cared for his adopted community and its people. He walked amongst them.

Champion President Reuben B. Robertson

R euben B. Robertson stood tall in Haywood County; as tall, figuratively, as fir trees cut for Champion's pulpwood.

His impact on this county and beyond was enormous.

Born in Cincinnati, Ohio, in 1879, a graduate of Yale University and University of Cincinnati Law School, he met a man named Peter G. Thomson who would change the direction of his life and, in the process change Haywood County. Thomson was a client of the law firm where Robertson was a partner.

Robertson married Thomson's daughter Hope in 1905, and soon after was sent to Haywood County to handle legalities of a paper mill being built by Thomson. His wife and daughter joined him, and they never left. Reuben B., as he was affectionately called, supervised every step of the building of the mill and eventually became general manager of Champion Fibre Company. Through the following years, he climbed the corporate ladder to the position of president and chairman of the board.

Those of us who knew him from afar regarded him as a benevolent grandfather who took good care of the mill, the town, and especially the people. Those who knew him on a personal basis agree. Under his leadership, the paper mill had no worker's union because it was not needed.

Reuben B. was sincerely interested in this community and its people, according to C. W. Hardin, a retiree who was Champion's official photographer. Accessible, his office door was always open. He was a philanthropist and a humanitarian. "He was one of the best-loved and most well-known men who ever lived in Haywood County and undoubtedly one of the nicest men I ever met. He was a first class gentleman who was fine to everybody.... always a decent person, always cooperative, kind and giving."

As the mill prospered under his leadership, the Haywood County area prospered. With good wages, good benefits and steady employment, employees were able to improve the quality of their lives and, most important, educate their children beyond high school.

Canton could offer its citizens more services, fueled by the mill's tax base and hefty contributions from the plant. Streets were paved. Water and sewer services were installed.

Champion was responsible for building a YMCA, a summer camp for employees' children named Camp Hope for Robertson's wife, a town library filled with books, and a company store with food, clothing and other necessities at low prices, an outgrowth of the mill's Relief Association, which assisted families in need for years. Donations to the school system included incentives for machine and welding shops to educate future workers.

During a typhoid epidemic, a small hospital was built and staffed to supplement medical care. Employees could bring their produce to a home canning building, agreeing that a portion be stored for assistance purposes. A lunchroom was built. An ambulance was donated to the American Red Cross during WWI for use overseas, and called the Champion Family Ambulance.

Wayne Carson, another retiree, offers insight into the character of this man, recounting acts of kindness. A cook at Lake Logan struggled to raise her family after her husband's death. Robertson quietly saw that her needs were met. Another employee with a large family became ill. Robertson let him know that his salary would be paid until he could return to work. They were only two among many.

Information gleaned from issues of *The Log*, the mill's monthly publication, illustrates Robertson's concern for safety. It describes safety squads, a fire brigade, and ongoing emphasis.

Anticipating times when river flow would be insufficient to operate the mill, he went to Champion's headquarters in Hamilton, Ohio and convinced the board of directors that a dam and reservoir should be built. In time, water release from Lake Logan, named for his son, was needed

Foresighted, he took great interest in conservation and forest protection when such concerns were rare. Two trees were planted for each one cut. Immediate proof of his policy can be seen around Lake Logan. Dr. Carl A. Schenck, manager of George Vanderbilt's vast forest lands, was amazed by the reforestation project, and allowed Robertson to attend his renowned school at The Cradle of Forestry, according to Carson.

Widely known for his work and his community spirit, he received the Distinguished Citizen Award from the North Carolina Citizens Association in 1957, and was named Man of the South in 1950 by *Dixie Business* magazine. A professorship at Western Carolina University and a dormitory are named in his honor.

"Mr. Champion" touched our lives and left us better off than we were.

Canton YMCA: Hub of Community

If the walls of the old Champion YMCA did not heave like an exhausted athlete's chest, they should have. The three-story brick building with its wide porch was always crowded, and something was always going on.

When Peter G. Thomson, owner of Champion Fibre Company, heard a suggestion that Canton needed a community center under the auspices of the YMCA he jumped in with both feet, becoming an enthusiastic supporter and donating a building near his pulp mill.

The "Y", opened in April 1920, was the second largest independently owned YMCA in the state. The building had a swimming pool and four bowling lanes on the lowest level, a large gym with stage, pool tables, a sitting area, and offices on the main floor, and the third floor had a kitchen and rooms for banquets, meetings, classes, or ladies' bridge clubs.

A masked carnival celebrated the first Halloween in the building, according to old records. An educational committee sponsored lyceum (lecture) courses and members were entertained with live musical programs and a magician. Plays, bridge tournaments, banquets, dances, sports, club meetings, bridal and baby showers were held there. The calendar was crowded. The Y was the center of community activity, the hub of the town.

Grover C. Suttles began as director in 1929, and kept the place jumping during his twenty-five year tenure. Elizabeth Thompson and her sister Bobbie Carter kept watchful eyes on the place and those who came and went. Jack Justice, Paul Rogers, George Price, Michael Haney, Woody Robertson, Walter Holton, Red Ivestor, German "Nazi" Miller; all familiar names, they are but a few of those involved in programs through the years.

Marie Bell, who made a piano ring, and James Haynie, with his guitar and singing voice, were also strong presences.

During WWII, the Y served as a morale booster and a place to stay busy. A Rockettes-type chorus line of young women actively entertained during those years.

Those of us who grew up in the '40s and '50s learned to swim there. Dances (mostly square dances) packed the gym every Friday night. Champion Y square dance teams for different ages evolved from those dances and cloggers traveled in and out of the state for exhibitions, competitions, and as entertainers.

Movies, bowling leagues, Tri-Hi-Y club for girls, Hi-Y club for boys, the Y's Men's Club, and Friends of the YMCA provided something for everyone.

Sports teams—baseball, basketball, and football—were organized and well coached, several times winning state titles. Those first Gray-Y teams, as they were called, had to mow lawns and sell newspapers to buy uniforms, remembers Charles Burnette.

Ross Kilpatrick went to the Y almost every day. Member of a championship football team, he recounts that the team competed in games as far away as New Jersey. "We were given the opportunity to travel, a chance we would not have had otherwise."

The Champion Y fast-pitch softball team for adults became formidable competitors and gained recognition throughout the southeast, even playing in the Softball World Series. Stands were packed when they played at home, and a faithful band of supporters followed wherever they went.

Suttles built the YMCA's summer program at Camp Hope in Cruso, used for both day camp and resident camp. The Y bus was a familiar sight, with twice daily trips to the camp. In fact, the entire town used the camp for picnics and other get-togethers.

Champion employees and their families had access to the YMCA at no cost. Others paid a $2.00 membership fee.

Gray-Y teams packed and delivered Christmas baskets. "That made a big impression on a lot of us. We realized how much we did have," said Charles "Skeeter" Curtis.

Looking back at the hours he spent at the Y, Curtis said it best. "It was friendships, being with each other, staying there all day. I don't know what we would have done for something to do and stay out of trouble. You had people there who seemed to take an interest in you. If you got in trouble, they approached you and tried to get you on the right track. Those who didn't have a place like that missed a lot of good things in their life."

A popular quote says, "It takes a village to raise a child." The old Y was an integral part of our village.

Camp Hope

Ever bathed and shampooed your hair in the icy water of the east fork of the Pigeon River? Trust me, it is an experience you won't forget.

Those lucky enough to spend a week or two or three at Camp Hope haven't forgotten those plunges, or the worn path through the woods paved with tree roots and small stones that led to the swimming hole.

Hardy ones jumped in quickly and swam across the pool to the big rock on the other side, gasping from the frigid shock. Couldn't swim? The late Turner Cathey tied a rope around the learner's waist so swim strokes could be practiced in the river current without the swimmer being washed away.

Camp Hope was a rustic place, and campers were treated to an outdoorsy experience; a fun-filled, forest-surrounded, friendly, unique experience.

Wooden cabins held four bunk beds each. Canvas flaps were lowered to cover screened areas if the night air was nippy, or if rain blew in and dampened the top bunks. A large, round fountain built of rock and located near the "big house" was used for washing up and brushing teeth. The bathhouse? You got it. The river. And multi-seated, unplumbed outhouses.

Morning bell rang at 6:45 a.m. Campers hurriedly dressed and filed across dew-soaked grass for flag raising and the Pledge of Allegiance, then into the "big house" for a generous, stick-to-your-ribs breakfast. Wait. What else went up with the flag? A counselor's stolen unmentionables, a tennis shoe, someone's forbidden candy stash. Innocent, giggly fun.

Days were full. Nature hikes by the river, weekly day long hikes into the mountains, fishing, swimming, games, archery, horseshoes, scavenger hunts, softball, and crafts. Lanyards woven by campers over the years, if combined, would stretch for miles. The camp bell summoned campers to eat.

Camp Hope had no outside lights and dark in the mountains was complete. In the evening, campers grabbed a flashlight to walk through darkened woods to the Counsel Circle. A rock wall, wide enough for seating, encircled the fire pit. This nighttime ritual was eagerly anticipated, a favorite part of the day.

Weiner roasts, marshmallow roasts, singing, vespers. Ghost stories. Shadows cast by the blazing fire weaving through trees, the surrounding darkness, sounds from the forest created an eerie setting. Walt Zachary and Melvin Henline teamed up, with Zachary the storyteller and Henline lurking in the woods to provide sound effects and jump out at just the right time. The woods rang with screaming children.

Days ended with the haunting sounds of "Taps" played by a musically talented counselor.

Friday nights were special. Parents visited excited campers who nervously awaited their cabin's turn to stage a skit or other entertainment for the weekly talent show. The campers planned, schemed, and practiced all week, hiding their show from the other cabins. One memorable performance featured Nancy Smathers Hall of Lake Lure as Clementine. Clomping along in someone's large brogans, true to the song, she fell into the foaming brine, a large washtub filled with water.

Frances and Dot Gidney, now Hannah and Wells, respectively, have good memories from Camp Hope. In retrospect, Frances realizes it was an adventure for her through which she was introduced to the beauty of nature and the outdoors. She learned good sportsmanship and how to get along with others and help each other, she says. "Camp Hope was a very caring, loving place with a Christian environment. I think it had a very positive influence on my life."

The camp, named for Reuben B. Robertson's wife, Hope, opened around 1924. Champion Fibre Company, at Robertson's initiative, bought twenty-five acres of land, an old farmstead. It was sixteen miles southeast of Canton, on a new road being constructed across the mountain through Pisgah National Forest. Robertson issued a challenge to people living in Canton and its vicinity. The land would be donated for a children's camp if they built a clubhouse.

The Y's Men's Club launched a successful fund raising campaign and constructed the assembly building and caretaker's home. Boulders and stones on the property and riverbank were plentiful enough for laying foundations. Work began immediately under the supervision of Champion YMCA. Canton Civitan Club built six cabins for $150 each.

Improvements stopped during the Depression, but camp went on. After WWII ended improvements resumed at a steady pace, including new rock cabins, bathhouse, tennis courts, a pavilion to extend the "big house," and a swimming pool. Out-of-state campers discovered the facility and joined the locals.

Later campers loved modernized Camp Hope as well, but those of us who knew a more primitive, rustic camp are glad we did.

Champion's Company Store

"I owe my soul to the company store," Tennessee Ernie Ford sang in his grim, coal mining recording "Sixteen Tons."

Champion Fibre Company's Reuben B. Robertson had a different viewpoint on establishing a company store for the paper mill's employees. His goal was to provide food and other necessities at reason-able prices for his employees. More than that, he hoped to encourage these mountain people, unaccustomed to receiving regular cash income, to manage their money wisely. He was aware that these workers looked upon debt as a deadly trap.

According to mill publication *The Log*, he saw this store as "a strong agent for social and commercial change in Canton, unlike traditional mill town company stores, which kept low wage workers caught in a debt trap to the company."

C. W. Hardin, Champion retiree who was Communications editor and photographer, agrees. "It was never intended to be used as a way to financially enslave employees," he said.

"The beauty of it was you could live out of the company store. You could get food, clothing, animal feed, over-the-counter drugs like castor oil, coal, kindling, wood, gasoline for your car. And you could get all this stuff delivered. I am sure it helped a lot of employees who fed and clothed their families from there," Hardin said. The store closed in the late 50s or early 60s, he believes, to make room for the number. 20 paper machine.

"Doogaloo" was the popular name for scrip negotiable only at Cham-pion's store that basically amounted to a salary advance. A round metal coin, it was bought or charged at the store office, then used to buy anything in the store.

"A variety of high quality, moderately priced goods were always avail-able and a challenge to downtown merchants' own marketing plans," *The Log* reported. A picture taken in the 1930s showed an orderly, clean, well-stocked store with bins brimming with vegetables and fruits, shelves stacked with dry goods, cans and other merchandise, and even a maga-zine rack.

Keitha Morgan Campbell worked in the company's nearby main office as did Mary Carroll Ray.

"I traded there," Campbell said. "After work, I ran over to the store, bought what I wanted to cook for supper, went home and cooked it. It was a real convenience. Their meat was always good."

"It was a nice place, a good thing to have," Ray said. "I remember that Daddy bought our Christmas gifts there. Everything was good quality." Ray recalls leaving her job in the mill office to go next door to the store for lunch. "We always went there for lunch," she said.

Especially popular was the soda fountain. "Howard Hemphill made the best chili," Campbell said. "When my son David moved away, he called me one day and asked me to get the recipe." Ask anyone what they remember about the company store and the usual reply is "Hemphill's hot dogs." He made good milkshakes, too. Older kids would make a beeline for the store's soda fountain after school before going next door to the YMCA.

A 1931 ad announced groceries, meat market, soda fountain, coal and wood yard, gas station and tires were available along with three delivery trucks with "snappy drivers," "a store crew that is hard to beat," and declared "the best is none too good for you." Another advertised oysters and fish as well as meats native and western.

Employees received a dividend from the store each year, just before Christmas. This was a refund distributed among workers for a portion or percentage of the money they had paid that year for their purchases. The dividend could be taken in cash or used as credit on accounts.

In 1932, annual trade discounts/dividends amounted to more than $20,000. Five years later, the store recorded 2,100 patrons with a trade discount amounting to $45,000.

Champion's Company Store was indeed a convenience, a fixture in a town with few places to shop, and, perhaps, a blessing for many families.

Champion Credit Union

C hampion Credit Union was organized on April 26 in 1932, conducting business in one small office inside Champion Fibre Company in Canton.

"The credit union was intended to help the little fellow who needed small loans at reasonable interest rates, people the banks couldn't help," said the late Joe Worley, manager of the institution for twelve years. "It was very conservative. Loans for big items, such as homes or cars, could not be offered at its inception."

The credit union's major accomplishments are measured in benefits to the mill's employees. The measuring stick includes notches for the number of homes built, acres of land bought, college educations financed, and vehicles purchased over the years. Notches are also there for intangibles financed for workers and their families, money for medical expenses, and other unexpected crises of various descriptions.

Mary Alice Roberts was originally the first and only employee, working part time in a small, narrow space located at the upper end of the time office, near the clock aisle inside the plant's entrance.

Eloise Evans and Georgia Ann Scroggs eventually joined her. Worley, whose father Letch was treasurer of the credit union for approximately twenty-five years, went to work there in 1953, became manager in 1977, and retired in 1989.

"We had three desks, three adding machines, an old Burroughs posting machine, and one cash box," Worley said. "We used the safe in the company's time office. We posted the payrolls and calculated dividends and interest on loans by hand."

Start-up money came from the employees themselves. To become a member, they were required to pay an entrance fee of twenty-five cents and deposit $5.00. After that, they could choose to have an amount deducted from their paychecks. A basic premise of the credit union, to promote habitual saving, was partially the reason for the fee.

One year later, mill employee Mack Harkins was quoted in *The Log*, stating that the savings and loan did more to relieve financial distress in Canton than any other organization, crediting the association with providing a definite saving plan. A poll among mill employees conducted in the late '50s or early '60s by the National Association of Credit Unions revealed that workers considered the institution the most valuable service offered to them.

Credit for instituting the credit union or coop banking goes to the younger Robertson, a man like his father Reuben B., who was motivated by more than profits earned from selling paper. Reuben Jr. learned of credit unions and their tremendous impact on employees in a chance meeting on an airplane with a fellow who was very knowledgeable about such institutions. He was so convinced that Champion workers could gain immeasurable benefits that credit unions were initiated at all three Champion paper mills, Canton, Ohio, and Texas.

Christmas Baskets

Frank "Happy" Smathers, a supervisor at Canton's Champion Fibre Company in 1928, would be gratified to know that a Christmas tradition he unknowingly began continues to flourish.

A member of his crew was diagnosed with tuberculosis that year. Dreadful news to receive at any time of the year, but hearing it just before Christmas seemed to compound its effect on the family.

Envisioning hardships imposed on the family, he and his crew pooled their money and came up with $3.00. Although this seems a small amount, it was enough at that time to purchase a good amount of food, which was gathered into a Christmas basket and delivered.

That single act of caring and compassion grew, and continues to grow, into a well-organized program of giving, funded by employee donations.

For thirty years, Smathers was president of the Christmas Basket. In 1958, the baton was passed to his son, Jack T. Smathers, president of the program until 1981.

Ownership of the paper mill has changed a few times over the years, as has its name, but those changes have not altered this long-standing tradition. Evergreen Packaging now owns Blue Ridge Paper Company.

In early years, Champion's Company Store employees filled the boxes with staples including flour, lard, and cornmeal, along with oranges and stick candy as treats, Smathers said. Deliveries were made using both company and personal vehicles.

The mill, proud of the generosity of its workers, men and women who gave personal time and money, gave the program its blessing and more. The company contributed by compensating those who spent personal time packing boxes and carrying them into the community with their regular wages, along with donating the use of company trucks, according to Smathers.

Filled boxes, usually more than 600, would line the gymnasium floor in Champion YMCA, adjacent to the company store, awaiting delivery.

In time, Canton area schools initiated a White Christmas project in conjunction with the mill program. School children brought cans of food to school, cans that also went into the boxes as supplements, Smathers said.

Male students at Canton High School assisted with deliveries, experiences that taught them life lessons. "They saw the need that existed in their communities," Smathers said. "They learned that everyone didn't have plenty. It made a big impression on them, especially the first time they participated."

Two of my classmates told of their shock and dismay at the living conditions they encountered after carrying a box to a cabin accessed by a log over a stream.

After mill expansion took the space occupied by both the Company Store and the YMCA, the National Guard Armory donated floor space for packing the boxes and continues to do so.

Company employees who saw where need existed in their home counties, primarily Haywood, Jackson, and Buncombe, named those receiving the baskets.

The Christmas Basket went beyond the food boxes. Schoolteachers submitted names of children in need of clothing and other essentials and mill workers would select children to take shopping. Area merchants like K-Mart, the old Hudson Department Store, and the Army Store, owned by the late Jack Feingold, were especially helpful, Smathers said.

Some recipients showed their gratitude in various ways. "I was walking down the street," Smathers said, "when I was stopped by a woman and her two teenage daughters. She said, 'You don't know me, but you clothed me when I was a little girl.'"

Editor's note: Current employees continue to carry the torch, making the event the longest running community assistance program in the county. Bruce Chambers heads the Christmas Basket this year and Jeff Messer, the Santa Pal. An employee, who was packing boxes as we spoke and preferred not to be named since so many mill workers are involved, spoke with immense pride as he said that 600 baskets were being filled and that 480 children will be clothed, citing K-Mart for its continuing assistance.

One might say that for many of us, Christmas and the paper mill's Christmas Basket are synonymous. The Christmas spirit is alive and well.

The Paper Mill Whistle

The mill whistle at Canton's paper plant has talked to its employees for one hundred years, setting the rhythm for their days.

Those first workers had largely regulated their days by seasons and sun, daily schedules set by most demanding tasks on the farm. Timepieces were a luxury few could afford before the mill began grinding wood and making paper, so the whistle was a necessity.

Its voice initially told them when to get up, when to go to work, when to eat lunch, and finally, when to quit for the day and let another shift take over. The twelve o'clock whistle still denotes lunchtime for those within hearing distance.

The main whistle, coupled with the wildcat whistle, has celebrated special events such as the end of World War II, granting of a permit allowing continued use of the Pigeon River, Pisgah High School's winning the state basketball championship, and the beginning of each new year. Ted Woodruff was fire marshal at the mill before he retired and knows the original schedule. "It blew at five thirty a.m. to wake people up," he said, "then at ten to seven and at seven a.m. When lunch break was an hour, it rang at noon, then ten to one p.m. and at one. The four o'clock whistle meant quitting time. After shift schedules changed, the whistle blew at twelve, twelve thirty, and three thirty. The whistle isn't blown on Sundays."

"The steam whistle now emits its deep-throated, one-pitched "whoooo" at seven a.m., noon, twelve thirty p.m., three thirty p.m.," said Danny King who works in the power plant where the manual control button is located. "Time is synchronized with Greenwich time," he said. "There are really three whistles, mounted on the roof east of the main smoke stack; the main whistle, the wildcat whistle with its variable pitches, and the old high-pitched fire whistle which today would be used only in an emergency." The wildcat is occasionally heard at noon on Saturday.

In 1905 and 1906, before the mill was complete and steam was not available to activate a whistle, an iron bell was used. The bell was mounted on a wooden shack known as the field office. After its retirement, the bell was neglected in a storage room until the late Reuben B. Robertson, chairman of Champion's board of directors, retrieved it and presented it to the Old-Timers' Club in 1955. "I rescued it from threatened oblivion and have kept it ever since, as a treasured memento of those early days," he said at the time. Wayne Carson, who heads the Old-Timers, also known as the Snug Harbor group, said if the organization ceases to exist, the bell is to be placed in the care of the Canton Area Historical Museum, according to an agreement with mill officials.

A fire in the mill was pinpointed by a code, still posted near the control button, King said. "The whistle warned employees there was a fire and told them where it was," Woodruff said. "One long blast, a pause, followed by a short blast meant fire was in the YMCA, company store, gas station and main office area. One long and two shorts meant number 20 paper machine. Six blasts and then one meant fire in the wood yard, wood preparation, and filter plant areas, and you had better move quick."

The whistle continues to talk to us. "It's time to eat." "The day is half over; I better get moving." "Check your watch." "The mill is producing paper and providing jobs." The sound is woven into the pattern of many lives. One might perceive the steam whistle as a comforting sound, a voice saying that all is well.

Ol' Mule Worked by Mill Whistle

"That mule was something else," Jack King of Canton, seventy-eight, told me. "If it was a falsehood, I would tell you. Some people will say I'm a 'liar by the clock,' but it is true."

Jack's father, the late E. L. King, was living in Sandy Mush in Buncombe County when he bought a mule from the late June Gibson of Canton. "June Gibson was a horse trader, and evidently that mule was born and raised in Haywood County," King said.

"Dad bought the mule and took it home. The next morning he got up, put it on a harness and put it in the field. It was a good mule and worked hard, but when the twelve o'clock whistle blew at the (Canton) paper mill, it stopped dead in its tracks. No amount of persuasion could get that mule to move another inch," King said.

"Dad finally took the mule off the plow and the mule went to the barn. Dad fed and watered it and let it rest. When the one o'clock whistle blew, the mule went back to the field, Dad put it on the plow and it plowed until the 4 o'clock whistle blew. Once again it stopped dead. Dad knew that mule was done for the day, King said."

"That mule was a Canton mule," he continued, "and whoever had owned it worked by the mill whistle. The mule got used to that, I guess."

"He'd work like a fiend until the whistle blew, and then you had to stop working and feed and water him. I'd lay down in the field and roll laughing."

"Dad kept him awhile, but he couldn't put up with that. He couldn't work that way, so he sold him to a man in Madison County, got him away from that mill whistle."

"We could hear the whistle clear as a bell on Sandy Mush, especially on a clear day," he said.

Did the mule have a name? "Not to my knowledge, he didn't, but that was about seventy years ago and a lot of water has run under the bridge since then," King said.

The Kings didn't hear of the mule again so its fate and working habits are unknown.

Mules have earned a deserved reputation. "Stubborn as a mule" is an oft-heard saying and obstinate people may be called mule headed. This animal lived up to expectations.

Curious about possibilities of training mules, I did a bit of research. According to what I found via the Internet, mules can be trained, and doing so is a lucrative business in some states, but none of the sites I visited electronically mentioned the use of a mill whistle. The claim is made that mules are smarter than horses and those that qualify have pedigrees.

OL' Mule

Author's note: While the mill was under construction, it was preceded by and later coexisted with logging camps to provide wood for the making of paper.

Sunburst Logging Camp, Railway

Puffs of smoke and the rhythmic clatter of wheels turning on rails announced the passage of a train huffing its way some thirteen miles from West Canton to Sunburst logging camp and back for almost twenty years, 1909–1926.

The roadbed, now NC 215, along which the Shay locomotive huffed and spit hot cinders while pulling cars of pulpwood for

Champion Fibre Company, passed by farms owned by Hargroves, Moores, Catheys, and Rhineharts, among others. A dirt road for other vehicles, built later, ran primarily alongside the Pigeon River and was subject to flooding.

"They (engineers) were awful good to us kids," said 99-year-old Florence Hargrove Wells.

Young children hung on wooden gates waiting for the train to pass because engineers would throw candy to them.

Older children would pack a picnic and ride the train to Sunburst. Transferring to one of the smaller Climax engine logging trains, they rode high up the mountains to logging camps at places like Beech Gap, Shining Rock and Middle Prong. Watching loggers hewing trees and loading the train, they didn't get home until almost dark.

Wells went along once, but that was enough for her. The steep track wound around, crossed the face of the mountain, and passed over trestles spanning deep ravines, rock cliffs, and rivers. She tells of the engine pushing flatbed cars part way up the mountain, stopping at a switchback (spur), pulling onto a side track, hitching up again, and pulling cars from the front.

The Tennessee and North Carolina railroad operated to haul wood out of the mountains, not to carry passengers, but those who lived near the tracks were welcome to hitch a ride, standing in the locomotive. Flag stations, positioned at intervals by the track, were pole-like contraptions with a flag lowered and raised by pulling on an attached cord. A lowered flag meant passengers were waiting so the train stopped. At each station was a little shack with seats, offering scant protection from the weather. Stations are recalled at Stamey Cove, Woodrow, Retreat, and Burnette Siding. A couple of water towers and stops for loading coal were necessary.

Wells remembers riding to school with her sister Berlynn and brother Walter, along with Moore children, on a jitney bus that ran on the tracks. The jitney had canvas curtains on the sides and might have held a dozen or so people. The jitney played an important role in passenger service between Canton and Sunburst.

Wells rode the train into Canton for piano lessons when young, then later on, to work.

Shay engines were considered top of the line in logging engines; powerful, designed for steep grades, and suited to rough terrain and heavy loads. The seventy-ton machine had its limits, though. It was not able to climb grades over sixty degrees or go around extremely sharp turns, creating the need for switchbacks and smaller engines to traverse the steepest grades.

Acquiring right of way property for the railroad meant Reuben B. Robertson and his attorney George Smathers had to negotiate with landowners, some agreeable and some not.

William Harrison Hargrove, a relative of Wells, surveyed the land.

Building the railroad by hand was no small feat. Manual labor used picks, shovels, axes, and other hand tools, assisted by horses, mules, wagons, and wooden skids. Motorized heavy equipment was not available. Building trestles was a work of art.

Champion Fibre Company originally planned for use of a flume, but lack of sufficient water capacity and gravity cancelled that idea.

Dynamite was used for large cuts through the rough mountainous terrain, with its heavy rock formations and rock cliffs. Huge rocks on the west fork of the Pigeon River are testimony to its use.

The route of the railroad followed the river for the most part, as NC 215 does today. Lake Logan Road follows the old roadbed.

When the Sunburst logging operation closed, the Sunburst village around the logging camp disappeared as well. The waters of Lake Logan cover the spot. The tracks were removed.

Hike these old logging trails with a sharp eye. Steel rods, wire cable, rusted railroad spikes, and other evidence can still be seen.

Woodrow, Retreat and Sentelle

Although none of the three are or ever were actual towns Woodrow, Retreat and Sentelle, all in the Bethel area, are shown on a map of Haywood County. At one time, the three were important locations for folks living in the Pigeon Valley.

The train from Champion Fibre Company's logging operation at Sunburst (now the site of Lake Logan) to the paper mill in Canton hauled pulpwood. Woodrow and Retreat were depots or stops for the train that ran up and down the valley.

The Woodrow depot was located on NC 215, a few miles west of the new Bethel Elementary School, I am told. Retreat's train stop was in Mauney Cove, off Lake Logan Road. Sentelle was on US 276, near the present Jukebox Junction café.

Woodrow was so named after former USA president Woodrow Wilson, according to Hugh K. Terrell, Jr. of Bethel, quoting what he had been told by his grandmother. "I suppose there were so many Wilson families living in the area that they used the first name," he said.

Terrell's grandmother the late Mrs. James W. Moore, who lived in the valley, was familiar with the Woodrow train stop. A store in a rock building, still standing, was across the road from the depot, she told her grandson. It would likely have been a busy place, with the two buildings situated close together.

Plans were in progress to incorporate Woodrow. Terrell said, "It was to be a little town, but it never happened."

Retreat was in Mauney Cove, near the junction of Edwards Cove Road and Lake Logan Road, according to Dave Edwards. He has called Edwards Cove home for eighty-nine years. "I have no idea why it was called Retreat," he said.

One of the late E. B. Rickman's stores near the Retreat train stop was run by a fellow named Carlyle Sheffield, he said. Since both Retreat and Woodrow were rural areas, having stores near the depots would have been convenient for those living in the areas at a time when road conditions were poor and transportation was scanty.

Ava Barrett remembers Retreat, although she too doesn't know the origin of the name. "I was just a little girl then and I liked to go to Retreat. We would stop at Walker Brown's Store because it was closer and I always got a few pennies to buy a little poke of candy. I was careful to make it last until we went to the store again. I remember that Warren's corn mill was there, too."

Sentelle was not on the train's route. Captain Billy Terrell had a store and a home there, Terrell said. Shortly after the Civil War ended, Captain Terrell went to Col. Joe Cathey's store to buy some tools. They evidently exchanged words over the north-south conflict, according to both Terrell and Charles Cathey.

Angered, Terrell told Cathey that if he wouldn't sell him what he needed, he would just go build his own store. He did: It was a narrow, two-story brick building and was called W. S. Terrell & Sons, Terrell told me.

R. A. Sentelle also had a home near the store site. In 1881 he was elected the first county superintendent of schools in Haywood County. His son R. Ennis Sentelle married Annie Terrell, daughter of Captain Terrell.

Students' Project Preserves Sunburst's Past

Sonoma, a small booklet patterned after the *Foxfire* books, was written in 1978 by Hugh K. Terrell's eighth grade English class as a creative writing exercise. The thirty-six students involved learned a great deal about writing, interviewing people, and putting a book together, but those lessons paled in comparison to the invaluable information they preserved about Sunburst, the huge logging operation that existed on land now covered by the waters of Lake Logan.

Armed with notebooks, tape recorders, and some trepidation about talking to strangers, they garnered their facts from people who had lived and worked at Sunburst. Most of their sources are now deceased.

Approximately 500 people lived in the town that grew up around the large, double-band mill that supplied pulpwood to Champion Fibre Company in Canton. Almost all the men who lived there (some with their families) were involved with the sawmill, the railroad, or logging.

"The houses at Sunburst were not like the modern houses of today, but they were equipped with sufficient facilities...many had electric lights and most had inside plumbing, but no bathtubs. You took a bath in a washtub," said Virgil Sizemore.

"The village at Sunburst had 100 to 125 telephones," Mrs. Tellie Beverage told them. "Telephones were in the woods, mess halls, depots, mills...usually on party lines and were crank operated." Using the crank, you got the operator.

In 1907, Reuben B. Robertson and his wife Hope moved to Sunburst. They lived in a twelve-room house at Spruce, upriver from the sawmill. The building later became a boarding house, run by Mrs. O'Dell Ross. Robertson had been sent by his father-in-law, Peter G. Thomson, from Ohio to oversee operations at the new mill.

Two other living accommodations were Hipps' Boarding House and the Sunburst Hotel. Small houses were scattered around the mill.

"We had a hotel close by, and we had a community store, a commissary, and this commissary had a drink fountain and anything you wanted to buy," said Mrs. Beverage. She called the store a "supermarket, in a way, because it handled everything for you, hardware to clothing." Lumber mill offices were located alongside the Commissary.

Hipps' boarding house also had a store, said his daughter, Mrs. Fred Hyatt, and he ran the community barber shop and a taxi service.

"The school, on a hillside above the band mill, had three rooms. They had two grades in each room. We had a big ole pot-bellied stove, and we'd sit up real close to the front (to keep warm). The older boys worked for months to dig out a depression in the bank to make a basketball court," Sizemore recalled. Professor Samuel A. Guyer was teacher and principal, assisted by his wife and daughter as well as Beverage and Georgia McAfee, an African-American who later lived in Canton.

"We...had a doctor," said Mrs. Beverage..."Sam Stringfield." He was the company doctor." He rode to Sunburst on a bicycle-like contraption that ran on the train tracks, which he pumped by foot.

The building of the railroad that carried pulpwood to the mill and the engines that ran on it were an important part of their stories. While Sunburst was the main operation, there were smaller camps scattered throughout the mountain for the loggers, all connected by the railroad. Railway cars with their loads of wood often overturned, as the trains moved up and down steep grades.

These excerpts from *Sonoma* paint only vignettes of the larger picture the booklet portrayed.

Sunburst Memories

Edie Hawkins Abbott and Vivian Deane Sexton Foster of Canton share a birthday—July 27, 1918—and recollections of childhood years living at Sunburst logging community, once located in the valley where the water of Lake Logan sparkles.

"We call each other on our birthday," the two tell me. The women were delivered three hours apart according to Abbott, both in their respective houses, by Dr. Sam Stringfield of Waynesville. Dr. Stringfield was the company physician for Suncrest Logging Company at Sunburst. Abbott was born first. "Dr. Stringfield walked across the road and delivered Deane," Abbott said.

Their collective memories alter my image of a temporary, rough and tumble camp deep in the forest with men and saws amid the sounds of falling timber and splitting wood, giving me a new perspective of a long-ago village where families lived and worked. The towns of Canton, Waynesville, and Clyde did not enjoy all the amenities of Sunburst then.

"I feel fortunate to have lived there," Foster says. "It was more progressive there. Sunburst was a very modern community."

The village of their youth was "up to date on everything," according to the two. Foster remembers her home, a frame house on a hill with two bedrooms, living room, a fully equipped bathroom, and the kitchen with its handsome, old-fashioned oak china cabinet. "All the houses were alike, like those in Fibreville," according to Abbott. The deep porches sheltered children at play while parents enjoyed visiting with friends in good weather. (Fibreville was a Canton community of mill-built houses for Champion Papers employees, until the flooding Pigeon River finally sealed its doom.)

Enclosed within a wooden fence, Foster's house had a yard where she could play in her sandbox. Summertime meant bright flowers and a vegetable garden. Her mother hung the wash, which she had scrubbed on a washboard, on a clothesline. Behind the house was a small, cold stream where she fished for minnows.

Winter brought deep, lasting snows in the valley's mountainous elevation. The millpond froze and some residents, many of whom had lived in more northern states, laced on their ice skates to skim the thickly frozen water.

Wells provided the mill houses with running water, while generators supplied the camp with electricity.

Sunburst was populated not only with local mill hands, but also with those who would eventually be responsible for operations at the new paper mill in Canton. One of those was Reuben B. Robertson who managed the paper manufacturing plant for his father-in-law, Peter G. Thomson. He and his wife Hope resided there for a time.

"They were upper class people, well-to-do folks," Foster said, referring to those who had come from Ohio where Champion corporate headquarters were located and other locales. "They were from different places. They weren't local. People lived pretty well (in Sunburst)." Abbott added.

"There was a nice commissary where I followed my mother when she shopped," Foster remembers. "She sewed, so she bought fabric to make our clothing and curtains, whatever we needed." Abbott recalls her own homemade clothing, including crocheted sweaters, bonnets, and "lacy stuff."

"We would walk to the post office. We walked everywhere" Foster remarked. A large hotel/boarding house served meals. She considered eating at the long tables in the dining room a special treat. "We had a big school on a hill with rows of houses lining the road on the way up. I remember my first grade teacher was a beautiful redhead. We had wonderful teachers."

Another fond memory for Foster is riding the train upriver to a smaller mill at Spruce, now Sunburst Campground. "We picked gallons of blueberries."

In time, Foster's father bought a Model T car. "My mother learned to drive and we traveled those dirt roads a lot." Abbott's father purchased a Buick touring car, and she loved to sleep in the back seat as her mother "drove everywhere on those dusty dirt roads. She went to Canton to buy groceries."

There were many buildings, Foster said, and something was always going on. There were lots of parties and square dances. She also remembers the thick forest surrounding Sunburst. "There were more trees then, beautiful trees," she recalls. "On the hill were two cemeteries."

"It seemed like everybody played something (musical instruments)," Abbott said, "guitars, mandolins, banjos. There were lots of good musicians."

Foster, daughter of A. Y. and Alta Armes Sexton, moved with her family from Sunburst when she was seven. She eventually married Ray Foster, an electrical engineer at the paper mill. Abbott was five when her parents, Maude and Ed Hawkins, left Sunburst. She married Jack Abbott, Canton businessman.

Their association continued. As young adults as they worked together on the switchboard and in the reception area at Champion Papers.

Fond Memories
of Spruce

"I want to tell you about Spruce because I'm afraid no one will remember it," said Vaughn Rogers, eighty-seven. He lives on family land on NC 215, up the mountain from Burnette Siding Baptist Church. "It was a beautiful place."

"There was about 1,500 people living there in rows of houses, bungalow type houses, up the right prong of Pigeon River, and in houses all over this place," he said. "It is hard to believe now that many people lived here, but they did." Wooden sidewalks made walking easier among the right prong houses. Electric power wasn't available but there was phone service—crank telephones, he remembers.

"There was no timber on here. It was all open fields with cattle on them and there was an apple orchard with all sorts of apples. It was a wonderful place," he told me.

Spruce occupied a large area, including the site of current Sunburst Campground, and Suncrest Lumber Company owned the land. Wood logged by Suncrest went to Champion Fibre's Sunburst Mill, now Lake Logan.

"I remember a flume down the left prong. At the end, there was a trough about thirty feet long and eight feet wide, with water knee-deep or deeper. Men in rubber suits got the wood and loaded it in on railroad cars. Trains went by here hauling lumber all day. I watched for them," he continued.

Across the river was a field called Soldier's Bottom, a training camp for World War I soldiers; this information was handed down to him. "I didn't see the soldiers because I hadn't come along yet, but I did see evidence of where they had been. Tent stobs were still in the ground. Now that's history," Rogers said.

Rogers' brothers went to Spruce's one-room school, but he went to Burnette Siding, another one-room structure used as both school and church. "Burnette Siding was a little village," he said. "Lots of houses were around that church, and a commissary owned by the Gwyn brothers."

He enjoyed riding with his father in a Model T Ford to the Gwyn commissary, as well as the ones at Spruce and Sunburst.

Families began moving away in the '20s, when Suncrest moved to Bandmill Bottom in Waynesville. "After all that went away, the Civilian Conservation Corps camps came in the early '30s," Rogers said. "The CCC did wonderful work building roads, trails and bridges."

Rogers worked at the CCC camp, served a stint in the U.S. Navy, and was employed by Unagusta, a furniture manufacturer in Hazelwood, during his working years. Behind his house sits a 1939 Chevrolet truck with 400,000 miles on it, driven to work in Hazelwood.

"It was a wonderful place," he repeated. "I am glad I lived there and saw it with my own eyes. I am a blessed man with good family, good children. I have had a good life."

Standing on Rogers' porch, with its view of the mountains accompanied by the lilt of rushing water from the Pigeon River below, listening to this man talk and marveling at his calm demeanor, gentle smile, and pervading sense of peace, one has to agree.

Dinner Buckets Inspired by the Paper Mill

Manufacturing plants often spawn other businesses to supply workers and plants with related needs.

In 1915, a small company was established in Canton to provide Champion Paper and Fibre Company employees with a product that catered to their needs:

A dinner bucket. Since mill workers routinely carried meals to work, a dinner bucket would be a logical product for a town dominated by a paper mill.

Restaurants were few; fast-food establishments weren't even a blip on the radar screen. If a variety of eating places had existed, it would have made no difference anyway. Those paper makers could not leave work to seek food, and probably couldn't have afforded it if it were available.

Union Manufacturing Company, according to a page copied from an unknown publication (probably a newspaper), was organized and incorporated September 3, 1915 "to manufacture and exploit this unique bucket."

The venture began after a Calvin F. Christopher of Canton invented a unique dinner pail, then patented it on April 14, 1914, according to the clipping.

The bucket, at least one of which still exists in this area, was apparently designed after careful thought and consideration for its use.

Rather than a domed design as usually seen today, it was rectangular in shape and measured on the outside 9.5"x5.5"x5" inches. It was stamped with the company's label.

When opened, it expanded to reveal "four convenient trays—compartment for knife, fork, and spoon, and with the other compartments to suit the taste of the user."

I have little acquaintance with dinner buckets, but the most unique feature, to me, was what I first perceived as a sort of chimney. It was a cup that also served as a clasp for the bucket. The lunch box has a rather unique design, especially for the time, and certainly functional. The handle, extending above the cup, had a wooden grip.

The clipping goes on to say that the bucket holds enough food for two or three people and is "made so as to be thoroughly aseptic - clean, dust-proof and germ-proof - and yet permitting of a unique system of ventilation, thus obviating the sogginess of contents so common to other pails."

One has to doubt the "germ-proof" claim, but the bucket, if cared for in a sanitary manner, could be easily cleaned.

T. L. Gwyn was the president of Union Manufacturing Company and W. T. Sharp was vice president, familiar names in the history of

Canton. J. O. Plott was secretary and treasurer and T. J. Wooldridge was manager. G. L. Hampton and T. J. Bailey, also familiar names, and M. L. Welfley of Asheville, were on the board of directors.

The building was located on Penland Street near Felmet's Garage (now Ronnie Mills' Riverview Farm and Garden store) and along the Tennessee and North Carolina railway line that ran through Canton and on "up the river" to Sunburst. The structure was eighty feet by forty feet in size, although a later expansion was predicted. "There will come a time when the building will have to be much larger. Anyone who makes a careful study of the dinner pail will become convinced, not only of its superiority, but of its ultimate success financially upon the market."

The story includes a picture of the building that burned several years ago. The company was producing around 150 buckets a day and had seven employees. The expectation was that the plant, described as having the most modern and up-to-date machinery made especially from original designs, would eventually produce 800 to 1,000 buckets a day.

Union Manufacturing began with $50,000 in capital, most of which had been provided by local residents.

The copy of the article, apparently an advertisement, was on page 63 of "Haywood County Industrial and Resort Edition."

Howard Sellars, ninety-three, remembers the "bucket factory" and its location. His father owned one of the buckets and carried it to work at the paper mill.

However, he doesn't believe that the business survived for too many years.

"A man from South Carolina bought the building and used it as a knitting mill. I think it operated for quite a few years," he said. He was a young child at the time, too young to remember what the knitting operation produced.

The bucket company had high hopes. Its owners considered "The Union Manufacturing Company (to be) headed by strong and successful business men—engaged in the manufacture of the world's finest dinner pail. Very properly called the "Union" bucket—the only one in the world thus catering to the hosts of union labor—there is no reason why this flourishing young industry should not grow into vast and undreamed of proportions."

Further information on this local venture is not immediately available. One can only speculate why the bucket mill failed to reach its high expectations. Marketing the product to a wide area would certainly have been difficult at a time when current media and advertising tools were not available.

Nature's Beauty

Pinkish-purple Joe-Pye weeds are standing tall and proud, decorating roadsides, vying for attention with prickly-looking thistles with their erect posture and deeper pink flowers. Waving around their feet are shorter blue asters, adding contrast with blooms that mirror the sky.

The landscape is changing gradually, subtly but surely, signaling that another season is approaching.

Beyond the flowers of fall, forests, whether they are Pisgah or the Smokies, are lush and green this time of year, deep into summer. A dense canopy of leaves shades the forest floor, allowing little penetration of sunlight. Results of summer's months of growth are highly visible.

A season with too little rain has left the woods dry, all but eliminating the usual moisture-laden touch of the atmosphere in the thickest, deepest parts of the forest, but faint trickles of water whisper the presence of small streams meandering among last winter's rotting leaves and summer's new growth.

Enticing.

Beauty abounds, from higher elevations showcasing spectacular views of range upon range of mountain peaks to the closer confines of the inner forest.

Easily overlooked is the miniature world of mosses, small plants growing in mats in damp, shady locations, especially near water.

These wonderfully soft green carpets soften the contours of the land, rocks and rough tree bark.

Examined carefully at close range, a clump of moss can give the impression of a minute forest in itself. Spores balanced on the end of thread-like stems could be called the trees, in one particular species.

Dark tree trunks rising from among the cascading whorls of tall, thick ferns and multicolored, faceted rocks surrounded by a carpet of moss is a visual feast.

Expanding the view, Nature appears to be a poor housekeeper, with decaying trees and fallen limbs littering the ground, but for a good reason. The natural cycle of forest life includes absorbing nutrients from tree stumps and dying plants as they return to the earth in which they sprouted. The forest absorbs and retains water, conserves soil, absorbs carbon dioxide, and provides habitat for animals. It is a complex and many-faceted eco-system with many benefits.

The hush of the forest encourages light, careful steps. After all, we are entering someone else's residence. A myriad of creatures, large and small, furry and slithery, tiny insects, lizards, and frogs call this their home. We can share, so long as we do so with respect.

Joe Pye Weed

READIN', WRITIN' AND 'RITHMETIC

Subscription Schools

" Subscription schools," also called "old field schools," provided the only opportunities for educating children following the Civil War in Haywood County. Prior to the War, at least eight academies (pay schools) existed. Apparently only two, Bethel and Waynesville, survived when the fighting ended.

Many of our settlers arrived here to make a better life for themselves and their families. Most had left other countries or areas where education was only for the rich, the privileged few, and they wanted it for their children. They wanted it so much that they went to great lengths to attain it.

These schools were organized by communities and groups of families who were willing to build a structure themselves to house the school, if need be. Generally, the area church was used as a school during the week, and the preacher was also the teacher.

A history of Haywood County schools, compiled by the school system using the input of active and retired teachers, offers some insight into these places of learning.

"These first structures were built of round logs, having a big chimney at one end and no windows. Students sat on the flat side of split logs supported by two legs at each end. The fortunate...had two textbooks—a *Webster's Blue Back Speller* and an arithmetic. The *Speller* began by teaching the alphabet and placed a strong emphasis upon vowel sounds as a key to pronunciation. Example sentences were designed to provide the student an exposure to a broad range of general information and moral overtones," *Haywood County Schoolin': A Rich Heritage* explains.

Two examples are "Botany is the science of plants." and "Smoke rises because it is lighter than air." Emphasizing morality, two others were "We look with amazement on the evils of strong drink." and "The wicked knows not the enjoyment of a good conscience."

Fortunate students used a slate and pencils for practicing their sums, while many had to use a board and charcoal for figuring.

The history goes on to list some of the subscription schools, which cost parents a small fee per student to pay the teacher. Sometimes this fee was paid in the form of room and board. Others were paid in commodities such as a ham, a bushel of corn, or even dried beans. A third payment option was manual labor. The county was dotted with the schools.

A settlement in the Bethel area, called Woodrow, organized a school in 1825. The windowless, one-room log building, located about a mile west of the present Bethel school, was poorly lighted and ventilated. Memories recounted by an older generation stress the role of a hickory, strong and heavy, to maintain discipline. The building was also used as a church.

A hickory stick, for those too young to remember, was a limb broken from a tree or shrub which stung badly when applied diligently to bare legs or thinly covered parts of the anatomy. At one time, most every mother kept one handy but might find it broken into small pieces by the one receiving the whippings.

R. A. Sentelle, who would become the county's first superintendent of schools in 1881, taught at another in Bethel having "forty odd students generally of good behavior." Sentelle recorded that he received $25 a month for a four-month term. These pay schools were generally open for four months, usually in the spring.

Capt. W. H. Hargrove, my great-grandfather, and the Rhodarmers, according to the late Mrs. Ida Reid and the late Mrs. Mary Hargrove, built Piney Grove School and Church in Stamey Cove. "We held our books on our laps and took turns warming our feet," the ladies remembered. Joe Hargrove, my grandfather, and a Mr. Monday replaced the slab seats with better seats and desks.

Hickory Grove, Chinquapin Grove, and schools in Henson Cove, Cruso, and Panther Creek were also located in the Bethel and Cruso areas in the 1800s.

Hyder Mountain, Flat Rock on the crest of Utah Mountain, Rush Fork in Crabtree, and James Chapel on Bald Creek in Upper Crabtree were named in the book. At least eight of these small institutions were located in Crabtree and Iron Duff communities. The late Dr. Nick Medford, a dentist, went to dirt-floored Chambers School on Iron Duff. "I always took biscuits, and whatever was available and often "crumblings," (milk and cornbread) which I stored in the springhouse. Good, too," he said. Lunchrooms were an unheard-of luxury.

Dutch Cove in Canton had a one-room log building. Pleasant Hill and Peter's Fork were in the Clyde area. Possum College School was located in the Fines Creek-Shelton Laurel area. Grace Lumber Company built Cecil Thelma School at the Cold Springs/Harmon Den community, and Lower Hurricane was also near the Tennessee line.

Add Henry's Chapel in Maggie Valley, Mica Dale and Quinlan Town on Allen's Creek, Cataloochee, Francis Cove, Peachtree, Turpin's Chapel, and Camp Branch to this probably incomplete list.

Subscription schools left much to be desired, but each one was part of a foundation laid for mountain people and for Haywood County's current school system.

Haywood Institute

Before the days of public schools, some Haywood County families went to great lengths to see that their children were educated. Haywood Institute in Clyde was one good example of their efforts.

Haywood Institute is noteworthy not only because its students received a better than average education, according to accounts by long-ago students, but also because its classes progressed from first grade through high school, eleven grades at that time.

The institute also had dormitories, operating as a boarding school, with students from Crabtree, Fines Creek, Iron Duff, Waynesville, Tuscola, Canton, and Bethel living there.

The school's forerunner, Pigeon Valley Academy, was established in 1885 on land donated by Mont and Nancy Haynes. Humphrey Posey Haynes and six other men had a two story red-brick building constructed. When the Academy went into debt, Humphrey Haynes bought it at an auction. Along with Joseph Collins, Jasper S. Morgan, Bailey Jones, Jephah Morgan, Fulton Osborne and B. F. Hill, all affluent land owners, he ran the school from 1890–1902 with the help of Pleasant Hill Baptist Church. Tuition and boarding fees were charged.

The church had already functioned as a school. In the 1880s, with the county struggling to recover from the Civil War and with opportunities for reading, writing, and arithmetic few and inadequate, Pigeon Valley Educational Association, composed predominantly of members of Pleasant Hill Baptist Church in Clyde, had organized a free school. Money from the national George Peabody Foundation funded this school. When the Foundation ran out of money, the Association took matters into its own hands and Pigeon Valley Academy followed.

The Haywood Baptist Association had dreams of establishing a Baptist academy. After looking at possible sites throughout the county, the Association concluded that Pigeon Valley Academy was essentially what they sought, already operating with seven Baptist founders and the assistance of Pleasant Hill Church. After months of meetings and negotiations, Pigeon Valley Academy opened the 1902 school year under the name Haywood Institute. With the change in place, the school received monetary assistance from not only the sponsoring church, but also from the Haywood County Baptist Association and Home Mission Board of the Southern Baptist Convention.

The history of the school is well documented, both by former students and local historian W. C. Allen. The late French Haynes, who earned her Ph.D. and became a college professor, called the school's courses of study "The fundamentals for entry to any institution of higher learning." Of the many doctors, lawyers, teachers, ministers and prominent businessmen educated at the Institute, she wrote, "The farm boys with their educated wives went back to the farms...and were leaders in community life, churches, schools, and clubs."

Well-chaperoned activities were almost as numerous as the classes. Many afternoons were spent walking through town, visiting various residents and businesses. There were hikes, house parties, candy pullings, corn shuckings, hayrides, picnics, ball games, and tennis clubs.

A party for all students was held once a month in the girls' dormitory so boys and girls could socialize, but individual dating, stolen moments between classes, and letter writing, were forbidden.

Rules were broken, of course, and former students write of usually humorous incidents.

"Some mighty fine citizens came from that school," said Bucky Brown, whose house sits near the school site.

After twenty-five years of successfully educating county children, public schools were built across the county; the Institute began losing students and the final graduating class collected their diplomas in 1927.

As the number of graduates gradually diminished and reunions grew smaller, the decision was made to perpetuate the school with two large scrapbooks placed in Haywood County Library.

The school was located on and around Brown Street in Clyde.

High School Consolidations

Almost fifty years have passed since Haywood County consolidated seven high schools into two. Promoting a sense of unity in each school was an awesome responsibility.

It was 1966 when Waynesville Township, Crabtree-Iron Duff, Fines Creek and part of student bodies at Reynolds and Clyde high schools merged to become Tuscola High School. In the other end of the county Clyde, Bethel, Reynolds, and Canton high schools merged to become Pisgah High School. Territorial lines determining who went to Pisgah and who went to Tuscola, intended to keep enrollments evenly balanced, negatively impacted Clyde students. Long-time classmates were separated by this line. Reynolds, an African-American school, had served the entire county.

Pisgah had more than 900 students and Tuscola had around 1,100.

These schools had been fierce rivals on football fields and basketball courts. Each had its own community, its own mascot, school colors and traditions. Each was proud of its identity. Some areas regretted losing their small rural schools that were the heart of the communities.

These were not numbers affected here. These were teenagers, boys and girls, who were being uprooted from familiar surroundings with familiar teachers, in small schools where most everyone knew everyone else, and replanted into brand new schools with different teachers and principals, literally hundreds of new faces, new routines, expanded class offerings, and longer bus rides.

You might compare the situation to rummaging through a kitchen grabbing foodstuffs, spices, various liquids, whatever was at hand, then throwing it all into one big pot and stirring it madly with no earthly idea of what you were creating. But that would be too impersonal. These were human beings with varied backgrounds, opinions, ambitions, feelings, and needs being mixed together. The quality of their education depended, in part, on their feeling comfortable in their surroundings.

School administrators dealt with the logistics. Teachers, school staffs, and the students had to assume responsibility for seeing their schools become cohesive units. Easy? Easier than expected.

Economics took care of school colors and mascots. Only Waynesville Township High School (WTHS) and Canton High School had enough band uniforms and athletic gear to accommodate enrollments. Clubs were reorganized and new officers elected. New student council elections were held. These considerations may seem insignificant in the total picture, but they were vitally important to students struggling to maintain the identities they had worked to establish.

Bill Milner was head football coach at WTHS, and came to Tuscola as assistant principal to Carl Ratcliffe. "A lot of them (students) were scared and didn't know what to expect. They fit in pretty readily, though," he said. "I feel like sports welded them together. If we hadn't had sports, they never would have gotten along."

Ratcliffe remembers the transition as very smooth with no problems. "They knew it was coming and prepared themselves for it," he said. "If they were unhappy, they didn't show it."

B. F. Maree was Pisgah's principal, but left the next year to move closer to his home in Rutherfordton.

Bill Stamey, Canton's town manager, was teaching history and coaching football when consolidation took place. "Basically, it went smoothly. Canton's football team had practiced with Pat Powell's Bethel team the year before. The boys got to know each other and we (coaches) got to know some of the kids. "Sports played an integral part in bringing the schools together."

Teachers were changing schools as well and had mixed feelings. Alice Cathey was teaching English at Bethel and asked her principal, the late Turner Cathey, to transfer her to Bethel Junior High. "I didn't want to go to Pisgah," she said. "He told me, 'Alice, you will like it' and he was right. We all went through an adjustment, but it went so much better than I had feared. It was a challenging undertaking." She believes that teachers and students alike decided they were all in this together, and they would do it. "I never saw any animosity," she said.

Wanda Conley Walker was a sophomore at Pisgah and her sister Betty was a senior. "It evolved into a positive experience, although it was a bittersweet time. We were so involved at Reynolds, and suddenly we became such a minority. We felt lost. It took some time and work, but we made enduring friendships and so many of our students went on to do so well," Walker said.

"It was a major adjustment for all of us," Betty Conley said, "but I am proud to say I graduated from Pisgah. I feel like a pioneer." Her son Bo Ellerbe plays football at Pisgah now, and her granddaughter Shanda is a ninth grader. "It wasn't a racial thing for us. It was encountering so many strangers. We had excellent teachers at Reynolds and we knew we could compete. Our socialization with other students was nil at first, because our classmates were so scattered, but we created friendships and everyone was treated fairly." She credits teachers for their role. "They were there for us and did all they could to reassure us. We had a ball, we loved Pisgah and we came together as one in a smooth transition."

Pisgah's head cheerleader that year was senior Karen Hall of Canton. Tryouts among students from all schools involved were held during the summer.

"It was more traumatic for parents, the school board, and the teachers than it was for us. It was no big deal. We were excited to meet new people. The curriculum was a step up and we had the opportunity to take classes we had never had available before."

"The only three things in place were the cheerleaders, the marching band, and the football team. Winning seasons for the three major sports helped a lot. It gave us all something to relate to and made everybody feel good. It gave us all a positive spin."

"We were all lost in those big buildings and didn't know where anything was. Then around Christmas we got a student council and things began to pull together."

"It was exciting, nervous, and good for the community, as it turned out," she said.

GOOD SAMARITANS

Salvation Army's Cecil Brown

"This is the story of a determined young mountain girl who fell in love with the mission of the Salvation Army (SA) and wanted to lift her people to new heights," wrote Frank Duracher in his book *Smoky Mountain High, The Consuming Passion of Cecil Brown.*

Cecil Brown grew up on a farm on Hurricane Creek but knew nothing of the Salvation Army until she visited her brother in Asheville at the age of 16. She had never before been out of the mountains.

Joining the Corps three years later, she served at several posts before being granted the assignment she saw as her destiny at age twenty-eight—establishing a Mountain Mission among her people.

Success in establishing the Mission might not have taken place without Cecil Brown, Duracher wrote. "She represents the rare leader who could have pulled off such a mammoth effort...although the mountaineers distrusted outsiders, they accepted her because she was one of them."

She was referred to variously as "Shepherdess of the Hills," "Maid of the Mountains," and a "legend." She was admitted to the Order of the Founder in 1947, the first person to receive the honor in the Salvation Army's USA Southern Territory.

"Everybody thought the world of her," said Wayne Moore, eighty-one. "We had five girls and they all liked to go to church there. She did a good job. She was willing to help poor people and she got some of the moonshiners straightened out." Moore attended church services at

161

Shelton Laurel, decided to join the SA Corps, and Brown made him a Sergeant Major (local officer), a title he still holds.

"There was real dependence on the Salvation Army," said seventy-three-year-old Dorothy Haynes. "Cecil visited the sick and tried to doctor them. She came to see my sister who had yellow jaundice and whatever she did made her better. She got Christmas gifts for people who didn't have much and she took in a lot of children whose mother was sick or had died. Cecil could relate to her people. She was strict and made us behave."

June Brown Ferguson was nine years old when her mother died. "Aunt Cecil became a mother to me," Ferguson told Duracher. She lived with her aunt until she married Reeves Ferguson.

Ferguson's memories of her aunt and of the missions are vivid. "We did lots of walking in the early years because the roads were bad. I was in high school before we got electricity. Before, we depended on oil lamps and a Delco battery. Those lamp chimneys had to be washed every day and if they weren't clean enough, we washed them again," she said. She remembers her aunt as a perfectionist.

"We stayed up all night and cooked before the Singing Convention. The top of the mountain was covered with vehicles and hundreds of people would attend. Logging trucks would come in carrying twenty-five or thirty people. We always had good groups to sing," Ferguson said.

"Cecil Brown and her sisters helped to bring about overdue modernization when they petitioned the governor of North Carolina, William K. Scott, to provide public services that were taken for granted elsewhere in the United States." Duracher wrote. In the 1950s, indoor plumbing, electricity, paved roads, and other modern conveniences finally reached the mountains.

Then in 1956, Brown was forced to retire when she was diagnosed with terminal cancer. She died December 4, 1958, and is buried in Hurricane View Cemetery.

Mountain Girl

Histories of the late Salvation Army Major Cecil Brown and the outpost known as the Citadel, in the small mountain community called Maple Springs, are so intertwined that one is incomplete without the other.

Citadel, commonly thought of as a fortress but also denoting a refuge, a strong, safe place, was an appropriate name for the compound spanning the border between Haywood and Madison counties. Four buildings housing a church, a trading post, living quarters, and the Haywood House (used as a dormitory) were built under the direction of Major Brown. The wooden, utilitarian structures were alive with people and events for years.

Major Brown was born Daisy Cecil Brown on December 13, 1906, in a two-room cabin on a farm in Hurricane Creek. She was consumed with determination to work among her people in the mountains of western Haywood. They needed so much, and she had so much to give.

Brown, then a SA Captain, had just completed her training in Atlanta when she was given a four-month opportunity, beginning in January 1935, to establish a Mission in the mountains. Previous attempts to bring organized religion to the isolated families living in scattered cabins reached only by crude trails had failed. Brown was armed with the powerful advantage of having lived among those she would serve, but these mountain people viewed "women preachers" with a dim eye. "No woman could shout and holler loud enough to make a good preacher anyhow," one mountain man said.

She began by visiting the twenty-three families who lived in the neighborhood of Shelton Laurel, which had a one-room schoolhouse. On a cold, snowy Sunday in February, she drove as far as she could, then hiked four miles in mud and snow to reach Shelton Laurel. When she arrived, she found fifty-four people awaiting her. By Easter, the Mission there was well established and she turned next to home, Hurricane Creek.

At the time, she reported to her divisional commander, "I'm getting along fine with my work, but it seems to rain every Sunday and this means a number of miles walking in the mud. I am getting to be quite a hiker. The most I have walked in one day so far is twenty-three miles."

People crowded into the Hurricane Creek one-room schoolhouse as they had done in Shelton Laurel. That community requested a revival, and some nights as many as 300 people crowded in and around the tiny building. Soon, a landowner donated land for a church, a nearby saw mill gave some wood, and sold the remainder needed at a discount. Area people rolled up their sleeves and set to work.

The notorious hamlet of Big Bend, then Poplar Gap/Little Creek, Bonnie Hill, Cold Creek, and Spring Creek, some of which were in Madison County, followed.

At Maple Springs, the Citadel, Brown and her fellow Corps workers had to adapt to some primitive living conditions that eventually improved.

A trading post opened that sold rugs, bedspreads, quilts and towels, woven by mountain women who were taught to weave at the Mission. Needed essentials were sold there, food that families couldn't grow such as coffee and sugar. A gas pump was available.

Fruit and vegetables were grown in extensive gardens and sold to Stokely Food Company in Tennessee. They preserved and stored their own food.

Mountain children attended classes there, receiving an education. Children who had lost one or both parents were taken in and provided with a home. Brown became a surrogate doctor out of necessity, carrying to the hospital those she knew she couldn't help.

Christmas was a special time. Brown made sure that every mission had a party and that there were gifts for everyone who flocked to the parties.

One of her most beloved accomplishments was an annual Singing Convention. Musicians traveled many miles to sing and play there. The event drew huge crowds, some of whom came long distances to enjoy the day.

Progress in the way of roads and cars and other modern conveniences began to lessen the need for the Mission. It was sold, partially dismantled, and Brown moved permanently to Shelton Laurel.

Major Brown's niece, June Ferguson, has among her possessions a handwritten diary in which this remarkable woman wrote daily. *Smoky Mountain High* is a 143-page book written by Major Frank Duracher to preserve the successes and accomplishments of Major Brown.

The Friendly House

O n Sunday drives to Lake Logan and the Blue Ridge Parkway on NC 215, my parents unfailingly pointed out Friendly House and its adjoining log cabin as we passed. I wish I had listened carefully to their comments.

The first female minister in this area was Reverend Hannah Jewett Powell. She named her manse, a house with local creek rock foundation, Friendly House. She was a Universalist in a region dominated primarily by Baptists and Methodists, and served only by male ministers.

The first Universalist congregation in Western North Carolina, perhaps the state, had found a home in historic Inman Chapel when it was completed in 1903, now listed on the National Register of Historic Places. The Reverend James Anderson Inman, an ordained Universalist minister, built the meetinghouse with the help of family and friends and preached there until his death. He had been introduced to the faith in Boston following his service in the Civil War, according to Ted Darryll Inman, his great grandson.

In September 1921, Powell arrived to carry on and expand what he had started.

Without a minister, church membership was dwindling until 1919 when Boston's Women's National Missionary Alliance recruited a Universalist minister in Greensboro, Dr. Harry L. Canfield, to assess the possibility of national support for work based at the chapel.

Canfield was enthusiastic about a mission in the area. At a meeting in Vermont, he met Powell and convinced her and the Universalist church that the Haywood County church needed their support.

Powell took up residence in Inman's old home the Manse, living there until Friendly House, located only a few yards below Inman Chapel, was finished.

Powell soon became an integral part of the community, heavily involved with providing far more than spiritual guidance for the families living in the rural setting. Her acceptance in the area was no small feat. She was living among a people who, reportedly, strongly opposed women preachers and liberal Universalist doctrines, and embraced a historical approach to the scriptures. "If people heard her preach, they accepted her," Inman said.

Apparently, her sincere desire to provide hard-to-get services endeared her to the community. She is said to have envisioned a mission that would become a religion, education, and social services center.

The Women's National Missionary Association of the Universalist Society sent funds for a preschool and kindergarten with summer school programs, library, and free health clinic. Barrels of books were said to have been shipped for the school and a missionary nurse arrived to supply health care. The health clinic was located in the old log cabin at first, Inman said.

Inman said the library had more books than Canton and Waynesville combined. "Some of those books are still around," he said. "She really cared about people. She was well liked in this community."

She was a familiar figure in Pigeon Valley as she traveled along miles of rough, unpaved mountain roads in a buggy pulled by a horse she called Lexington, or Lex.

Around 1940 Powell acquired a car and hired Willis Warren to drive for her, a job he continued for ten years, he estimates. Warren, now ninety, lives with his wife Dora, eighty-eight, on Rivermont Drive. He said, "She kept me busy. I was all the time driving people to the doctor. I lived upstairs in the Friendly House until I married, and there was always someone beating on the door at night needing help. She never turned anybody down. They depended on her."

"I don't know how the woman lived," Dora said. "She would give away the last bite she had." When her meager salary of around $70 was gone before the next check arrived, she would borrow money from Warren. "She always paid me back, he said, "She was honest."

Another of Warren's jobs was cranking the gas pump in the well house each morning to fill a 500-gallon reservoir, a task he continued after he married and moved. It was the only house around with running water. He drove Powell to nearby towns or to Sunburst's company store for supplies. Even though he no longer lived on the premises, someone always got word to him at night when a trip for medical attention was required.

Powell had her hand in many pies. She went to Sunburst Logging Camp to teach children and wives of the loggers, both black and white. She conducted night school at her house for people who could neither read nor write. She became minister to hundreds of local people.

Powell had to have been a strong, determined woman although she was not very large physically.

She retired sometime in the late '30s, according to the Warrens, and returned to her hometown in Maine. "She didn't want to leave and came back to visit, and often stayed with us," Warren said.

Her successor requested in the 1940s that the Universalist mission work in Haywood County be terminated. He had lasted only three or four months. "We (Universalists) don't have any business being here," he said, according to the Warrens.

Inman Chapel has had no minister since. It is used for weddings, funerals, and an annual homecoming and dinner on the grounds the first Sunday in June.

Friendly House and its well house remain by the side of the road, unused and in need of much repair. The log cabin is gone, moved to a nearby location. The community no longer needs Powell as it once did, but those who remember her and all she did for those she must have considered "her people" indicate only respect and fondness for her.

Shepherd of the Hills

A home for mountain children who had none was a priority for the late Rev. Robert Perry Smith, D. D., a Presbyterian minister whom some called "Shepherd of the Hills."

Traveling by horse, mule, buggy, or on foot in the Crabtree area of Haywood County during the winter of 1903, he encountered many homeless children who tore at his heart. He attempted to help them in any way he could, but establishing a home where they could live and be cared for on a daily basis became a personal mission.

"In my travels over this territory, I saw numbers of (homeless) children barely existing by the scanty hand of poverty," he related in *Expe-*

riences in Mountain Mission Work, a book he wrote at the request of the Appalachia Synod of the Presbyterian Church.

Having known struggles of his own as a child, Smith is pictured as being deeply empathetic for these children. Left fatherless at age twelve after the Civil War, he worked on the family farm in Reedville, South Carolina to help support his mother and the younger children.

Most of what is known about Crabtree's Mountain Orphanage is told in Smith's own words in his book, published in 1931.

Soon after he came here, he apparently attended a trial and saw an eighteen-year-old boy sentenced to prison. When the judge asked the defendant if he had anything to say, the boy replied, "Judge, I ain't got nothing to say, only I ain't never had no chance in life." Smith felt that the boy's pathetic words spoke for thousands of young people, living without a chance in remote places in the Appalachians.

Smith's dream took shape in 1904. Using his own funds and the assistance of a few individuals, he built a little four-room white and green cottage on a knoll in Upper Crabtree, obtained some second hand furniture, and hired Mrs. E. H. Bales to live with the children. The Mountain Orphanage, as it was called, cost about $500 to build and was the forerunner of the current Presbyterian Home for Children, located in Black Mountain.

Six children and Bales moved in when the Orphanage opened its doors on Friday, January 19, 1904. Two others soon joined the first six. The cottage was surely crowded, but after living hand to mouth and sleeping in cold barns, the children probably didn't mind.

Old photos show small children, most with bare feet, on the porch of the home along with Bales. Calling the cottage a scantily furnished, plain structure, Smith wrote," It was better than no home at all." The woman in charge was mother, housekeeper, teacher, and all else with a promise of $20 a month, half of which was to be used to buy food, clothing, and other needs. Donations of food and clothing helped ease the rather bleak existence.

Smith said it was the first home ever established in the Appalachian Mountains to care for homeless children, if he had been correctly informed. That spring he spoke eloquently and repeatedly of needy children at a meeting of Asheville Presbytery, finally gaining ongoing support for the home from a reluctant membership who feared it was too big a burden for a small mission Presbytery.

More children came until the home was crowded beyond sanitary limits. Others came begging for shelter, creating the need for a waiting list. Since the state's public education office required that the home must also serve as a school, some of the children for whom there was no room did attend classes.

Since school had been hit and miss for him as a child, Smith regarded education a primary need. He had persevered, eventually graduating first from Davidson College, then Columbia Theological Seminary in Columbia, South Carolina. When he came to Asheville, his title was superintendent of home missions, according to Bernard R. Smith of Asheville, his grandson. He lived for some time on Ashland Avenue.

Within five years, it became painfully obvious that the home was inadequate to meet the need of the Western North Carolina Mountain area. Dr. Smith, in his renamed position as secretary of home missions, observed that literally hundreds of mountain children were homeless and uncared for, many of whom he knew by name.

His sincere concern for these youngsters and their plight had become widely known and had gained substantial support. Two men acquired a tract of land at Balfour, near Hendersonville. A facility that would house forty children was constructed, and in 1910, the Mountain Orphanage left its Crabtree location. This location was outgrown also and its wood-frame buildings were considered a fire hazard, so the now-called Presbyterian Home for Children made its final move to Black Mountain in 1923. The Home celebrated its 100th birthday this year.

Local history buff Clarine Best of Crabtree, has no personal recollection of the Mountain Orphanage, of course, but she knows where it was located. Standing in the parking lot of Crabtree Methodist Church, one can see the knoll on which Smith constructed that first small building for Haywood County children left homeless in the aftermath of the Civil War.

The house was next occupied by Dr. Bob Walker, and then later torn down. Some lumber from the original structure is still around, though, having been used in the construction of two nearby private residences.

JUST MEANDERING

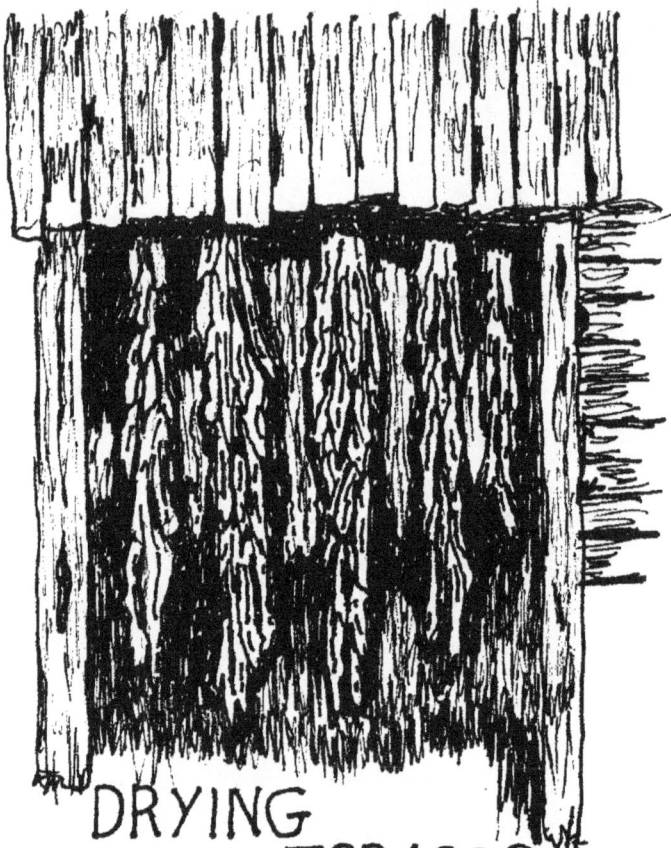

DRYING
TOBACCO EHB

Tobacco Was Prevalent in Western North Carolina Fields

Long, narrow plant beds, covered with white muslin, once dominated rural landscapes across this county in early spring. The muslin protected tender tobacco plants.

There was a time when tobacco was the only source of income for many. A good crop meant money for winter staples, shoes, perhaps a new plow and a bolt of cloth, and maybe something for kids at Christmas. A harder than usual winter followed a failed crop. Later, tobacco provided a college education for many, including two of Tom Harvey's children.

Drastic changes in the tobacco market have brought decline to a crop once all important. Like so many old ways, this crop is gradually fading from the scene. Old barns deteriorate, no longer sheltering drying tobacco leaves. Tobacco warehouses sit dim, dusty, and silent, but redolent with the lingering scent of the golden brown leaves.

Carroll Best of Beaverdam, seventy-four, and his wife Lucy grew tobacco for fifty-three years. "It takes thirteen months to make a tobacco crop and it's put many a shoe on kids and bought a lot of real estate," Best said. "We depended on it when I was a kid, for shoes and stuff. The first land I bought was paid for out of a tobacco crop. It didn't bring that much (money) then but it sure helped." His first year of not

173

growing tobacco is surely different, but he can't get it into the barn anymore and good help is hard to get, he says.

"Raising tobacco is hard, manual labor," stressed Harvey of Bethel, retired agriculture extension agent, even for those with modern machinery and pesticides, neither of which was available for those first growers. And bad weather could devastate a crop and a family.

Tall, yellowing tobacco plants were a beautiful sight. Brown, wrinkled leaves hanging in a barn to dry were even more beautiful.

Entire families worked year-round in the growing process. Burning beds to kill weeds and insects, clearing, tilling, and sowing seeds were a winter chore. Pine needles or broom sage topped with staked-down cloth protected seedbeds until young plants could be transplanted by hand into carefully laid out furrows. A summer of plowing, hoeing, then "topping" and "suckering" (removing mature and budding seed heads) followed. I personally remember gum deposited on hands and clothing, removed only with vigorous washing and strong soap, and the sting of those "packsaddles," a woolly-worm-looking pest. Phew! Tired yet? Can't rest.

Stalks were cut, speared on tobacco sticks, and left to dry in the field. Burdened tobacco sticks were hung in barns to air cure until November. The drying process completed by warm days and cool nights, brittle leaves became pliable from rain-carried moisture. Tobacco was "in case." Hurry. Strip leaves from stalk and separate by grades gathered into "hands," neat piles tied off with a tobacco leaf, before building a basket full. A nice-looking basket was a source of pride, Harvey said.

Hauling tobacco to market was a family affair charged with anticipation. Warehouses were noisy and thick with tension as auctioneers began chanting and farmers hoped for good prices for a year's labor.

Growing burley (air-cured) tobacco in Western North Carolina has a long history, but this powerful emblem of our state is waning.

Haystacks Displayed Hard Work

Haystacks rising in mown fields were a sign of harvest time, the waning of summer.

These carefully constructed mounds could be picturesque, an art form inspiring paintings by the likes of Claude Monet and Vincent Van Gogh. "Like finding a needle in a haystack" is an old adage referring to difficulty in locating something. Haystacks could be regarded as a symbol of security, satisfaction with a harvested crop, and knowledge that forage was stored to feed livestock during long winter months.

To farmers, completion of the rounded pyramidal shapes also meant the end of long, hot, dusty days spent working in the field; an annual back-breaking, wearisome chore completed.

Haystacks have all but disappeared from our landscape, replaced by tightly wrapped bales and, predominantly, rolls of hay.

Modern machinery accomplishes in half a day a job that took three men a week to complete, according to Ernest "Shorty" Chambers, seventy-seven, who lives on the Clyde side of Stamey Cove on land where his father farmed and built haystacks for winter survival.

Chambers had to work in the field, but wasn't included in the actual building of the stacks. "That was Daddy's job," he laughed. "He didn't want them to fall down." But he can tell you how the job is done, as can Tommy Worley, sixty-three, of Beaverdam who helped his uncle and cousins in the hay field.

"There ain't that much to it," Chambers said. "We used horse-drawn mowing machines to cut the hay and horse-drawn rakes and pitchforks to gather it into windrows of loose shocks (stacks) so it could cure out." Curing was important. Wet hay generates heat and rots, so stack building didn't begin until hay had lain in the field, turned and turned again, until it was dry. A pitchfork is a three or four-tined implement with a long handle. Mowing machines used a sickle bar for cutting, Worley said.

"Long, sturdy poles, usually locust or chestnut, were set a couple of feet into the ground," Chambers said. "Heavy brush was piled around the pole to keep hay off the ground." Some used boards to make a "platform. "Heavy chains or ropes were wrapped around shocks and horses drug hay to the stack pole," he said.

"Three men were a good size team," Chambers said. Two pitched the hay around the pole while another stood on the hay, working around the pole to pack it down so there would be no air pockets and to keep an even stack." When the stack tapered to ten to fifteen feet high, the man on top slid to the ground. Finally, the haystack was raked with pitchforks to smooth hay in a vertical position so rain wouldn't penetrate the stack.

"They wouldn't let just anyone on top of the stack," Tommy Worley of Beaverdam said. A strong fellow with a three or four-tined pitchfork who could accurately maintain the shape was needed. The stack would be fourteen or fifteen feet in diameter or smaller, and he would be responsible for keeping hay piled half the diameter around the pole, Worley said.

Worley remembers that a Halloween prank resulted in two burned haystacks. "They represented fifty to sixty dollars' worth of hay," he said. "Children weren't allowed to play on haystacks. You got your fanny beat for digging holes in a haystack."

Well before our time, hay would have been hand-cut with a sickle, a curved blade fastened to wooden handle, or a scythe, with curved blade fastened to a long, contoured wooden handle, sometimes called a cradle scythe. Crude pitchforks were fashioned of wood.

Cattle would feed some from stacks, but when hay stored in the barn was depleted, a farmer climbed to the top of a haystack, using a ladder or pole, and pitched the hay onto a horse drawn sled or wagon to be carried to the barn.

"I never had the experience, but I have been told that wet hay can get so hot that it will set a barn on fire," Chambers said. Worley agrees, saying when hay stored wet begins to mold or rot, spontaneous combustion is a real possibility.

A stack might weigh a couple of tons, according to Worley who says that haystacks began disappearing in the mid '50s and were a thing of the past by the mid '60s.

HAYSTACK

Tobacco Farming: Auctions

Notes of the tobacco auctioneer's song are fading and cavernous warehouses, once home to lively, all-important auctions, might display antique dealers' wares rather than golden leaves.

Burley tobacco auctions were an important event around here when the leafy crop was a major source of income for mountain folks. Good prices for tobacco meant growers could pay their taxes, buy the family a little something for Christmas, and for some, provided the only significant source of income until the next year. Later on, tobacco money paid college tuition for many mountain children. Farmers could grow nothing else that would legally bring in that much money.

Warehouses in Asheville, where Haywood County farmers usually did their selling, were huge, drafty, dusty buildings. "It was the coldest place in the world in the winter," said Neal Stamey of Bethel.

"It was a ritual of fall," said Robert Cathey. According to Cathey, who described his crops as being among the smaller ones. The warehouses were a half-acre to an acre in size. Sale day was "quite a show with lots of activity," he said. "If you weren't wearing bibbed overalls and boots with a chew of tobacco in your mouth, you felt out of place."

Rows of tobacco were laid out in hands on baskets on the warehouse floor, separated by class. Leaves stripped from the bottom of the tobacco stalk were classed as sand lugs, Tony McGaha explained. From the center of the stalk came the leaves in shades of red and gold called smokers, and narrow leaves from the uppermost area of the stalk were classed as tips, he said. A hand of tobacco is a group of leaves tied together at the stem end with a couple of carefully chosen leaves. Hands were laid in tobacco baskets with the stem ends pointing to the outside.

The auctioneer, calling his singsong chant, moved quickly along the aisles selling to buyers as farmers looked on anxiously, hoping for a good price. Auctions were fast paced; the leaves of gold sold quickly.

McGaha is an extension agent with Haywood County Cooperative Extension Service. His family grew tobacco, and money from its sale sent him to college. Auctions in cement-floored pole barns with enclosed sides are part of his history. "Buyers would run their fingers through the hands to look for leaves tipped with mold, moisture, or hidden stones to increase the weight, because there were always people who wanted to rub the system the wrong way," McGaha said. At one end of the barn, a pot-bellied stove would blast heat where those who wrote the checks were located. "It was hot as blue blazes and very smoky," he said.

McGaha provides a certain perspective on tobacco growing and getting ready for sales, emphasizing its importance to farmers. "It was a pride thing for farmers to have a good crop or a big sale," he said. Growers would wear their best overalls to the sale, as if they were going to town or church.

"Pulling leaves (from the stalk) was time consuming and people took great time and effort to do it right and get it neat. For us, it was all family labor or neighbor helping neighbor. My grandfather would choose the prettiest leaves to tie the hands. Everything had to be just so-so. He took great pride in having it look nice. We always wanted to sell before Thanksgiving, but avoided the first and last sales in order to get the best price."

This dying ritual, another disappearing aspect of our culture, was primarily a man thing, but Cathey said some wives came with their husbands to be sure they got the check. He added, with a self-conscious laugh, that he also remembers seeing many women hovering in the check-dispensing area. They were not wives, but rather ladies of ill repute who hoped they might get a share of the freshly-written checks.

Ginseng: An Old Appalachian Treasure

One of author Mark Twain's characters declared "Thar's gold in them thar hills," referring, of course, to the precious metal. There is "gold" of a different description in our hills. Ginseng or "'sang," as the old-timers call it, grows primarily in the Appalachian Mountains.

Ginseng is a plant, a much-coveted herb that is thought by some to be a panacea. A staple in Chinese medicine, it is used to treat high blood pressure, anxiety and other emotional problems, anemia, shortness of breath, and a host of other symptoms. Ginseng is thought to promote longevity, act as an aphrodisiac, battle symptoms of aging, and is used as a beautifying agent and an ingredient in weight loss formulas, to name just a few uses. Comparing it to gold may seem far-fetched, but last year it sold for $850 a pound and may earn $1,000 a pound this year, I am told. Roots have been exported from North America to Asia for centuries. "It takes a lot of ginseng to weigh a pound," a mountain man told me as he handed me a dried, twisted root. It was light as a feather.

Men who hunt and dig 'sang responsibly, who will not be named, have shared information with me. Revealing their identity might make them potential targets for ginseng poachers, like those who stole a long-tended crop from retired State Patrolman J. D. Silver, affectionately known as "Hi Ho," who intended to partially fund college educations for his children with its sale.

One said that most of that he finds is "growing in deep hollows where the morning sun comes in." Ginseng likes shady woodlands with rich soil and a cold/warm growing cycle. The plant also prefers to grow in a littered environment surrounded by undergrowth, not in open spaces.

He has found a few plants three to four feet tall, but one to two feet is the usual height. Leaflets grow from varying numbers of prongs, emerging from the fleshy root. Year-old plants have one prong with three leaflets. As the plant matures, it branches out with two, three, or four prongs, each of which can have three to five leaflets. Roots younger than five years old should be left untouched.

"I have found plants with five prongs on the same root, but those are rare," one person told me. Harvested in the fall, the plant is centered with red berries that contain seeds. Responsible diggers take care to preserve ginseng, planting the berries where they find the plants.

The prize is the root which grows in all directions, not straight down. Digging is usually done with a stick rather than with a tool with a sharp edge. Carefully, the stick is stuck in the ground surrounding the perennial plant and soil is gently lifted. Once harvested, the root is allowed to dry thoroughly. Roots are irregularly shaped: some are long, some fat, some forked. "Three pounds of green roots make a pound of dry roots," I was told.

Anger with irresponsible diggers was expressed by one. "If they are smart, they plant the berries where they found the plant," he said, "Some dummies carry all the seed out or dig the plants when they are too little. Dummies dig it before it is ready. What they are doing is destroying the ginseng."

The herb was a source of rare income for pioneers. The money it brought in fed families, and bought clothing and other necessities.

'Sang was, indeed, a form of gold for them and knowledge of the plant has been passed through generations.

Once plentiful, ginseng is becoming difficult to find because of overharvesting or careless harvesting. Laws and regulations governing harvesting vary from state to state. It is illegal to harvest American ginseng roots on all National Parks Service land. In North Carolina, taking ginseng without permission from private property in a felony.

Ginseng

Ramp Smell Is a Badge of Honor

Ah, spring. Blooming flowers perfume the air and delight the eyes. The rites of spring is normally a poetical phrase. However, one rite is lauded not by poets, but by those who anticipate the appearance of the dual leaves of a distant cousin of the lily.

Ramps. Wild leeks. Those odiferous, malodorous vegetables are ready for harvesting. Seemingly a cross between onions and garlic, some regard them as vile while others call them delicious. The plant favors moist, rich soil underneath the cover of thick deciduous trees in the hills, and emerges only in the spring from a blanket of dry, brown leaves. Even though their smell endures for a few days, those who partake say it is worth the odor and consider it a badge of honor.

However you regard these innocuous-looking spicy bulbs, it is time for that Southern Appalachian ritual, the ramp convention or festival.

Festivals are like the ramps. They spring up all over. Waynesville's is likely one of the oldest, according to Joe Sam Queen, who hosts his own mini festival during the ACC basketball tournament.

Frank Lauer and his associates at the American Legion Post in Waynesville, where the Waynesville festival takes place, say 2005 marks the 75th festival in Haywood County. Originally, the event was held at Black Camp Gap and was the brainchild of "politicians and the good old boys," Lauer said.

"Ramps are good for your nervous and digestive systems," Lauer said, "and were an old-time settlers' staple, combined with branch lettuce, for medicinal purposes." He didn't make that up, he says. The Waynesville festival has a scientist and a botanist on hand to testify to the benefits of eating ramps and answer questions. Queen calls it the "spring tonic of Appalachia."

The Waynesville Ramp Festival was moved to the American Legion post on Legion Drive about thirty years ago to provide easier accessibility and more space. The first Sunday in May is the traditional date, with festivities beginning around noon.

RAMPS

"We are renowned worldwide for holding the record for the most ramps eaten in ten minutes," Lauer said. Randy Surrett held that record for many years, downing ninety-four ramps at one sitting, but has passed his reign to his son, Randy, Jr. "It is a point of honor for the family," Lauer said.

The program is always basically the same. Music, clog dancing, politicians working the crowd, and ramps, both raw and cooked. They are said to taste best mixed with eggs, accompanied by country ham, red-eye gravy, and homemade biscuits or cornbread. They are a meatloaf ingredient in Waynesville, and are often fried in a batch of potatoes.

"Ramps are harvested on private property by the Waynesville group and a replanting program is used to assure that there will be ramps available for future generations to enjoy," Lauer said.

Grand Hotels

They came "to take the air." They came "to take the waters." And they came to stay the summer.

Tourists, especially those from coastal areas of the Carolinas, discovered a summer refuge in the lush, green coolness of Western North Carolina's mountains in the late 1800s and early 1900s.

An era of grand hotels in Haywood County emerged to accommodate the lowlanders.

What a grand time that must have been. Accounts tell of lavish parties, scrumptious dinners, croquet on the lawn, carriage rides, horseback riding, billiards, card games, and strolls around the lawn.

Since the trip from coast to mountains by stagecoach and later by rail was long and arduous, the summer people were aptly named as they brought children, servants, and steamer trunks, settling in until fall. Some liked it so well that they built homes and stayed permanently.

These were people of wealth, certainly, enjoying lavish dinners served on white linen cloths with china, crystal, and silver gleaming in the soft glow of oil lamps. Afterwards, there might be dancing on a verandah or in a pavilion. Or ladies might sip wine and gossip over a card game, while gentlemen took themselves elsewhere to smoke an after-dinner cigar.

During evening, children were neither seen nor heard, entertained in nurseries provided by hotels or by family servants.

White Sulphur Springs Hotel was the first, and probably the grandest. The original building was a plantation-style private home, enlarged around 1878 before assuming its new identity as a hotel. Fourteen years later it was destroyed by fire, but quickly rebuilt. The new structure was brick, with three stories of rooms. Its popularity necessitated the building of a three-story annex, giving the hotel a total of ninety rooms. Therapeutic mineral waters flowing from nearby springs were a big draw. Guests either bathed in the waters or drank from the springs.

Eagle's Nest Hotel, a fifty-room frame structure with a rock foundation, topped Junaluska Mountain, as it was called then. The owners touted its fresh, pure air. Popular with tourists who enjoyed the views from the mountain, this hotel also burned but was never rebuilt.

Piedmont Inn was a rambling, white frame building on Eagle's Nest Road that attracted some well-known guests, such as Eleanor Roosevelt. Still open but in a decline both structurally and financially, it was sold and razed in the 1980s to become Laurel Ridge Country Club.

Other hotels and boarding houses abounded in Waynesville, Canton, and Clyde, but none were as grand as these.

Then the Depression showed its ugly face and the magical summers of Waynesville's Grand Hotels were essentially ended.

MR. VANDEBILT'S SPRING HOUSE

Vanderbilt's Hunting Lodge Retreat

B uck Springs Lodge: George Vanderbilt's retreat and hunting lodge near Mount Pisgah.

As with all his endeavors, the Lodge was a grand place, according to recollections by old-timers in Haywood County.

"I never understood why it was torn down and not preserved," said Ora Burnette of Bethel, eighty-seven years old. "It was one of the best places of interest in this area."

He should know. He worked there in summertime from 1933–35 to earn extra money for school. His great-grandfather James Henry Burnette helped build the lodge. His grandson Seth, who lives in Charlotte now, penned an interview with him in 1992. Their conversations are recorded in a copyrighted booklet called *Pigeon Valley*, compiled by Cheryl Haney's eighth grade class at Bethel School.

"It was a huge log building, furnished with the very best," Ora Burnette said. "He (Vanderbilt) had hunting trophies all over the walls. The one that caught my eye was a huge polar bear hide that lay on the floor. I am sure he killed them himself because he traveled all over the world."

"The poplar logs used to construct the building were cut in exact lengths at the head of Pisgah Creek, and hauled up the mountain in wagons pulled by horses and oxen," he said."

"The main lodge was approximately fifty feet by thirty-five feet wide. The inside of the lodge had a living room, which was the biggest room, and it had two large bedrooms and some rooms for staff. There were other buildings scattered around; a tool shack, a building for staff, a kitchen on the side of the main lodge, and a school house built just for Gloria, Mr. Vanderbilt's daughter," Seth Burnette wrote. "A breezeway connected the main four-bedroom lodge with a two-bedroom suite and a combination kitchen and dining building."

Ora Burnette told his grandson of the big fireplace, made to burn eight-foot logs. "It was nine feet wide and about six feet tall, he said."

He also remembers what he describes as fine musical instruments of every description, including violins.

"I earned twenty-five cents an hour," Ora Burnette recalls. "I worked on roofs (split oak shingles) with a rope tied around my waist because if I had fallen I would have gone into a gorge about two hundred feet down the mountain. It was built on the edge of a rock cliff that faces toward Hendersonville."

Another of his chores was rounding up the sheep. Sometimes he found that bears had eaten part of the herd. "There were deer and bears all around. Vanderbilt shipped in two carloads of deer, and put one load in the Pink Beds area and took the rest to Asheville (Biltmore Estate)." Old postcards show flocks of sheep on the lawn at the Lodge.

"Vanderbilt was known for his landscaping abilities, and the area outside the lodge was no exception," Seth Burnette recorded. "It was all natural, with shrubs and wildflowers."

The site is off US 276 on the Blue Ridge Parkway, on what Burnette calls the Buck Spring Trail. About one and a half miles past Pisgah Inn is a road that turns right into the Pisgah parking ground. Rock steps lead to the lodge site, he said.

Many hikers and sightseers must have unknowingly walked on or around the site with no inkling of the grand lodge that once stood there.

Skip Shelton of Hendersonville is among volunteers gathered by the Carolina Mountain Club to help clean the site. "We have cut out some trees and other growth. We found a few rock foundations and walls that must have been along the driveway. One foundation, probably a root cellar, is relatively intact," he said.

George Cogburn lives on family property on Pisgah Creek. He recalls his father, Robert H. "Bob" Cogburn, telling how he helped build a dam on Flat Laurel Creek and install a "ram," a pump that pushed water uphill to the lodge. He also helped construct Gloria Vanderbilt's schoolhouse, furnished some lumber used to build the lodge, and later maintained a vegetable garden for Vanderbilt near the lodge.

Cogburn's Uncle Lonnie worked on the road to the lodge, hauling water from the Wagon Road Gap and Frying Pan Gap areas to power the steam drills used to build the road that is now the Blue Ridge Parkway. "They dynamited mountainsides to build the road," he said. "It was a big undertaking."

Cogburn and Burnette both say that Vanderbilt was interested in the community, and provided residents with jobs that paid more than others around. With their alert minds, well-spoken words, and excellent memories, the two men provide a wealth of information concerning Buck Spring Lodge and other factors that influenced the life and growth of Haywood County.

The site could become an archaeological dig and eventually a historical interpretive site, Shelton said.

Multitalented, Industrious Colonel Smathers

John Charles Smathers and his Turnpike Inn claim prominent spots of importance in the history of Western North Carolina.

The late Wilma Dykeman called Smathers the last of the illustrious pioneers of Western North Carolina in her book *The French Broad*. John Preston Arthur's *History of Western North Carolina* calls him a fine example of the old-time pioneer, following a listing of Smathers' talents and achievements.

The Turnpike Inn property on US 19/23 straddles the Buncombe and Haywood County line. George Smathers gave the 1,000-acre site to his second son John, who created the essential destination for travelers, especially drovers driving their stock to market, and summer visitors.

Smathers was "lively as a cricket and busy as a queen bee, farming, building, sawmilling, trading, and running his famous Turnpike Hotel," wrote John Parris in *Roaming the Mountains*.

"Turnpike John" or "Colonel Smathers," as he was sometimes called, was born at Pigeon River, now Canton, in 1826. He married Lucinda "Lucilla" Johnson of Haywood County and the two raised a family of thirteen children at the Turnpike Inn, which the couple built and ran, along with a general store.

A prosperous inn, a busy store, and the rearing of a large family would keep most people busier than they wanted to be, but not Smathers. His property included a blacksmith shop, saw-mill, wagon works, cabinet factory, and a complete grist and flouring mill, the second flouring mill built in Haywood County.

Extending his enterprises, he operated a second grist and flour mill and a store in Clyde. In Waynesville, where the Smathers lived for four years, he had a third store and a hotel.

"Colonel Smathers was a man of remarkable character and a jack-of-all trades," wrote Parris. "He was a rock and brick mason, a carpenter and shoemaker, a tinner, painter, blacksmith and plumber, a harness and saddle-maker, a candle maker, farmer, hunter, storekeeper and bee raiser, a glazier, butcher, fruit grower, hotel-keeper and merchant, a physician, lawyer, politician and rail-splitter, a cook, school master, and gardener, as well as a Bible scholar. When he was eighty-four years old, he could still run a good foot race and throw most men in a (wrestling) match." Parris was quoting, in part, the words of George W. McCoy, whose account of Smathers was published in the Sunday edition of the Asheville Citizen-Times on December 30, 1950.

His great-granddaughter Mabel Smathers Green, who lives on the property above the inn site, remembers him as being a thrifty person. "I lived at the Inn until I was fourteen," she said, "and it was neat growing up there."

The late Frank Smathers, a federal court judge, wrote of his grandfather, "...when there was a difficult or dangerous thing to be done in the neighborhood of Turnpike, North Carolina, Colonel J. C. Smathers could always be counted on. His neighbors looked to him in those troublous Civil War times, and were met with a cheerful resourcefulness that inspired confidence and restored sometimes sagging morale."

"Although Grandpa was unable to serve in the Armies of Virginia, he was, nevertheless, an ardent and active soldier on the home front of Western North Carolina, raising wheat, corn, cattle, hogs, and horses for the heroic armies of his beloved Confederacy," he wrote.

When the news of Lee's surrender at Appomattox reached Smathers, he is said to have dropped his heavy hammer on the anvil in his blacksmith shop and told his helpers, "Now men, we'll start tomorrow morning making more and better plowshares."

Of German ancestry, John C. Smathers was the grandson of John and Mary Agner Smathers, who left Rowan County to settle in Dutch Cove in Haywood County.

The Turnpike Hotel: A Magnet for Travelers

The old Turnpike Hotel stood tall and proud on a slight knoll overlooking clay tennis courts and long-gowned women in broadbrimmed hats enjoying their leisure. The image of her great-grandparents' hotel, painted in oils, was copied from an old photo and hangs prominently in Mabel Smathers Greene's living room.

The white, frame structure was two stories high with wide porches on both levels, rows of distinctive dormers, and a number of chimneys. Built in the early 1800s, the hotel had twenty-eight rooms. Alongside the imposing building that some called a Southern plantation was the first hotel, a ten-room building constructed in the early 1860s. Later called the annex, the initial hotel was connected to the other by a covered walkway and housed the kitchen and dining area.

John C. and Lucilla Smathers, mentioned earlier, built the popular and prosperous hotel with its two-story general store, blacksmith shop, sawmill, wagon works, cabinet factory, and a complete grist and flouring mill.

The need for the hotel went far beyond that of a summer destination for visitors enjoying the mountain air and delicious meals of food grown on the property.

"Sixteen miles west of Asheville is a model country hotel, at Turnpike. For long years it was a stopping place for the stages on the way from Asheville to Waynesville," wrote Zeigler and Grosscup in *The Heart of the Alleghenies*, in 1883. Before the railroad was built, before the tourists came for the summer, it was the stopping place for drovers bringing cattle, hogs, and turkeys en route to Southern markets along the dusty Western Turnpike: a toll road. Cattle would be pastured and fed grain and fodder and the farmers could rest, eat, restock supplies, and get necessary repairs to their wagons before resuming their journey.

Other travelers on horseback, riding a horse and buggy, or in a stagecoach would stop for lunch, supper, or to stay overnight.

The store served a wider territory than the township of Turnpike with its forty or so residents and the travelers. Smathers bought wheat in the western counties, ground it into flour during the winter, and bagged it. His older sons transported it by horse and wagon to Greenville and other South Carolina cities. The flour was traded for shoes, calico, salt, coffee, sugar, and other items. In his extensive trading business, Smathers also bought hams, bacon, shoulders, or whatever else for which there was a market, selling to people throughout the area. An ancient photo shows four covered wagons leaving for South Carolina.

The railroad figured largely in the success of the hotel, for a time. Engineers and workers constructing the railroad, which ran between the hotels and the store, stayed at the hotel during the week and were joined by wives and families on weekends. Completed in 1882, this improved transportation brought more and more summer visitors to the Turnpike; its greatest business was from 1885–1898. Then Waynesville and the Sulphur Springs area became a mecca for those coming to the mountains for the entire summer, and the Turnpike was an overnight stop before arriving at Waynesville.

Lucilla Smathers was an able partner for her husband. She planned the meals and oversaw housekeeping chores at the hotels while tending to her children. She grew flowers and kept chickens, ducks, guineas, quail, and turkeys and gathered their eggs, Frank Smathers remembers in his illustrated *The Last Pioneer of Western North Carolina*, a booklet about his grandparents. She was also determined that her children would be well-educated. When she died May 5, 1911 at age eighty-two, neither her husband nor the hotels were ever the same. Smathers died July 21, 1918. He was ninety-two years old.

Closed around 1920, the buildings fell into disrepair and were eventually vandalized. The hotel burned in 1989, in a fire likely started by vagrants.

The First County Fair

T he first county fair staged in Haywood opened on November 1, 1905, according to local historian W. Clark Medford.

"There had never been seen such a conglomeration of people - in wagons, buggies, carts, horse-back (an oxcart or two) and on foot," Medford wrote.

"The opening day was a gala affair," Medford wrote. ""Most of the county, it seemed, was there, also many from other counties."

The event wasn't a hastily thrown-together affair, and the planning process had evidently been under way for a lengthy period of time. Organizers had expended many hours of their days, along with a great deal of effort.

Exhibit buildings were built, along with a racetrack and seating.

Horse racing must have been a major attraction. An old photo shows a fine-looking oval dirt track, and the property was described as having a steep, sloping incline toward the rear, "which could be used for the grandstand from which to view the horse races."

Fair-goers included women, who customarily stayed close to home, prompting Medford to write, "...contrary to most such public associations in those days, there were many women attending." He commented on their attire: rather long skirts, stiff-collared shirtwaists, stacked-up hair, and big ornamented hats. Some men wore their finer clothing as well: cut-away coats, rather tight trousers, derby hats, celluloid collars, a few fancy canes, and waxed mustaches.

"Crowds of thousands" were said to have attended the fair to see the races, and the exhibits of farm products. Farmers had brought in poultry, livestock, apples, vegetables, berries, nuts, wheat, rye, or whatever they had raised or harvested, and prizes were given.

The fair was successful for its first few years as it retained its rural characteristics, but its popularity probably contributed to its demise. Inevitably, word spread far beyond the county and some unsavory entrepreneurs appeared on the scene, with their equally unsavory attractions.

Attendance dropped and some regular exhibitors lost interest. Financial difficulties arose, Medford said.

The carnival features of the fair became increasingly popular—too popular according to the fair's critics. As some folks said, the event had become "a big, nasty and gambling carnival." Stories circulated about the "sexy midway," the rowdiness, and the folks being fleeced by gambling.

Somewhere around 1915, the fair was dropped from the county's agenda, according to Medford. Attempts to revive it in 1934 failed.

After a hiatus of almost 100 years, the fair has been revived in a new location. In 2005 a bicentennial celebration was held in the Haywood County Agricultural and Activities Center on NC 209 in a first-class, year-round facility, according to Sam Smith, administrative assistant and board of directors member for the center. The center has two heated exhibit buildings, a livestock barn, and a covered arena. Waynesville Lion's Club added a horse barn with thirty gated stalls.

"We can handle everything from the fair to rodeos, even concerts," said Guy Angel, another longtime board member.

Pigeon Gap Spring

"Beautiful Spring" headlines a story in the July 7, 1924 issue of _The Carolina Mountaineer and Waynesville Courier_.

"A movement of the Waynesville Women's Club to beautify springs along main highways in Haywood County has resulted in a pretty little fountain and resting place for motorists near the top of Pigeon Gap...on the new Waynesville-Woodrow road," a reporter wrote.

Travelers on horseback or driving a wagon, perhaps herding livestock, on the new, dusty road would have welcomed a drink of cold water before continuing their journey.

The spring still exists at the crest of the Gap, or "Apple Mountain," as some continue to call the rise on US 276 between Bethel and Waynesville. Calling it beautiful in its current condition requires a stretch of imagination, but a bit of clearing, simple yard work really, would expose the still-lovely wall protecting the site. A bronze plaque imbedded in the wall reads "Erected by the Community Club of Waynesville," and is dated 1924.

"In a cool nook, stonework has been placed about the cold water that gushes out from the steep bank providing cool seats and drinking place for travelers and heightening the scenic effect of that part of the road. From the spring proper a pipe carries the water farther out to a miniature fountain back of which is the semi-circular stone wall and resting place," the story reads.

Starved for water, there is no gushing stream. But later on, after the drought releases its stranglehold, perhaps it might return. To my way of thinking, this is a historical treasure that calls for recognition and restoration, but its location is now on privately owned land.

Blanton Burnette, eighty-one, remembers driving the undulating road that preceded US 276 from the Bethel/Cruso area into Waynesville. He was courting his wife, Fannie, and always stopped at the spring. "That was a curvy road. I believe that was the first paved road I ever drove on," he said. He didn't observe a gushing flow at the spring, but said it was good water.

"The club women do not expect to stop with the work already done there, but plan to further beautify the place with shrubbery and provide seats and swings in the grove adjoining...Ultimately the club women expect to establish similar stopping places at other highway springs."

Further research has not yet revealed the existence of more beautified springs.

The old news report relates that "C. W. Dicus, the contractor, suggested the beautification and did the building...the ornament has so far cost almost $300 of which $100 was furnished by the board of county commissioners."

Author's Note: In 2014, Joey Rolland, in collaboration with Bethel Rural Community Organization, Haywood County Historical & Genealogical Society, and interested individuals, restored the watering hole or spring as an Eagle Scout project. The wall and monument were cleared of overgrowth, cleaned, and polished. A small bridge was built to make the site more easily accessible. Visitors can park outside the gated barrier at the Estates at Boulder Creek, and walk the short distance to the renovated site.

Civilian
Conservation Corps

High Arch and Triple Arch bridges on NC 215 with their fine rockwork stand in silent tribute to the valuable work of the Civilian Conservation Corps in Haywood County. They are but two examples of many benefits reaped from President Franklin Delano Roosevelt's peacetime army, initiated in 1933. Our access to and enjoyment of places like Pisgah National Forest and Great Smokies National Park lands was greatly enhanced by CCC.

One CCC camp was on Cold Springs Road in the Harmon Den area, called the twelve-mile stretch, according to Rodney Snedeker, Forest Archeologist with the USDA Forest Service. "They built roads and trails, planted trees on both east and west sides of I-40, and built the fire lookout tower on Sutton Top (near Mount Sterling)," he said. "The camps were supervised by U.S. Army personnel, but on the job, workers were directed by the commanding agency in the area; either federal or state forest, and agriculture service."

Enrollees at the Sunburst camp, actually located in Spruce, numbered 211, according to Scott Ashcraft, USDA Forest Archaeologist. Vaugh Rogers of Lake Logan area, eighty-seven, was one of ten locals at the camp. "We lived in green barracks and were issued army clothing," Rogers said. "We did road work, logging, and built buildings, including the Ranger Station on Big East Fork. I really enjoyed working there." At times, they traveled over the mountain into Transylvania County where they built sheds and other structures in the Pink Beds and worked around the Cradle of Forestry. "I bet some of those sheds I built (Pink Beds) are still standing," Rogers said.

"My grandfather, James R. Boyd, Sr., leased 840 acres for the camp at Black Camp Gap from 1933 to 1935," Dick Boyd of Waynesville said. "The men wore army uniforms and shaved every day. They were certainly glad to have work. They cleaned the land, logged the forest, and were involved in road work on Soco Road. A Masonic marker built from thirty-three white stones from all over the world stands near the site. I believe they had two or three barracks." Boyd owns 272.5 acres of the original tract.

Raymond Caldwell of Waynesville remembers the camp in Cataloochee Valley. He was thirteen and living in Cataloochee. "The army officer in charge was from Brooklyn, N.Y. and the superintendent was Farraday Green, a local resident. The camp workers earned thirty dollars a month and sent twenty-five home," he said. "The camp was near the first bridge below the old Palmer house, and they worked on the south side of the creek. They set out a field full of white pines, and some cedar trees. Some of the trails they built followed old Indian trails. The stack rock retaining walls they built are still as beautiful as they ever were."

"They did a great job," he said. "They built good buildings, a lot of rock buildings. They did a lot of rock-work." He remembers they lived in structures with wooden foundations and tent tops. Burrell McGaha, local blacksmith, sharpened tools for them. Caldwell's father was a road foreman at a camp in the Davidson River section.

Uneducated young men in the Corps could attend basic education classes at night. One of Roosevelt's New Deal Programs aimed at lifting the US out of the Great Depression of 1929, CCC was called one of the most successful, especially in the hard-hit mountain region of North Carolina. Initially, CCC was open to unemployed single men between eighteen and twenty-five, who had to sign on for at least six months. Its mission was simple work not interfering with normal employment, and confined to forest land and its conservation.

CCC had considerable and lasting effect on Western North Carolina, with large projects like construction of Blue Ridge Parkway and numerous recreation areas, forest planting, massive road and bridge construction, and watershed restoration, according to Snedeker and Ashcraft. CCC ended when the US economy began growing during World War II.

CANTON, CLYDE, HAZELWOOD, LAKE JUNALUSKA, MAGGIE VALLEY, WAYNESVILLE

Hazelwood,
Industrial Town

The Village of Hazelwood hasn't always been a village. Once the industrial center of the county, Hazelwood was a small but thriving town.

W. H. Cole, credited with founding the town, moved to the area from Tennessee in 1893. He established a sawmill operation, the first in a series of events that would lead to the chartering of Hazelwood as a town by the state legislature in 1905.

E. E. Quinlan came along and built another sawmill, this one on Allen's Creek, an area that became known as Quinlantown, and a lumber depot. His interest in fine wood resulted in his establishing Unagusta Furniture Manufacturing Company. He was Hazelwood's first mayor.

Dick Bradley, former co-owner with Joe Cline of landmark Cline-Bradley Hardware, opened in 1935 by Bradley's father, W. H. Bradley, is knowledgeable about the various enterprises and tells interesting details about each.

A. C. Lawrence was the first industry in Haywood County, opened in 1888. The company's business was the tanning of leather for shoes. "They made quarter-inch thick shoe soles in their cut sole division and shipped them all over the country. The soles came with glue and tacks and we sold many of them," Bradley said.

Royal Pilkington, maker of tapestries used for furniture upholstery, came to town in 1925. Locals called it the "rag mill," Bradley said. "They shipped fabric to the Piedmont area, where the big furniture manufacturers were located," he said.

Dayton Rubber Company opened its plant in 1942. Heinz Rollman of Welco Shoes and Ro-Search leased space in the rubber plant before building its own facilities. Welco/Ro-Search is the only survivor among Hazelwood's early industries, and makes boots for the military.

These were the big boys of the industrial site, but there were others. Harry L. Liner Jr.'s Hazelwood Lumber Company became affiliated with Lowe's, and is now Waynesville Builder's Supply. Robert McKay's slaughterhouse and freezer locker business evolved into the present McKay RM Construction Company.

The town had, at one time or another, a blacksmith, a silent movie theater, a school, churches, a popular variety store, grocers, doctors, and other businesses as well as another landmark that still endures; Hazelwood Pharmacy.

Then Hazelwood began to lose its industries to fire, environmental issues, and company relocation. The tax base dwindled.

The issue of a merger with Waynesville came up at least four times. Attractive to some for economic reasons, it was fought with tenacity by others who didn't want to give up their town.

In 1988, Plott Creek residents requested annexation by Waynesville, despite Hazelwood's efforts to include the area within its town limits. When the annexation was finalized, Hazelwood was almost completely encircled by Waynesville, like a hole in a doughnut.

In 1994, beset by water and sewer problems and other economic woes, Hazelwood's Board of Aldermen with Mayor Mary Ann Enloe requested annexation by Waynesville, a move approved by a four to one vote. Waynesville's town board accepted unanimously and on July 1, 1995, Hazelwood was incorporated into Waynesville.

Hazelwood Dodged
a Bullet

"A series of explosions sent fire raging through a chemical packaging plant here Wednesday afternoon, releasing a plume of
toxic smoke high into the air and forcing the evacuation of nearly 2,000
residents for several miles."

The date was April 22, 1982, the site was Benfield Industries Incorporated in Hazelwood, and the report was from the Asheville Citizen.
Tom Benfield's 3.5-acre packaging plant was in flames, fueled by a wide
range of flammable chemicals.

Kenneth Moore, Waynesville alderman, was Hazelwood's police
chief when the fire occurred. He remembers working desperately to
evacuate everyone within a mile's radius of Hazelwood. "Waynesville's
fire department and law enforcement officers and Dan Crawford, State
Bureau of Investigation agent, were among the first to arrive to help us
get everyone out unharmed. We were especially concerned about those
with respiratory problems." Moore remembers the thick, black smoke
that caused burning sensations in noses, throats and eyes. Eventually,
seven fire departments would be fighting the blaze throughout the night
and numerous state and local agencies would be involved.

Health authorities said air samples indicated a substantial concentration of toxic chlorine gas in the smoke. Diligent firefighters were
successful in keeping the flames from exploding two large storage tanks
that held waste, solvents, and creosote.

The danger of the situation was compounded since no one, probably
not even Benfield himself, knew the amount and varieties of chemicals
stored in the structure made of wood and sheet metal.

Most residents fled to homes of relatives and friends, Moore said,
while others were taken to the National Guard Armory in Clyde and to
Hazelwood Elementary School.

Tony Winchester was at his home on Railroad Street when he heard
the town's disaster siren go off; school was just out and children were
walking home. He looked up to see a small plume of smoke that rapidly
grew larger and shot straight up into the air. He heard the continuous

explosions as vats of chemicals were ignited, releasing brightly colored puffs of smoke within the black cloud. Wooden railroad ties were burning beneath a tank car filled with propane gas, he said. "My sister was driving home on US 276 from Bethel, and she saw more of the smoke than we did because the wind was blowing that way, and she said flakes of ash were falling like snow."

The smoke was visible in Asheville and beyond as it drifted past Mount Pisgah.

Two Waynesville firemen were rescued from their perch in a cherry picker truck with a mechanical breakdown. Carolina Power & Light (CP&L) sent a truck to snatch them away from advancing flames while their colleagues sprayed them with water.

The fire was so uncontrollable that one fireman commented, "This is like spitting on a bonfire."

Aluminum siding on houses across the street from the plant melted and curled up.

According to the United States Environmental Protection Agency, which designated the area a Superfund cleanup site, Benfield Industries was a bulk chemical mixing and repackaging facility from 1976 until 1982, handling and storing such things as paint thinners, solvents, sealants, cleaners, de-icing solutions, and wood preservatives. The list of specific chemicals that contaminated the soil and groundwater is hair-raising.

Although the EPA has implemented the prescribed treatment processes, all traces of contaminants have not been removed and the site is tested and reviewed every five years.

As Winchester said, locating such a plant that close to residences and other businesses was an invitation to disaster. Good fortune prevailed and Hazelwood dodged a potentially lethal bullet.

Dayco, Champion
Were Once Bookends

The deteriorating sprawl of buildings, tanks, and smokestacks once known as Dayton Rubber Company is being demolished, razed to make way for a shopping center.

When this county was anchored in the east by Champion Paper and Fibre Company and Dayton Rubber in the west, job security was at an all-time high and tax revenues from the two manufacturing giants swelled county coffers.

Watching heavy equipment reduce to rubble a workplace that employed over 2,000 people in the 1960s is anticlimactic when compared to the emotional experiences of those who had spent their working lives in the factory, when they learned their livelihood was gone. This big blow came in 1966, when the icon announced its closing.

"You can't see that part of your history torn down without having some feelings about it. It is an emotional thing for me," said Barbara Wright, who was employed in human resources for thirty-eight years. Every worker passed through her office, at one time or another. "The atmosphere was like that of a family, and a livelihood was provided for a lot of people, she said." Wright described the workers as dedicated, loyal, hard-working people who were proud that they produced good projects, qualities not always easily found.

Dust rising from tumbling yellow bricks that walled the main office symbolically carries memories of steady jobs, food on the table, homes, education for children, health and retirement benefits, perhaps a shiny new car.

Dayco, as it was known later, was a virtual breeding ground for strong community leaders who willingly shared their talents to enhance life in Haywood. Haywood Community College will forever be indebted to the late A. L. Freedlander, who was company president, general manager, board chairman, then chairman of the executive committee and a director, for his interest in and contributions to the school.

The plant opened in 1941 with sixty-five employees. It produced a variety of rubber products for the automobile, textile and printing industries, and eventually, plastics. Research and Development was a busy place, resulting in many new and improved products.

Shortly after the plant opened, World War II was declared and military needs changed production lines. Pontoons and life rafts for American soldiers rolled off the lines.

The last vestiges of Waynesville Dayco are gone now, except in the minds of those who worked there. A large shopping center occupies the site.

Clyde's Stockyard

C lyde is a quiet little town with scant evidence of the days when it was the locale of the biggest stockyard in the Southeast. "It was a booming town," resident Bucky Brown says. "Clyde became the principal shipping point for cattle, tobacco, and produce," wrote W. Clark Medford, deceased, local historian and author.

Around 1889, Before the new highway pierced the center of town (before paved roads) and shortly after Western North Carolina Railroad was extended west of Canton, buildings, loading chutes, holding pens, and structures with scales for weighing livestock were built near the Clyde Depot.

Brown, seventy-nine, remembers the stockyards in the late 1930s. His family owned Brown's Grocery and he worked there, helping his mother.

"Thursday was auction day, the biggest day in Clyde," he said. Some 200 farmers brought their cattle in trucks and the auction took place in a barn at the foot of Charles Street. Remembering the sounds of the auctioneers' loudspeakers and the cattle and the dirt roads, he laughs as he says, "It wasn't a place for women in high heels."

"Cattle were classified, weighed and auction started at one p.m. The animals were loaded in railroad cars for shipping," Brown said. He shows old publications with advertisements for a number of businesses, signs of a bigger and busier town.

"Our icebox was filled with Cokes and Nehis, the only bottled drinks at the time," he said. My mother made big ham sandwiches and sold them for a quarter. Drinks were a nickel." He recalls that Granny Ford, who bought her groceries at Brown's store, prepared big meals to feed cattlemen in her home.

"She started cooking on Wednesday," says granddaughter Joan Browning of Canton, who spent a lot of time with Ida Ford. "She had a huge dining room table and it was always filled with people. She also rented rooms to people from out of town who came to the auctions."

"It was a big operation that moved as many cattle as any of today's stockyards, maybe more," said Horace Sellers of Canton whose grandfather owned the land where the stockyards were located. He was ten years old in the early '40s, helping Smathers move cattle in and out of boxcars along with other chores, some not so pleasant.

"None of the roads were paved," he said, "and moving livestock created lots of dust or mud if it was rainy. I think most of the (railway) cars went to Chicago."

Information supplied by Clyde Town Hall indicates that farmers came from all the western counties, South Carolina and East Tennessee, herding their livestock with the help of trained dogs, before trucks were available for hauling. Some brought sheep, turkeys, apples, chestnuts, and tobacco to be shipped. They could stay overnight at the Clyde Inn, the Pennington Place, or at Mrs. Ford's.

Sellers believes the stockyards were closed in the early '50s. And Clyde's heyday was over.

Clyde's Big Gun

"I'll meet you at the big gun in Clyde," has been a frequent remark since the highly-visible landmark was mounted in Clyde's town square almost fifty years ago.

Acquiring the three-inch, fifty-millimeter anti-aircraft gun and getting it moved to Clyde from a Norfolk, Virginia naval yard is credited to Milton "Bucky" Brown, then chairman of the now-defunct Clyde Chamber of Commerce.

"My son is the reason for its being here," Brown said. "I served in the U.S. Navy during World War II and have always been interested in anything relating to the navy, so I took my boys to the Naval Reserve on Merrimon Avenue in Asheville when they were young."

Brown was aboard an ammunition ship that supplied ammunition to the Seventh Fleet, the USS Gadsden, in the southwest Pacific. "That was practically our entire cargo," he said.

The Naval Reserve facility in Asheville had a gun similar to Clyde's on display. "'My ship had guns just like that one on it,' I told my boys," Brown said. "David, who was six and a half or seven years old then, asked 'Why don't we get one of those and put it in our back yard?'"

"I said, 'Okay,' just kidding him. But he didn't forget it. Several times he asked me, 'Daddy, when are we going to get that gun?'"

"Finally, I decided to try to get one. Tom Mallonee, Administrative Assistant to US Congressman (the late) Roy Taylor, came by the Chamber once a month. One day he was in the office and I told him I needed a three-inch fifty-millimeter gun," Brown remembers.

Mallonee, a retired naval commander, wasted no time in relaying the request to Taylor. "I got a letter from Tom in three or four days," Brown said. "Tom said, 'I've got you a gun in Norfolk. All you have to do is come and get it. We will even load it.'"

"Chester Sellars, who is dead now, had a low-boy truck and he volunteered to go after the gun. He wouldn't let us pay him," Brown said.

The next order of business was finding someone to unload the gun, which weighed several tons. "I went to Champion Papers and talked to a fellow who was a contractor doing work at the paper mill. He said they would be glad to bring a crane and get the gun off the truck. After they unloaded it, I told him to come on over to the office and I would write him a check. He wouldn't take any money, either," Brown related.

A fellow from Candler heard about the gun, and said he would like to sandblast and paint it at no charge, Brown remembers.

"We had a nice plaque made with names of those from Clyde who died in combat during World War II mounted it next to the gun, and had a very nice dedication service," he said. "The late Ernest Messer, North Carolina Representative, gave a nice dedication speech. A big crowd gathered around here that day."

Years later, another man volunteered to repaint it. "I don't know where he found them, but he even attached some three-inch, fifty-millimeter shells to the base of the pedestal where the gun was mounted," Brown concluded.

The gun has been moved from its highly-visible perch alongside the railroad tracks on Broad Street in Clyde, facing four-lane US 19/23. It has been incorporated into a new park in the town square, located near its former resting place.

The Shook House

"I am going to tell you a tale of two houses," said Sarah Queen Brown, as we entered the Shook Museum in Clyde, once a tired, gray house with sagging porches, struggling to stay erect, hoping for someone to breathe new life into its walls.

The heart of this renovated, historic structure is the house that Jacob Shook built. Virgin timber from the wilderness on his vast acreage was the source of eighteen-inch wide boards on walls, ceilings, and floors of his three-story, frame pioneer box house. Irregular, hand forged nails, clearly visible, hold it all together. Workmanship and materials create an impression of sturdiness and timelessness.

The house was built in the late 1700s, according to oral history, Docent Sharon Shook said. The earliest written documentation of the house is from a journal written in 1810 by Bishop Francis Asbury, the first Methodist bishop consecrated in America. Asbury, who rode thousands of miles during his years of service, spent the night at Shook's. He may have conducted religious services in the third floor chapel, one of the house's most distinguishing features. Records of events that occurred more than two hundred years ago are sketchy, at best.

Climbing the steep, narrow stairs to the rustic, spare-looking chapel was a personal journey. I attempted to visualize my grandmother, Mary Shook Hargrove, great-great-great granddaughter of Jacob, ascending the risers with one or more of her children stretching their short legs to reach the top, as I have been told. According to oral accounts, many others made that journey to worship in Shook's house when no churches existed in the immediate area. Some wrote their names on the wall.

Faintly seen letters on the chapel wall state that the Holston Conference met there in 1888 and include names of those who attended.

Shook's campground meetings were popular events. Families came in their wagons or with tents, some even bringing cattle, and stayed as much as a week for the opportunity of hearing music and visiting preachers, and enjoying the fellowship. The site, donated by Shook, holds Louisa Chapel Methodist Church and Pleasant Hill Cemetery, where he and his wife are buried. Shook died September 1, 1839.

A Revolutionary War veteran, Shook probably glimpsed his property-to-be as he passed that way with General Griffith Rutherford and returned to claim it as his.

Raising eleven children on their farm, Shook and his wife Isabella Weitzel owned the house and surrounding land until their deaths.

The second house is an addition wrapped around Shook's original structure. Levi Smathers bought the house, expanding it by adding additional rooms, another chimney and two wrap-around porches. Other changes included relocating the front door and the stairs. His son, D. I. L. Smathers, inherited the house, eventually leaving it to his daughter Mary Smathers Morgan, the last occupant of the Shook-Smathers house. Morgan loved to entertain and made additional changes, touches of elegance, particularly in the dining room with its finely crafted plate rail on the walls and wood beams on the ceiling.

Dr. Joseph S. Hall, Shook descendant and retired history professor, who lives in Washington, DC, bought the house after it sat vacant for twenty years and is responsible for the careful and thoughtful restoration of the oldest standing frame house west of the Blue Ridge.

The silent walls of the house guard many secrets: the extent of Jacob Shook's involvement in the founding of Methodism in Haywood County, the origin of its Georgian cypress wood doors and three-over-two windows, the identity of those who wrote their names and comments on the chapel wall, the number of worshipers who climbed the chapel stairs, and the influences that created the remarkable man who played a star role during this county's infancy.

Clyde Historic Hotel

A landlocked ocean liner perched on a grassy, treeless knoll overlooking Clyde.

Bunny Brown's description of the building known variously as Clyde Inn, Yankee Hipps Hotel, Skyland Home, and now Skyland Camp for Girls is apt, judging by sepia-tinted photos dated 1897 and a detailed sketch on 1990 guest stationery of the 107-year-old, three-story frame building.

Originally, two curved, tapering chimneys, resembling smokestacks of an ocean-going vessel, rose from the front roof. Flags flying above them completed the impression of a huge ship. A French mansard roof, new to this area, topped the structure.

Built by Lorenzo P. Hipps of Crabtree in 1898, early history of the hotel is sketchy. The venture faltered. The site was isolated, activities were limited, and the stench from Clyde's stockyards wafted across the Pigeon River and up the hill. The somber building later saw other usage, once as a dormitory for Haywood Institute.

"I wish these walls could talk," Brown said as we walked along one of two porches encircling the structure, looking at the dark brown siding spider-webbed by tiny cracks. So do I. The place reeks of history, untold tales, and interesting events.

Ten guest rooms with fireplaces, each opening to a wrap-around porch, occupied the second floor. Living room and dining room, which shared a fireplace, and the kitchen, were public rooms. Children skated among the rafters of the third floor unfinished attic.

Panes of colored glass flank the front door. The hotel has plaster walls with bead-board wainscoting, and hand-rolled brick. Six rental cottages remain. There was no electricity or plumbing.

Susan Courtney Harris of Jacksonville, Florida forever changed its destiny, arriving with her five children after use reverted to a hotel. She loved the place, returning each summer.

One day in 1916, she had donned an apron to make sandwiches in the kitchen when a cook told her the hotel was being auctioned at that very moment.

Wife of Robert A. Harris, Norfolk Southern Railway executive, she reacted quickly, appearing at the front door to face a crowd of black-suited men and the auctioneer. "I will give you three thousand dollars for the whole kit and kaboodle," she reportedly declared. The group was speechless. Women weren't supposed to do such things, and probably none of the bidders had that much money, Brown said. "Sold to the woman in the apron," the auctioneer said.

Harris walked to the nearest phone in Canton to tell her husband what she had done. "Woman, you have one year to make a profit or it goes back on the auction block," he replied, according to Brown, who knew "Granny" Harris.

During the winter in Jacksonville, Harris persuaded neighbors, relatives, and friends to bring their children and spend the summer at her hotel. The next summer she opened as a camp for girls, assisted by some of the same people.

Skyland Camp for Girls

"I thought I was climbing the stairway to Heaven," said "Bunny" Brown, recalling the days when she was a camper at Skyland Camp for Girls in Clyde, beginning in 1943 when she was eight years old.

She and husband Timothy own the 40-acre site now, a unique summer camp with a distinctive flavor.

For eighty-eight years, youngsters have spent part of their summers at Skyland Camp and loved it so much that some of the campers are the fifth generation in their family to come there, while others have returned as counselors.

The stairs we were climbing, with timeworn risers, lead to the second floor in the 107-year-old, three-story "big house," where meals are served and younger campers sleep. Actually, the girls have always preferred to sleep on cots encircling the sloping floor of the wrap-around porch, and climb through windows into their rooms.

Older girls live in six rustic cabins, once guesthouses for rent when the property was a hotel.

Bunny arrived at Skyland in 1943 as an eight-year-old and has been there in one way or another ever since. After returning each year as a camper, she became a counselor at sixteen, eventually married the camp director's nephew Timothy, and took over as camp director in 1973.

"My family loved you long before I even knew you existed," Timothy tells Bunny.

Campers arrived by train in those early years. "I got on the evening train in Jacksonville, Florida, and got to Clyde around noon. We were so excited that we ran up the hill (a good distance) and someone in the Weaver Green family brought our luggage up. Ernest Green called our bags "duffies" and charged ten cents a bag." Campers are predominantly from North Carolina, Tennessee, and Georgia, but also come from as far away as California. "All over the country," Bunny said.

Brown's first year as camper was a gift from Santa Claus. She was to go to another camp in Western North Carolina, but an emergency closed it that summer and she enrolled at Skyland instead. "I call that fate," says Bunny, who believes she was destined to be an integral part of the camp and its family.

Sitting on a knoll overlooking Clyde from one direction and Chambers Mountain from another, the buildings have changed little structurally, except for the additions of plumbing and electricity, since Susan Courtney Harris bought the property in 1916 and organized it as a camp. Huge old trees shade the area, and the old stack rock walls are picturesque.

In Harris' time, before electricity, each camper was given a kerosene lantern. Lectured sternly on the dangers of fire, she told them if the lanterns flared up to throw them over the porch railing into the yard. A new game was born. The girls learned to cause flaring so they could throw lanterns to the ground and watch them explode.

A new, heated swimming pool has replaced the cold water swimming hole fed by Skyland Brook. The horse barn, original to the property, has been moved and spruced up a bit, and a new horse ring is among the volleyball field, riding trails, tennis courts, archery range, and other activity areas for campers.

The Browns own property on the slope of Chambers Mountain, used as an "out camp," for hiking and camping in tents.

Now retired, Brown has turned the camp over to her daughter, Sherry, thus passing its management to a fourth generation. Plans are underway for a 100-year celebration in 2017!

Naming of Clyde

It seems the origin of the name of Clyde, one of Haywood County's earliest settlements, is unclear. Located between Canton and Waynesville, various names have been attached to the small town that was incorporated in 1889.

A local historian, the late Clark Medford, indicates that the area was first referred to as Shook; an appropriate name, since Jacob Shook was one of Haywood County's first settlers. He located here in the late 1700s, acquiring a large tract of land.

Shook became Lower Pigeon River, understandable since Canton was a settlement known as Ford of Pigeon.

According to a locally written history filed in Clyde's town hall, three possible sources for the name are listed. A foreman named Clyde worked on construction of the railroad that reached the town in 1883. His name was called so often by workmen laying the rails that he became the town's namesake. Shook donated land on which a depot was built.

Another account involves an unnamed man from Scotland. Supposedly, he left his home on the Clyde River, crossed the ocean, and settled in Haywood County. The area reminded him of his former home, so he decided it should be named Clyde.

Iron for the old bridge that crossed the Pigeon River came from the Clyde ironworks in Ohio and was stamped in several places with the company's name. The structure washed away in a flood. This third and last scenario is reminiscent of Canton's receiving its name from a bridge that crossed the Pigeon River. Iron for that bridge was stamped Canton, Ohio.

In 1890, the town's population consisted of ninety people.

By the early nineteen hundreds, Clyde had various businesses. The town had a gristmill and several boarding schools, including the Haywood Institute. Having been noted as a health resort, people from other states summered in Clyde. A firm that manufactured liquor barrels was located there. It was the major livestock market west of Asheville, and it was a busy place with two hotels and two livery stables. The Yankee Hipps Hotel is now operated as Skyland Camp for Girls.

The current population of Clyde is almost 1400 and the town considers itself a bedroom community, with residents living in Clyde and working elsewhere.

Infected by Mountain Fever

Cataloochee Ranch and Ski Resort on Fie Top Mountain, overlooking Maggie Valley, has long been a popular destination for both new and loyal mountain lovers, nurtured by the children of Tom and "Miss Judy" Alexander Alice, Judy, and Tom Jr., and their children.

The ranch was developed as a prime destination for tourists, to be sure, but its evolution is a love story, an atypical romance between a man and the mountains.

"For me, the craving for mountains is an incurable disease," wrote the late, Atlanta-born Tom Alexander Sr. "I actually become mentally and occasionally physically ill when away from this environment too long."

Before he settled Cataloochee Ranch, and later an adjoining ski resort, atop Fie Top, he wore many hats: forest ranger, Marine, game warden, district forester, and rancher. Liked and respected by the mountain people he came to know, he was a rarity, embraced into their fold.

Miss Judy, Judy Morton Barksdale, daughter of an Army physician from Richmond VA, stationed at the Veteran's Administration hospital in Oteen, met Alexander on a "pack" trip and married in June 1929. The two were an unlikely but formidable team. Alice Aumen wrote of her mother, "She was thoroughly coached in how a Southern lady should run a house...and inherited a love of gardening from her father."

She would use all these skills and more in raising her children and living in often-primitive conditions, apparently adapting with relish to her new environment while adding touches of elegance to her surroundings.

The Alexanders operated a primitive fishing camp in the Three Forks area of the Smokies in the late 1920s. Then in 1932, they ran a much-visited rustic guest ranch at the lower end of isolated Cataloochee Valley before they bought and developed the ranch on Fie Top. After five years in Cataloochee Valley, they watched their neighbors and friends leave the valley, forced to go because their land had become government property. They soon followed, moving away as well.

After two years of managing timberland in Florida, simmering mountain fever infected Alexander and his family again. A trip to Maggie Valley led to a drive to Fie Top.

Halfway up the mountain, he encountered Verlin Campbell and his son, Kyle. Introducing himself, Alexander must have been startled by the first words he heard from Verlin Campbell. "You're just the man I'm looking for," Campbell said, declaring that he had the finest tourist place in the world and wanted Alexander to see it.

Alexander had found his nirvana—a mountain sitting on the Cataloochee Divide, southeastern boundary of Great Smoky Mountains National Park.

Tom and Miss Judy converted a stone barn into the ranch house, adding a massive fireplace that became a gathering spot for guests who often enjoyed square dances in the big room. Stables were built and log buildings became guest cottages.

After extensive development of their property to accommodate guests, the Alexanders added the first ski resort south of Virginia in 1961.

The Alexanders and their ranch were contagious, infecting their children and many of their guests with mountain fever.

"After a little time with Miss Judy and Mr. Tom, you knew that you had been given a gift—a gift of sharing the beauty of Western North Carolina, of being with two people who accepted you just the way you were, who expected and got the best from most people, and who, I think, always gave the best back to all," wrote a guest and her husband of the Alexanders.

Purchase Knob: The Ferguson Family's Legacy

Love affairs between people and their mountain land are not uncommon in this area.

A prime example is Purchase Knob, in the Hemphill area. The beauty of the 535 acres that butt the Great Smoky Mountains National Park drew the late Voit Gilmore and Kathryn McNeill here, and they were smitten. Although they had busy lives in Pinehurst, in 1964 they built a house full of windows to capture the magnificent views from Purchase

Knob, and enjoyed as many months here during the year as their lives allowed. They bought the property from Med Leatherwood.

Gilmore, who wore many hats—journalist, world traveler, public servant, and travel agent—penned a brief history of the Ferguson family who first loved the land.

Hugh Glenn Ferguson of West Jefferson came to the Purchase with his family and two dozen relatives for a reunion on July 4, 1965, at the Gilmore's invitation and provided information for the history.

According to this account, John Love Ferguson, who grew up in the Crabtree Creek section of Haywood County, looked up at Purchase Knob during his youth and fell in love with the place. In 1874, he bought the Love Speculation tract for the price of $447 in cash and one horse. He and his wife, Emily Angeline Conley, moved into an old, round, pile cabin near a spring, which had been occupied by a Mr. Holcolm. In 1884-85, Ferguson built a frame house and moved his wife and two small children there. A third child was born in 1885.

John Ferguson had a series of four women move up to the Purchase to help with housework and tutor his children. Hugh Glenn Ferguson was one of the sons.

John Ferguson contracted with workmen who cleared the entire mountain slope by girding trees so they would eventually fall over and decay, and farmed around the trees. Two and a half miles of fence surrounded the farm area.

He raised vegetables, fruit, and grain, and had ten cows, which produced enough milk for ten pounds of butter per day. The butter, stored in cool houses at the spring and under the barn, was sold for twenty-five cents per pound at Waynesville resort hotels. He also raised sheep, selling wool and mutton, harvested apples and hauled them down the mountain to market, forty bushels to a wagonload.

Hugh Glenn Ferguson told Gilmore that his parents and his family lived a solitary but happy life at the Purchase until 1903, when fifty-three-year-old John Love Ferguson decided the Purchase was too steep to climb anymore. He sold the Purchase to John Boyd and Clarence Campbell.

Gilmore observed that the Fergusons still loved the Purchase as no other place on earth.

The Gilmores eventually divorced, but Kathryn continued to spend summers at the Purchase for years. The 79 pages of *Purchase Knob*, a book she authored, reflect her unabashed love for her mountain land. "There's a summer place, a farm, forever imprinted on my memory, spacious in its views, lovely in its close-ups, on the gentle slopes of Purchase Mountain in the southern Appalachians...These Appalachians are ancient mountains, some of the oldest on earth. Worn down by the ages from water, frost and the work of the wind, they are gentle, livable mountains. Having a home on top of one is as close to heaven as one can get," she wrote.

The couple decided that, in time, the land would be donated to the National Park Service. Their wish was that it be used for environmental education. They saw it as both preservation of the land and as a gift to the American people.

The Appalachian Highlands Science Learning Center at Purchase Knob was one of five National Park Service education and science centers officially established in 2001, and Great Smoky Mountains National Park includes the site within its boundaries. Paul Super is the science coordinator at the Center, and the first ever GSMNP resource manager stationed in the North Carolina half of the park. He shared Gilmore's history of the Ferguson family with me.

Museum of North Carolina Handicrafts

The Museum of North Carolina Handicrafts in Waynesville's historic Shelton House delivered its usual sensory impact to those of us who walked through its doors this spring. The house and its collections are always a feast for senses and mind, but this year the museum had a rejuvenated look about it.

Collections sheltered within its walls include various histories, each seeking its own voice. The house itself, built sometime between 1875 and 1880 by Stephen J. Shelton, Haywood County sheriff, was constructed with an eye for details. Its Colonial-style architecture is reminiscent of a Charleston farmhouse, perfumed by mountain air rather than the scent of the sea, with jib doors and windows opening to wide verandahs from four of the twelve rooms.

Mantels, doors, and furniture carved from walnut trees that grew on Shelton's 67-acre farm are scattered throughout the main living quarters of the house. The house also contains other treasures, like the massive cabinet and desk crafted by local master carpenter Henry Napoleon Francis, which was once used in the old courthouse from 1884–1928, and the flax wheel used by Mary Ann Love, wife of Colonel Robert Love. Museum Curator Jackie Stephens, cataloging and researching museum contents with a new and knowledgeable perception, said, "I am frequently tempted to stay overnight in the museum and sleep in that magnificent walnut bed upstairs."

A collection of Native Peoples' artifacts gathered by Shelton's son, W. T. "Will" Shelton, who bought the house from his father in 1905, fills one room. His story is as interesting as the collection he brought home from Shiprock, New Mexico, where he was lauded for accomplishments as head of Bureau of Indian Affairs for the Navajo, and from Cherokee, North Carolina, where he worked both professionally and as a volunteer. He added a dairy to the property, and enhanced the house with his passion for growing dahlias.

Other rooms showcase a comprehensive collection of handicrafts made by North Carolina artisans from across the state; too many to list, too lovely to describe, and too many stories to tell.

Mary Cornwell, former Haywood County Extension Agent, is a vital part of the story. She and her twenty-seven Home Demonstration Clubs, with plenty of help from others, launched a fund-raising drive in 1976 to establish a handicraft museum. Cornwell was also the director of the Village of Yesteryear at the North Carolina State Fair in Raleigh for forty years.

"She conceived the idea for a museum out of her concern for a permanent preservation and display of various talents of 500 or more crafters she knew," said Jim Trantham. He assumed Cornwell's responsibility for the Village in 1990, about ten years before her death, and chairs the nine-member board overseeing the museum where his own hand-crafted dulcimers are seen.

The original site was to be a log cabin on Haywood Community College grounds, but Shelton descendant Charles Ray and his wife offered their house at an attractive price. With more room and beautiful grounds, the house was the perfect location; and grateful crafters have filled its rooms.

Frog Level: The Former Commercial District's Revival

Frog Level was hopping in 1884, having become a vital commercial center after the old Western North Carolina Railroad, on its journey west, laid the last ties and rails that would extend its length to Waynesville. Along its route, more convenient and efficient transportation was opening proverbial doors into the previously isolated area of Western North Carolina, spurring development where there had been none. It was Frog Level's turn to grow.

Waynesville's downtown area alongside Richland Creek, swampy land with a few scattered buildings, was transformed into a hustling, bustling center of commerce. Uptown is slightly elevated, running along the ridgeline of what was once called Mount Prospect, and includes the county courthouse.

Already a destination for summer-long visitors seeking cooler atmospheres, Waynesville could offer tourists a more pleasant ride from the heat of the low country on as many as six passenger trains, a welcome alternative to long carriage rides over bad roads. An old photo shows women in long gowns and their families stepping from the train into surreys waiting to carry them to White Sulphur Springs and Eagle's Nest hotels, Balsam and Piedmont Inns, and other lodging places.

A depot with waiting room, loading ramp and long, covered platform had been constructed. Dewey Stovall Jr., seventy-four, remembers its roof of orange Spanish tiles.

A gristmill, general stores, coal yards, and a livery stable were some of the businesses located in Frog Level in early days. And more would come. Meals were served and rooms rented at the Suyeta Park Hotel, located on a rise above the railroad tracks.

The mill, powered by water diverted from Richland Creek, was first called Waynesville Milling Company. Later the name was changed to Noland Mill. The stone foundation that once supported the mill wheel remains, although it and the millrace are almost hidden by vegetation. Flour and cornmeal were sold in a general store operated by a Mr. and Mrs. J. R. Carswell, who lived there with their eight children during the early 1920s.

Stovall, who continues to operate the family Waynesville Candy Company, lived nearby on Love Lane. Farmland once bordered Frog Level and Richland Creek, he says. He remembers the evening serenades, too, with frogs as musicians. "There was lots of chirping and peeping around here, especially when Richland Creek flooded in 1941," he said.

A wealth of information, Stovall can walk mentally on Depot and Commerce streets and trace the history of each building—or empty space—and name the businesses located in each through the years. R. L. Lee sold coal in the only rock building, painted white. Two doors up was The Taproom, a bar later known as the Longhorn Saloon. Around the corner was the Royal Café. The late Euel Taylor sold Buicks at his first car dealership, in a structure no longer there. Stovall's building was originally a general store owned by Suncrest Lumber Company, and its second floor was used as a boarding house. Grady Honeycutt operated a mobile grocery in a panel truck, selling door to door, particularly in outlying areas. A railroad spur ran behind businesses immediately bordering Richland Creek, making loading and unloading boxcars an easier job.

During the 1930s and '40s businesses included furniture stores, three coal yards, hardware stores, auto dealers, wholesale grocers, farm and garden suppliers, lumber companies, department stores, and food markets. Business was flourishing until automobiles forced a decline in rail service. The passenger train delivered its last human cargo in 1949, and the decline of Frog Level's heyday began.

As businesses closed or sought locations with more foot traffic, the empty buildings and absence of people drew unsavory characters and Frog Level was a place to be avoided at night, Stovall said.

But times are changing and Frog Level, now designated a National Historic Area, is experiencing an influx of new businesses. Upbeat young people who are excited by the historic district's new life staff the attractive Western North Carolina Visitors Center down the street from Stovall's.

The Imperial Hotel

The Imperial hotel and Sid's on Main opened two years ago in January 2012, a bright face on Main Street in Canton. The new kid on the block, eagerly awaited and quickly accepted, has become a gathering place.

Good food, a welcoming atmosphere and a pleasing ambiance have infused the building, and the town, with new life and gaiety.

The grand old lady known as the Imperial Hotel, clad in a beautifully refurbished façade, has again assumed its role as the social, civic, and visitor center in Canton. The historic building is a vision in its new finery, a long-nurtured vision by a descendant of one of the town's bedrock families.

Attorney Pat Smathers, former six-term mayor of Canton, envisioned a restored hotel with the benefits it could provide his hometown. As a young boy, the gables and turrets rising above the flat roofs of Nicholls's Clothing Store, Medford's Florist, and Sellers' Jewelry Store piqued his interest. He heard the stories and colorful history of the place where mill workers, businessmen and professionals gathered, relaxed, and socialized, where young people danced and mingled.

He and wife Sherry and five other investors purchased the property from W. T. Sharpe's living heirs, and converted former guest rooms into twenty-three low-income apartments. In the 1990s, the couple acquired total ownership of the former Imperial Hotel property.

The heart of The Imperial, its infrastructure, is no newcomer. Built around 1876 as a private home, it predated the incorporation of Canton as a town in 1889 by thirteen or so years. The arrival of the Western North Carolina Railroad in Canton as a temporary terminus in 1882 indicates that the railroad and the house were both under construction at the same time, underscored by the use of railroad tracks as support beams in the house.

William H. Moore and his wife Rhoda built the house in a sparsely populated area known as the best location to ford the Pigeon River. The property deed pinpointed its location as Turnpike Road.

The original two-story dwelling had a sharply-pitched roof with a variety of gables and turrets in the favored Victorian style. An original photo shows covered porches on both levels. *Canton: The Architecture of Our Home Town* by former resident Camille Wells relates, "Its varied surfaces and materials were painted in two or more colors." A backyard garden from this earlier time continues to sprout a lonely cornstalk or two.

Unbeknownst to the residents, the mountain area was poised to undergo drastic change. Impetus for change arrived in 1882, when the railway was extended to the immediate area, and in 1906, when construction of Champion Fibre Company's paper mill began.

W. Turner Sharpe, one of four businessmen credited with Canton's growth, saw the need for dining and housing facilities in an expanding town. He bought the house in 1910, added a four-story tower to the west side of the building, and opened a hotel. A stable area for horses and buggies was located behind the building.

Management of the business was turned over to Edward and Mae Geir of New York. The couple gave the hotel its name. Advertised as "one of the state's best two-dollar hotels," patrons included travelers, businessmen, salesmen, and visiting executives of Champion Papers. Teachers also boarded there.

In 1916, Sharpe and the Geirs doubled the hotel's size by adding a forty-room annex to the rear of the structure and enlarging the lobby and dining areas.

The Imperial became well known for offering quality rooms and food, and having modern amenities. Connection to the paper mill's generators was arranged to provide electricity and water closets were added, a fact mentioned in official Canton Town Minutes. It was one of the state's first hotels to have electricity. The Imperial met the call for good dining, space for meetings and social events, and excellent rooming facilities.

Sharpe also built a three-story brick commercial building immediately adjacent to the newly constructed tower. It was used initially as the town's post office, then later as an A&P Grocery Store. Upper stories were used for meetings and boarders. The Knights of the Pythias Hall was located there, at one time.

In the 1930s, demand for more commercial retail space in the boom town era of a rapidly-growing Canton took precedence over The Imperial's status as a hotel. Sharpe essentially hid the hotel's Queen Anne appearance behind newly built, more modern-looking storefronts in the 1930s.

Spicy stories and maybe a ghost or two usually accompany older buildings, especially those who cater to public use. The Imperial is no exception.

A speakeasy was an unadvertised amenity during Prohibition. A trapdoor in the current dining room is a reminder of the basement area, where guests could slip downstairs to imbibe illegal beverages and gamble at card games in relative safety and anonymity. A device at the reception desk activated a warning buzzer in the basement room, warning staff and guests to hide the evidence.

Sharp-eyed sheriff Welch, likely responding to persistent rumors, visited the premises from time to time. On one occasion, he arrived determined to conduct a raid, according to a former employee who was stationed at the front desk. He found no evidence in the basement, but ascending the stairs, he spotted a wire attached to the wall and severed it with his knife.

In a short while he returned, and the desk attendant sounded the alarm, or so he thought. Welch laughed and said to the man, "Go ahead. Mash the hell out of it. It won't do any good."

Around 1937, new management took over the hotel, renaming it Canton Hotel. The business was closed in 1960, after completion of I-40 north of Canton allowed travelers to bypass both the town and the hotel. Some boarders continued to use the 1930s annex for living space.

Maintaining the existing apartments entered on Park Street, the Smathers began restoration in earnest in 1999. Brick façades of old storefronts were removed, and porches were restored. The interior maintains its vintage look with pressed tin ceilings, the use of original colored glass panes in some doors, and three shallow coal-burning fireplaces. An angled side door opens directly into the bar, which once housed a newsstand. Antique mirrored shelving is displayed as a bar backdrop, bought by Smathers and stored for later use because he knew exactly where it would fit. Small group dining occupies what might have been a seating area. In the basement, a portion of the original house foundation reveals metal railroad track used as support beams. Virtually a treasure trove, the labyrinthine basement that once housed the town's newspaper printing press continues to yield objects and materials from the many transformations of the structure.

Sharpe's adjacent three-story building now connects to The Imperial. The street-side room provides space for large gatherings and is used for receptions, class reunions, charity auction events, business seminars, meetings, and parties. Patio-area tiles were formerly the floors in Nicholls's Clothing Store.

The Colonial Theater

Pinch me. I must be dreaming.

The thought ran through my head this past winter as I sat in the Colonial Theater, a beautiful, freshly painted, gilded, and refurbished building with clean, comfortable seats.

On the stage was a full orchestra. You know; Tuxedos with white shirts, bow ties, and cummerbunds. The musicians were playing brightly shined brass instruments. There was a grand piano with a pianist. And, don't forget, a conductor.

The music filling the auditorium was classic, Henry Mancini classic; big-band sounds and show tunes. The beautiful music had melodies and rhythm. It was music with a definable beat.

"Where did all the beautiful music go?" asked the conductor, as he described Mancini's music through the 1960s. He said a mouthful in that one question.

The theater was full of people who hummed, swayed, and tapped their feet to the familiar tunes. Especially the Red Hat Society ladies in the purple dresses filling the back row, along with a wannabe in her pink hat and lavender gown.

I spent innumerable hours in that theater as a child, and then more as a teenager. It was different then; not so clean, not so bright, with torn seats.

There were no orchestras. We saw westerns, newsreels showing the aftermath of World War II, plastic musicals, cartoons, and The Three Stooges. You get the picture.

One sat gingerly on the seats, never touching underneath the arm rests because you might find a wad of someone's discarded bubble gum. Remnants of popcorn and candy wrappers rustled under your feet.

You sat in the balcony if enough seats were available for you and your inevitable crowd, primarily because you wanted to know why it was that your parents didn't want you to sit in the balcony. You tried to keep an empty seat beside you in case that cute boy you thought you loved at the moment showed up.

You screamed because you thought *The Blob* was going to fall out of that box. You laughed and cried. You wished you looked like Ava Gardner, danced like Ginger Rogers, and had legs like Cyd Charisse. You fantasized about James Dean.

Okay. Enough reminiscing about the wonder years of growing up in a small town where movies were the only Saturday entertainment, unless you liked sitting on wooden bleachers and watching the weekly softball games across the street from the Colonial. That is where our parents gathered to watch the town's championship team beat the socks off another opponent.

The point is that Canton has this beautiful theater where fine entertainment is available. One can enjoy classic movies, Folkmoot performances, country music, or orchestral presentations, such as the one that Saturday night. The possibilities are limitless.

Darrell Tilley, a Waynesville neighbor, remarked, "This theater is an asset for Canton, for Waynesville, for the county, for all of Western North Carolina." He was right.

The soda shop where buses came and went no longer exists in the adjacent, corner building. Gone are the smells of hotdogs and hamburgers, the sound of the jukebox, the whir of a milkshake in the making.

It is now a lovely room called the theater annex, complete with carpet, tables, and a kitchen. It opens to the theater and is well suited to most any gathering whether it be a corporate meeting or a wedding reception.

Canton people are proud, especially the town employees who contributed so much to the transformation of this building, who have fulfilled the vision and created this jewel. And rightly so.

It is an asset to be used, enjoyed, and admired by all, most certainly for those of us who paid a dime to see the movies and did some growing up in that building.

Old Rhodarmer Pool

The water in Rhodarmer's swimming pool was icy cold, I am told. The Pigeon River, with its popular swimming holes was probably warmer.

In the late 1930s, a swimming pool was such a novelty that people came from all around to swim and sun. They came on the gravel road by car, if fortunate enough to have one, by bicycle, and on foot, carrying their towels and swim suits.

Sounds to me as if they should have been carrying blankets to warm themselves after a frosty dip.

John Rhodarmer built the pool. Since there are no family records or pictures and most of those who swam there are no longer living, details are sketchy. However, there are still a few who remember.

Remember, this was the World War II era and that has been awhile.

I have listened to others talk about the pool all my life, and wished I could have gone. Repeatedly I have been told it was the place to go; the water was cold and it was a long way from Canton in those days.

It was a big pool, with depths from four feet in the shallow end and ten feet in the deep end.

Anita Churm remembers good times at the pool. She was too young to go alone, but her parents took her and a picnic lunch and spent the day.

My husband rode his bicycle from North Main Street, a distance of 3.5 miles. He, too, was young and very small but liked diving from the 20-foot tower. He was always a daredevil. Fortunately he was also a good swimmer, and could dive with the best of them.

Church groups used the pool for gatherings. Pug Parker went often with the Boy Scouts, and rode his bicycle at other times. There were large crowds, he said, especially on weekends.

He, too, remembers the wooden diving tower and the diving board located halfway up the tower. He also recalls a fence surrounding the pool.

Water was piped from a pond on the property, according to collective memories. Word is that Rhodarmer's wife called the pond Lake Doubt, because she doubted that it would ever hold water. Originally the pool was built level with the ground, but a 2-foot brick wall was added to discourage the snakes and wild animals from testing the waters.

The boys' changing room was a dirt room underneath a storage building for apples and potatoes, Parker recalls, and girls changed in the house.

There were picnic tables, benches, see-saws, a small concession stand for drinks and candy, hand-built barbecue fireplaces, horseshoe pits, and a badminton area.

Admission was a quarter or a dime, depending on whom you talk to.

Someone else owns the site now, along with the house and the changing shed, all sitting on 25 acres.

When the current owner and her late husband bought the house, they toyed with the idea of renovating the pool; but all things considered, they decided it was a daunting undertaking and discarded the idea.

The last time I saw the pool, approximately 50'x75', it was a rectangle of chipping cement. The bottom was covered with leaves, twigs, and tree branches, and looked as if it could surely use several gulps of that cold, fresh water. Surrounded by trees and shrubs, it was hidden from view unless you knew where to look.

Then came a spring flood, with muddy water pouring down the mountainside and overwhelming the nearby creek. The deluge was so fast and furious that it undermined the pool, and the old reservoir became an unsightly hazard. It was eventually filled with dirt, innumerable truckloads of dirt, and sown with grass.

However, it is a bit of not-so-distant history, and stirs a pot of memories.

For those who don't remember, like me, it is easy to imagine how it was with the hot sun beating down on a pool full of swimmers and yard covered with sunbathers, the picnic tables loaded with goodies. If you think very hard, you can imagine the excitement stirring youngsters who were going to swim in a pool, teenagers who might just see someone special, and adults who just wanted a leisurely break.

A Few of Canton's Unique Characters

The driver of the semi laboriously maneuvered his big rig into a parking space and opened the door to step to the sidewalk. "Hey, Shorty." The driver turned to see a short, stocky figure clad in bib overalls gesturing at him. "Hey, Shorty. You got my parking place. You got to move." His words were somewhat garbled, but he got his point across.

Apologizing, the driver climbed into the cab and repeated the time-consuming task of moving the rig. Did he glance in his mirror? If he did, he would have seen no vehicle, only the little man, about 5 feet tall, occupying the spot.

Every town has its characters. Harmless, unique threads woven into the pattern of life that gives each place its own special flavor. Familiar faces, "enjoyed and appreciated" as Town Manager Bill Stamey said.

He was one of Canton's, "driving" his way around town daily. He was his own vehicle, short legs and small feet shuffling along at a steady pace. His "steering wheel" was often a bucket lid. Other times, it was imaginary, but he moved his arms appropriately. For some reason, his ears were stuffed with cotton. He liked his "chaw" of tobacco, evidenced by traces of the brown stuff leaking from the corners of his mouth.

He did put nickels in parking meters, and "parked" until time ran out. And the driver of the truck was not the only person he told to get out of his parking space. At times he directed traffic, motioning cars to move around him. He liked the softball games. He responded 'Hey, Shorty' to everyone who spoke to him.

Ted Woodruff remembers him well. "A bunch of us boys drove to Asheville and saw him patched up with bandages with his overalls badly torn, standing by another man. We stopped to see about him and found out he had hoboed his way onto the train, and jumped off while the car was moving."

Southern Railway employees had found him and patched him up, they learned. Finally convincing the employee that they knew him, they brought him home.

"We called each other 'Shorty'," Woodruff said. A group of men working at the paper mill collected money to buy him a pair of shoes. "His mother had died and he was living alone. He had cardboard lining his shoes, his toes stuck out, and the weather was turning cold," Woodruff said. "Two of us went to his house, got him to wash his face, and took him to town to buy shoes and socks."

Later that day, Woodruff saw him talking to "Daddy Rabbit," another of Canton's characters. His old shoes were in a box under his arm and he was proudly showing off his new shoes.

Daddy Rabbit favored the area around town hall, and the bridges over the Pigeon River.

Tall and skinny, he limped when it suited him, a limp that grew more pronounced as he became aware that someone was looking at him or if he hoped to hitch a ride. His constant grin revealed some gaps where teeth should have been, and his eyes were crossed.

Clad in mismatched pants and shirt, he topped his garb with an Indian headdress and carried a five-and-dime store bow and arrow. Sometimes he traded the bow for a guitar that gradually lost its strings, or carried both.

Calling "howdy" to everyone he passed on foot and waving at every passing vehicle, he was seeking responses. Daddy Rabbit just needed a little attention. He would perch on a bridge and strum his guitar with flourish but no sound.

He lived in a secluded, dirt-floored log cabin halfway up Crabtree Mountain at the end of Thickety Road with his family, according to Paul Allen who lives out that way. People in the community would take them food and second-hand clothing, Allen said.

"People liked them and tried to take care of them," Stamey said, speaking of both characters.

The "Goat Man" wasn't local. He might pass through town once a year, according to Allen. He lived somewhere in Georgia during the winter, and headed this way when it got warmer.

Six goats pulled his small, wooden, covered wagon, with several others trotting behind. Pans and buckets hung from the wagon and from his body. The constant clanging announced his arrival.

A rough looking, bearded old man, he wore a worn felt hat and shoes that had seen better days, according to Allen. He set up camp once in

West Canton when a wooden wheel broke. The wheel was mended at a local car dealership before he moved on to Clyde, Lake Junaluska, Waynesville, and beyond. He would cross Balsam Mountain, but not Soco. He was afraid the bears would get his goats.

There were others, like the twin boys who liked to "direct" train traffic and the man driving a junk-laden truck who would chase down anyone taking something from his hoard, but none to equal the human vehicle, "Daddy Rabbit," or The Goat Man.

Labor Day Tradition

Labor Day brings a seemingly endless parade of marching bands from all over Western North Carolina, cars of smiling, waving town and county officials and politicians, lavishly decorated floats, fire trucks occasionally sounding their sirens, loaded with excited children , wagons filled with hay and people, clowns, balloons, and bicycles. Boy and Girl scouts are herded along by their leaders, and at the end, there are dozens of horses. Miss Labor Day and her court adorn a float. The excitement of the Stephens-Lee High School band from Asheville, with its pulse-pounding rhythms, extravagant routines, and dancing majorettes, is infectious.

Nose-tickling cotton candy, popcorn, hot dogs, hamburgers, and hand cranked ice cream are available. Square dance taps reverberate on a wooden platform. The whine of a steel guitar and thump of a bass fiddle, voices solo and in harmony resound from the temporary stage, and lively calliope music from the merry-go-round are punctuated by screams from the Roll-o-Plane, the Ferris Wheel, and the Swings.

The talented James Haynie, now deceased, hee-haws his way through the notes of "Johnson's Old Gray Mule" while propped on his crutches, and accompanies himself on a guitar.

Crowds and crowds of people pack the streets, the bleachers around the performance platform on the high school baseball field, and the adjoining area, with amusement rides and vendors.

The air carries a distinctive perfume, created by mouth-watering odors from cooking food mingled with the oily smells of motors powering carnival rides and the crush of jam-packed bodies. The twinkle of colored lights on the rides brightens the sky, especially at night.

Champion old-timers are in the parade and crowding the porch and lawn of Snug Harbor, their mill-provided clubhouse on Park Street.

Growing up in Canton, it was akin to Christmas and Thanksgiving combined.

Historical facts chronicling this long-running event are sketchy, scattered, and sometimes contradictory.

The first Labor Day celebration was in 1906, according to a town history compiled by Kay Levine, former librarian of Haywood County Public Library. Pearl Coman was the first Labor Day Queen. Champion Fibre Company is said to have organized the event to honor its employees, and chartered four rail coaches to take them to a Labor Day picnic at Lake Junaluska.

The Log, a Champion publication, related that Champion Savings and Loan Association organized a celebration for the people of Canton and the community at Lake Junaluska on Monday, September 5, 1932.

Southern Railway ran a special train to transport passengers to the lake. Round-trip tickets cost a quarter. Participants were urged to pack lunch baskets for the day.

Ninety-three years old, Howard Sellars remembers walking the railroad track, hand-in-hand with his mother, to a Labor Day gathering in an area called "The Park" in lower Fibreville. A young child at the time, his impressions of the day were "a big crowd...lots to eat" and a contest involving a greased pole.

Lake Junaluska

Lake Junaluska is a unique community. A Methodist conference and retreat center, it occupies a special place in the hearts and minds of many, both residents and visitors.

Centered in a mountainous county known for its generous portions of natural beauty, the manmade creation echoes and complements its surroundings.

James Atkins and George R. Stuart, prominent Methodist ministers, are credited with seeing the need for a church-related assembly ground in the South that would be similar to two located further north, according to assembly history. With their support, a resolution was passed in 1908, at a laymen's conference of the Methodist Episcopal Church held in Tennessee, to create such a retreat.

An assembled commission bought 1,200 acres in Haywood County for what was generally called the Southern Assembly. A dam was built to capture the waters of Richland Creek, creating a 200-acre lake to enhance the property. The name Junaluska was chosen for the reservoir, echoing that of a nearby mountain peak named for a Cherokee chief.

Its inaugural use was in June 1913, when the Second Missionary Conference of the Methodist Episcopal Church met in Stuart Auditorium. The auditorium, a round, open-air building with a dirt and sawdust floor, was the only structure on the grounds. Participants had to stay in nearby Waynesville.

Although the unincorporated community has changed and grown in appearance, the purpose of creating a place conducive to spiritual growth, personal renewal, and Christian education has never wavered.

A modernized George Stuart Auditorium still stands as the focal point of the Lake Junaluska Conference and Retreat Center. The Reverend Billy Graham filled the meeting space in 1952, returning at least five more times. The list of renowned speakers includes Eleanor Roosevelt, wife of President Franklin D. Roosevelt. The building has been the site of the emergence of the leadership of The United Methodist Church, including election and consecration of bishops, and ordination of deacons and elders.

Other annual events include the Smoky Mountain Folk Festival, a two-day event that has featured the finest traditional Southern Appalachian music and dance for more than 35 years, Junaluska Singers concerts, and the closing ceremony of Folkmoot USA.

One other original building, Shackford Hall, is still in use. Both it and the auditorium are included in the National Register of Historic Places.

They have been joined by the stone Memorial Chapel, built in 1949 as a memorial to men and women who served in the armed forces during World War II and attended southeastern United Methodist church, stately Lambuth Inn, Terrace Hotel, the World Methodist Museum, the Heritage Center, the International Growth Center, The Library, and a fitness center, along with numerous other buildings for lodging, administration, recreation, dining, and meeting areas.

Areas of particular beauty include the Susanna Wesley Gardens and the Bryant Native Gardens, as well as the Rose Walk, which borders a portion of the popular 2.6-mile walking trail encircling the lake. The Junaluska Cross, considered a beacon of light and hope, was built in 1922. Supported by a 5-foot stone base, the cross is illuminated by some 200 light bulbs and stands twenty-five feet high. Below the cross is an amphitheater built in 1988.

Recreation areas include a swimming pool, tennis courts, a golf course and, of course, the lake itself.

Houses border the lake, both old and new; historic houses, many built as seasonal homes, show interesting architectural features.

Overshadowing the physical aspects of Junaluska are the personal stories and experiences, the friendships built, religious transformations, and budding romances that became permanent unions; the altered lives.

The beauty of Lake Junaluska and its surrounding views are overwhelming, but its impact on human lives in over 100 years is the true foundation of this gathering place.

Lake Junaluska Memories

Canoeing the length of Lake Junaluska in the heavy mist of morning, across the narrows and gliding through cattails up Richland Creek, is an enduring memory for Frances Crum Munroe.

"I never got off the lake except to eat and sleep... We roamed the lake," Munroe recollected as she rocked on the porch of her family cottage in 1988. "We would meet early in the morning, sometimes six a.m., in our canoes.

"We waterskied on boards, even a door from a bathhouse, until a boy smashed into the dock and demolished the door. Another boy skied standing on his head," Joyce Carter Patton recalls. "It was a special time and a special place."

Although not contemporaries, Joyce Carter Patton of Canton and Frances Crum Munroe of Asheville echo the same sentiments about living at Lake Junaluska in earlier times. Patton lived there year-round and Munroe was, initially, a summer visitor.

Seasonal residents, especially children, became close friends as they shared the days of summer year after year. "We were so close knit," said Munroe.

The lake community enjoyed a sheltered environment, a safe place where children could roam and play. Pranks were harmless. In the middle of night, boys tied a long rope to the bell in the bell house, ran to a hiding place, tugged the rope, and watched as house lights came on around the lake. Or bulbs were removed from the cross until a system was rigged that delivered a slight shock to anyone trying to darken the area.

The crowning of the Queen of Junaluska in August was the highlight of summer, both agree. Elaborate coronations included pages, maids, and knights of honor, all young people who lived at the lake. The event was so significant that it rated coverage by the Associated Press. Munroe was honored with the title in 1938, and Patton in 1953.

The Fourth of July was a big day, with swim meets, baseball games, a boat parade, and evening fireworks. Patton said, "Elaborately decorated boats and canoes were lashed together, and pulled around the lake by the big boat." She was referring to The Cherokee, an excursion craft with seats on upper and lower levels also used to ferry passengers from the train station across the lake.

The lake was dotted with boathouses during those days, and most everyone had watercraft of some description. Patton cranked her five-horsepower motor and puttered across the lake with her dog every morning to collect their mail. The train stopped at the old depot, now a private residence. Mail stuffed in a sack was hung on a post with a hook. Outgoing correspondence was lifted from the hook to the train and replaced with the incoming, to be sorted at the nearby post office.

Young people gathered at several spots, cementing their friendships with shared experiences. The main gate was manned by young men collecting about fifty cents per person for a day pass, more for weekly or monthly passes. Liner's Junaluska Supply Company, with its tasty hot dogs, stood across the way from the gate. The lake's boathouse had a long pier, leading to a wooden dock outfitted with diving boards and lifeguards for swimming. The lighted cross was also a popular meeting spot. People gathered on someone's porch for hand cranked ice cream. Other activities included nighttime frog gigging and walking Dellwood Road into Waynesville to the movies. The Soda Shop, with a porch for dancing, was often crowded following evening services in the open-air Stuart Auditorium. "We stood there with the plug to the jukebox and when the last amen was said, we would start dancing," said Munroe.

The arrival of Duke University students for summer classes was another high point of summer, both remember. Munroe's father was a professor at Duke, and taught classes in Mission (now Lambuth) Inn.

At summer's end, tears flowed as friends hugged and promised to write during the winter, knowing they would be together the next summer.

When the summer people left, life was often lonely for Patton, whose family was among the twelve that were year-round residents. There were still good times, though, with sledding on the golf course and ice skating on the lake at the upper end, where the ice was thick and the water shallow.

Her father, Ernest Carter, delighted in gathering pets acquired for the summer and then left behind, putting them in crates with some cornbread to eat, and shipping them to their owners.

It was a special time in a special place.

Snow: Transient Blanket of Peace and Beauty

S nowfall.

Heavy, gray clouds unburdening their low-hanging mass. Fat flakes beginning their descent, drifting lazily, then more quickly, and the ground disappearing under a white, downy comforter. Snow is falling.

The atmosphere is intensely bright, even under a gray ceiling unrelieved by sunlight. Snow reflects any available light.

Profound silence: The air is still, resting. There is an otherworldly sense of peace and quiet to be absorbed through every pore, with every breath. The sound of silence pervades as earth snuggles under its blanket of snow.

Unspoiled snow, not yet marred by living creatures. Tree limbs bow their heads from snow weight. Lacy shrubs adorn the landscape. Tiny shoots of brave daffodils are gradually immersing in frozen water, hiding a hint of spring.

Cold Mountain is hidden from view, obscured by heavy layers of mist.

Higher in the mountains, cascades of water have transformed into cascades of ice. Thick, heavy icicles bar the entrance to a shallow cave. The bleakness of winter's landscape has been whitewashed.

The headwaters of the Pigeon River flow through channels edged with thin borders of tatted ice, crafted by a master seamstress. Boulders in the river's path are shiny under their icy sheeting.

A sharp crack splits the quietness as a limb loses its battle with the weighted cover, disturbing a squirrel that skitters overhead, leaving a trace of falling snow in its wake.

Plop. A clump of snow slides from slippery evergreen needles and lands with a muffled thud.

Beads of ice decorate limbs and needles, drops of water frozen as they seeped.

Snow crunches under boots following the angular tracks of a bird, maybe a crow, before they end abruptly. A flutter of wings sends another flurry of snow. There are other tracks. Precise indentations might have been left by a deer. Smudges in disturbed snow are likely a rabbit.

The mountain peaks are beautiful etched in ice and snow against a bright blue sky, but not today. Gray clouds are still heavy with a wintry mix.

Snow begins to fall again, melting on an upturned face, and the silence intensifies until a slight wind begins its lowing song, creating a sharper nip in the air as it blows across ice and snow.

Change is in the air. The wind, cold, and snow are emitting signs that they may assume their other persona, viciousness that cuts to the bone.

It's time to leave, reluctantly. Time to head home for the warmth of a fireplace and a hot beverage, then a belly full of soup concocted from last fall's harvest. Time to reflect on the rare treat of being amongst the beauty and peacefulness of mountains blanketed with snow.

The soul of the earth and its people needed this quiet time.

COMMUNITIES

Wellstown

Growing up in Wellstown, once a small community in Canton, is a source of fond memories for some of Robert and Molly Henderson's eight children, who lived with their parents in one of Wellstown's modest homes in the '30s–'50s.

Wellstown could not, by any stretch of the imagination, have been called a high-rent subdivision. Some thirty to forty houses were built by Charles T. Wells, small homes of rough-sawn lumber with no heat, indoor plumbing, or, initially, electricity. Fairly typical for their time, the structures provided housing for the influx of laborers and their families, lured by the 1905 construction of Champion Fibre Company.

"At the time, we felt like we had it all; it seemed like good living," said Glenda Henderson Gravatt of Canton, who described Wellstown as a farm-like community.

Rent was $15 a month, collected by Wells' wife, Adeline, better known as "Addy" or "Granny," who usually arrived in a car driven by grandson Johnny Wells. Charlie Wells had a store in Canton where he sold caskets, among other things. This was the forerunner of Wells Funeral Homes in Haywood County.

Johnny remembers water was piped to houses from a spring-fed reservoir, with an outside spigot to each house. Cook stoves were the major source of heat. Walls were lined with heavy paper from the paper mill for warmth.

Initially, there was a community well house with water trough for animals where residents washed clothes, stored milk and eggs to keep them cool, and dipped water to carry to their houses, according to Ginger Reid of Canton.

"It was a very friendly place, where you trusted your neighbors and took care of each other," Gravatt said. "It was a safe place. We had a good time growing up."

She and brother Roy, also of Canton, remember tending big gardens, cattle, hogs, and sheep, and gathering berries, chinquapins, hazelnuts, and walnuts from nearby woods. They sold some produce and eggs.

Roy Henderson said, "We worked hard and couldn't play until all the work was done. We were taught to respect our elders and to not cuss." He remembers hog-killing time when his mother ground raw meat to render lard, then fried sausage before canning it.

"We had quilting parties, played ball, ran in the woods, waded in the creek," Glenda said.

Church was held under an apple tree, a gathering place for residents, when a circuit-riding preacher happened by. Eventually Charlie Wells donated a house for use as a church that sat roughly in the middle of what is now Food Lion's parking lot. Called Sheep Pen because it bordered a pasture for sheep, the church grew, moved, and is now West Canton Baptist Church, according to Reid. Children attended old Patton School in West Canton.

When those first families moved out, Wellstown began deteriorating, with its water source condemned by the state, pranksters and vandals burning empty houses, school kids stealing outhouses for bonfires.

Wellstown is only a memory.

Lower Fibreville

The houses of lower Fibreville are gone, bulldozers having accomplished in August what the Pigeon River started last fall; the very river that ran Champion Fibre Company, which constructed the houses for its workers. A vital ingredient in Canton's past has become history.

"I feel as if I have lost my identity," said Haynie "Poochie" Greene, who grew up in the mill village. "We were such a proud bunch of people with a sense of family who bonded there. All we have left are memories."

Fibreville was a residential community of thirty-nine paper mill workers' houses when first built in 1906. Later development added an alley with more houses. "There were (eventually) sixty-one houses and 108 children," said Susie Burnette Paquette who lived there until 1955. She has Champion-drawn maps of Fibreville with occupants' names listed on each house.

"The houses were owned by Champion," said Weldon Goolsby. "Rent was seven dollars a month," he recalled, "and the mill supplied all the utilities." A crew supervised by Ben Grube took care of all maintenance needs.

"On Sunday afternoons we all, boys and girls, played ball in the park at the end of the village," Goolsby said. "It was a close-knit community."

One bitter, snowy winter the older boys built a snowman that was at least fifteen feet tall, Paquette remembered. "They used long ladders to reach the top," she said.

The houses were similar in appearance with wood siding, gabled roofs and porches. Two rooms wide, some had two bedrooms; others, three. Bathroom facilities were added in 1916; bathtubs replaced galvanized washtubs in 1949. Champion sold the houses to the occupants in the 1950s.

Fathers worked shifts in the paper mill; mothers stayed home, tending children, houses, vegetable and flower gardens. Children of all ages played throughout the village, in the park, in a vacant lot regarded as a neighborhood playground, in and on the river and gathered on porches. Homemade boats were known to sink, leaving the paddlers to swim to shore. Children walked to old North Canton School over a swinging bridge or crossed the hill through "booger holler," so named because a thick forest of trees darkened the path, to Canton High School. A boy's club and another for girls met on Thursday at Champion's YMCA for the weekly jamboree. Many danced on YMCA square dance teams.

Boys built a brick grill for wiener roasts in the park, talented musicians gathered at Haynie's house to play various instruments and sing, and sledders raced down steep Fibreville hill in winter.

Pigs lived in a community sty. Goolsby was responsible for pulling a donkey cart through the streets to gather table scraps to feed the pigs. Thanksgiving Day was traditionally hog-killing time.

They watched the river, accustomed to its rise and fall. People would flee to higher ground when it rose, especially during the 1940s floods. Rivaling those of 2004, the '40s floods rotated some houses to face a different direction.

Those who lived there like to talk about their village, seeming to hold their memories, both personal and communal, close to their hearts. Listening to them, I get a pervading sense of security born of living among so many close families in equal circumstances, a fact mentioned by each in his or her own way.

Beaverdam Community Targeted as Nuclear Waste Depository

No admittance to an area one hundred and five square miles. Encompassing the entire Beaverdam community in Haywood County, Buncombe County's Sandy Mush area, and a slice of Madison County, the section of land extended almost, but not quite, to Hot Springs. There would be no access to Crabtree Bald, the Rough Creek watershed, or the Newfound Mountains. No residents. No churches. Off limits. The region would be designated Property of the United States Department of Energy.

This scenario loomed as a horrific possibility after a January, 1986, announcement by the United States Department of Energy that an area in the three counties was among twelve potential sites for location of a high-level nuclear waste repository, named the Elk River Complex SE-5.

Jack and Eileen Rice of Beaverdam were horrified when their pastor, the Reverend Kyles Wallace of Beaverdam United Methodist Church, broke the news on a Sunday morning. Before the congregation went home, a grassroots action group called Beaverdam Against Nuclear Dump (BAND) was organized. They weren't alone. CANT (Crabtree Against Nuclear Trash), Western Carolina Alliance, Blue Ridge Environmenral Defense League, Champion Papers, HALT, and others joined the fight.

"We were told we would have to leave, although we were in the buffer zone around the repository, and would be allowed only limited access to cemeteries. We counted two hundred fifty families who would be displaced in Beaverdam alone," Eileen Rice said.

U.S. Congressman at that time, Bill Hendon was a mainstay during the three-month comment period that ended in April, the Rices said. So were former U.S. Congressman James McClure Clarke, the late C. W. Hardin, former Canton mayor and state representative, and scientist Garrett Smathers, Canton's consultant on environmental issues, to name a few.

Secretary of the Interior Donald P. Hodel and Hendon flew by helicopter over the eastern boundary of Great Smoky Mountains National Park, only six miles from the proposed repository. They flew over the Blue Ridge Parkway, the Cherokee Reservation, where they stopped for lunch to meet with Reservation officials, and the potential repository site before landing in a field near the Rice home. Hodel held a press conference and attended a reception in his honor at that location. Hodel, who had brought Vice President George Bush with him, went from the reception to a community meeting at Sandy Mush Community Center. The Rices and the Greenes met briefly with Bush at Grove Park Inn, and felt that he was receptive to their remarks.

The Rices (Jack is a former county commissioner) and Mr. and Mrs. Ronnie Greene drove a water wagon, a vehicle filled with two dozen quarts of water from Canton's Rough Creek watershed, to Washington. Smathers had done his homework, and deemed the water the purest in North Carolina.

Their visit to the capitol included appointments with thirteen members of congress, to whom they gave jars of Haywood's pure water, and the Department of Energy, with constant coverage by national news networks.

Haywood's ammunition in the fight included proximity to the national park, the fact that rock in the repository area was not as stable as the DOE believed, related dangers involved with hauling and handling nuclear waste over I-40, other highways, and mountain roads, and the potential dangers of a nuclear spill into Haywood's water, all of which flows out of the county.

The mountains must have quivered from the collective sighs of relief when a May, 29th announcement declared, "DOE Gives Up on Dump."

Only a fraction of the activities and people involved in this harrowing event have been mentioned.

Rough Creek Watershed

C anton's Rough Creek Watershed, no longer used as the town's source of water, is aptly named. It is a rugged but beautiful forest. A moderately strenuous hike, beginning in Rice cove off Beaverdam Road, continuing up and over a mountain, eventually leads to the valley floor through which flows the cold, clear, fast-running waters of Rough Creek.

Most of the forest is natural growth, but in 1926 a reforestation program augmented what nature began, according to a yellowed newspaper clipping.

During the spring of that year, some 2,500 trees were planted on the watershed to increase the water-retaining capacity of the 870 acres.

A newspaper account written by Tom Higgins, published on September 26, 1957, tells the story. The reforestation project was conceived by the late W. J. Damtoft, head forester at Champion Paper and Fibre Company, who enlisted the aid of the late A. J. Hutchins, superintendent of Canton City Schools and an experienced woodsman, to bring the idea to fruition.

Hutchins, always willing to dedicate time and energy to civic activities, responded by gathering sixty high school students who were willing to plant trees. Damtoft, the state's head forester Mr. Holmes, Hutchins, and his crew trekked to the area over virtually untouched terrain. They carried with them the Champion-donated trees and planted them, a daunting undertaking.

Seedlings were set out yearly for the next ten to twelve years; for the following decade, every two or three years. Thirty-five thousand trees had been planted by hand at the reforestation program's end.

The result was a healthy forest, with a thick ground cover dropped from the trees that retained water. Those thirty-year-old, hand-planted trees—white pines, Norway spruce, and cottonwoods—had flourished. With a 90 percent survival rate, they had grown to enormous size, according to Higgins' observations. He mentioned one cottonwood, a species not native to this area, which was at least eighty feet tall, and five feet, four inches in circumference.

The Norway spruce was deemed the tree best suited for the purpose, since its shedding left a mattress-like mulch that captured and held the most rain with very little runoff.

The watershed's potential and supply ability had increased considerably.

A potentially disastrous fire was averted in 1941, when Hutchins and a crew of boys harvesting rock from the watershed to build Canton' High School's football stadium spotted a small wisp of smoke from a ridge near their newly-planted trees. Grabbing the tools they had at hand, they began raking a firebreak. Joined quickly by a forest ranger's crew, the flames were extinguished before they reached the cove and the maturing trees.

I was told that at one time, several families had lived in the valley; enough to support a church and a school, Higgins said. He was shown evidence in a small clearing of a long-ago cane-grinding site where molasses were made.

No families will dwell in the area again. The Southern Appalachian Highlands Conservancy bought Rough Creek Watershed in the early 2000s, and thankfully placed it in a permanent conservation easement; meaning the land can never be logged or developed. The Town of Canton retains control of the land for now, and can use it for recreation purposes. Eventually, the easement will be placed in the hands of the state. The Clean Water Management Trust Fund (CWMTF) worked with the Conservancy to obtain funds to buy the land.

Approximately 2.08 miles of Rough Creek's mainstream and an additional 5.29 miles of tributaries are permanently protected. "The waters of Rough Creek are among the most pristine in Western North Carolina," said Bill Holman, executive director of CWMTF, during dedication ceremonies. "This project ensures that the outstanding quality of these waters will stay that way."

Much of the credit in achieving the conservancy goes to Garrett Smathers, retired National Park Service scientist, a Waynesville resident who grew up in Canton. Garrett speaks of additional biological value in the 900 acres. The Watershed is also home to at least twenty-four rare plants and twelve natural wildlife communities, four of which are considered rare, including turkey, bear, and owl habitats.

In short, the area is an island of biodiversity, now protected from influences that could pollute the pure water and eradicate the rare flora and fauna that surround it.

Walters Dam: An Engineering Marvel

Walters Dam and powerhouse turned on the lights in Haywood County in 1930. Seventy-seven years later, the hydroelectric plant continues to supply power for this area and beyond.

The existence of the facility in northern Haywood County's Pigeon River Gorge is remarkable in part because of its rugged location and the time period in which it was built. The site's elevation and mountainous terrain in a hard-to-reach location with no rail access presented challenging construction techniques for the builders of the plant, and attracted national attention. Contractors leased a narrow gauge logging railroad line and extended it another five miles to the dam site, requiring a year's time.

Carolina Power & Light began its massive construction project in the remote, almost inaccessible area in 1927, completing it in 1930. The building of the hydroelectric facility was, and still is, an engineering feat. The plant has endured and continues to generate electric power with only a few minor changes, according to Mechanical Supervisor Dean Shults, at the plant for twenty-five years. "The tunnel was drained in 2001 and three new isolation valves were installed, but the original turbines and controls are still in place," he said.

The dam was the highest east of the Rockies until after World War II. The complex, including dam, powerhouse, and connecting tunnel, was designated a North Carolina Historic Civil Engineering Landmark in 1980, qualifying because it was more than fifty years old and "made a significant contribution toward development of a large region of the nation and to the civil engineering profession." It also meets the standards required for designation on the National Register of Historic Places.

The arch-shaped concrete dam, centered with a spillway, has an 861-foot head and impounds waters of the Pigeon River and Cataloochee Creek in Waterville Lake, near the Tennessee state line in the Harmon Den area of Haywood County. The dam is basically 207 feet tall and 900 feet across. The water intake tunnel connecting with the power plant is 6.2 miles long, and was blasted from solid rock. Horseshoe-shaped, its diameter is the equivalent of a fourteen-foot circle or pipe.

During construction of the tunnel, one crew started at the intake area near Cataloochee Creek and another started at the powerhouse. When they finally met, the tunnel was only 0.5 inch off engineering plans.

"That still raises some eyebrows," Shults said. "I am still amazed at the engineering achievement accomplished in three years." Shults, obviously proud of the Walters plant, particularly expresses amazement at how quickly it was built. Commissioned to build November 26, 1926, actual construction began in 1927 and the plant's operation commenced in 1930. The powerhouse, a brick building with tall windows, is named for Charles S. Walters, Vice President and member of the Carolina Power & Light Board of Directors, and is a source of power to several communities throughout the area.

Two 115,000-volt power lines connect with Canton and Asheville. One 138,000-volt line extends to the tri-cities, the Bristol, Johnson City, Kingsport– area, in Tennessee. One 161,000-volt line extends to the Tennessee Valley Authority.

Waynesville businessman Benjamin J. Sloan and his partners had laid some of the groundwork for CP&L when they built a power plant on Leatherwood Shoals in the White Oak section under the name of Haywood Electric Power Company, but power consumption outgrew that facility. In 1918, Sloan partnered with A. C. Springs of Charlotte with intentions of constructing a major hydroelectric power dam below the mouth of Cataloochee Creek, and obtained necessary options from Waterville to the mouth of Cove Creek and up to Crabtree Creek. After Sloan's death, his son Hugh and his partners sold their holdings to CP&L, who eventually realized Sloan's dream.

Waterville Village

Nestled in a valley along the banks of Big Creek, Waterville Village was built in the late 1920s to accommodate Carolina Power & Light employees at the nearby Walters hydroelectric plant. On-site housing was necessary in order to recruit qualified operators, since no primary roads entered the area. Driving to work daily was not an option.

Construction workers building the powerhouse, dam, and tunnel lived in numerous temporary camps, built by CP&L and dismantled when the project was completed

Finished in 1929, the village for one group of Waterville residents was on the slope west of Big Creek and the railroad. The other was on the east side of Big Creek. In the valley between the creek and the railroad were the school, two-story clubhouse, and other structures associated with the plant.

The railroad, which centered the village, was later removed and replaced by State Road 1332.

The nation was in the midst of the Great Depression and this rugged rural area was economically depressed, but those who lived in Waterville enjoyed good living conditions.

"It was a pretty place with those white, well-kept houses. It is still a pretty place," said Hal Brown of Newport, Tennessee, who once worked and lived there. "It will always be home to me."

According to CP&L documents, the company village originally had nine family cottages, a two-story boarding house, a guesthouse, a small post office, a clubhouse, a school, and a swimming area. A landscaped area, the village had lighted, concrete sidewalks and steps connecting the buildings. Rock walls terraced the hillsides and creek banks.

Telephone service was available for each wood-furnace heated home, as well as water and sewer lines. The community had its own water filtration system and fire protection facilities, with fire hydrants and hoses placed among groups of cottages. Garages were located near the powerhouse.

"We paid only twenty-five dollars a month for rent," Brown said, "and that included utilities. The houses were nice; well built, with five rooms, with two used as bedrooms."

Getting groceries was no problem, Brown said. "There was a store at Mount Sterling, about one mile up, or someone from the plant went into Newport twice a week on company business, and you could give them your grocery order and they would buy it at the Super Dollar and bring it back."

"Big Creek was damned up with logs to make a swimming hole. The dam washed out later, but people still swim there. That is cold water. There was a covered shed with a concrete floor near the creek that we called the 'pig stand.' At least once a month, we would cook a pig or a bear for the community. We had some pretty good musicians, so there was always some singing and dancing. When we weren't having a picnic, we visited each other or played cards. I remember a tennis court, too." The shed can still be reserved, according to Brown.

Brown laughingly admitted that a few stills were scattered around, but emphasized that the "moonshine was to sell, not to drink. Transportation did away with that," he said.

The nearest church was Mount Sterling White Baptist Church. Bernice Brown was the first teacher in the village school, and taught grades one through eight, Brown remembers.

Brown was plant operator when he retired November 7, 1992. "Everybody knew everybody real well. They were fine people, pleasant and friendly. We all worked shifts. It was like one big family." Families who lived there were large, he said, so the village was well-populated.

Waterville has changed over the years. As jobs were phased out, residential buildings were razed. Three homes and the clubhouse, used for meetings, remain, according to Dean Shults, mechanical supervisor at Walters. Roads provide access to the remaining houses, replacing the concrete sidewalks. Access to Waterville is available via a paved road.

Although not a part of Waterville, CP&L, now Progress Energy, built two dam operators' houses on the slope overlooking the dam, permanent houses which are still in use.

The area surrounding the village was "wild country," according to Brown. On the edge of Great Smokies National Park, it is still wild if you venture too far from Interstate 40, paralleling the Pigeon River, or from the Walters Powerhouse location.

Dutch Cove

German immigrants established some of the earliest settlements in what later became Haywood County, along the Pigeon River and Hominy Creek, arriving here before 1800.

"They brought with them the customs, characteristics and language...of their people in Rowan County" where the first contingent of Deutsch, or Palatinate immigrants, arrived a generation or more earlier, wrote Sadie Smathers Patton in her genealogy of the Smathers family, who were among those settling here.

"They were industrious, economical, and willing to endure any amount of toil to secure permanent homes or establishments over which they had complete control," she wrote.

The first stream of immigrants from Germany to England, and then to America, began in the 17th century. Their discontent had begun a century earlier during the Reformation, followed by the wars in Martin Luther's time, the Thirty Years War, and the conflicts that marked the long reign of the French king, Louis XIV. "No portion of Germany suffered so much as that part called the Lower Palatinate on the eastern boundary of France," she wrote. Easily accessible to French soldiers, the predominantly protestant population was a thorn in the side of the French king, who made them a primary target.

A rural-oriented people who avoided settling in towns, they had fled harsh living conditions, war, persecution, and religious intolerance. Their fierce seeking out of locations where they could control their own destinies is explained by the conditions from which they escaped, and offers insight into the independent, self-sufficient nature of mountain people.

Like the Scotch-Irish, as soon as shelter was provided for families in a community, both a church and a school were built.

Originally known as Fulbright's Cove, the settlement in eastern Haywood County was eventually named, appropriately, Deutsch Cove, Deutsch meaning Dutch. The name change came about as these immigrants heavily settled the cove. The area continues to be known by the same name, but with an anglicized spelling; Dutch Cove.

Surnames underwent similar changes in spelling over the years. Smathers was originally de Smet. French Huguenots associated with the Protestant movement. The de Smets had fled for their lives to Germany, England, Holland, and Switzerland, where they intermarried with the natives. Subsequently, de Smet became Smeter, Smetter, Schmetter, Smither, Smyther, and Smadders before the final spelling of Smathers.

In their frontier home, the Smathers lived among relatives and friends who had also migrated from Rowan. They included Fulbrights, Schneiders (Sniders, Snyders), Millers, Christoffels (Christophers), Redsleafs (Rhodarmers); all people with a common background and similar characteristics.

Patton further describes these people as being energetic and having common sense. Their farms were neat, and their homes were plain but comfortable cabins. They were not satisfied until they felt all work had been done properly, until all had been profitably arranged.

The distinctive traits of the early German settlers are said to have endured for a generation or two longer among the Deutsch people living in the coves of Haywood County before being assimilated into the culture around them.

FORCES OF NATURE

Wet and Wild Floods

The Pigeon River has rolled along quite calmly for a number of years now, occasionally topping banks by a few feet in the bottomland along its route and licking at Old Clyde Road, where the river makes a sharp turn.

Running brown with mud when heavy rains deluge its east or west forks, or both, the river has carried heavy trees and other debris to gather against bridge pilings and lapped at bridge bottoms. But the Pigeon has shown little sign of its flooding potential. Actually, it has behaved rather well compared to its earlier history.

The Pigeon went on recorded rampages three times in the 1800s and six times between 1901 and 1928, damaging crops and property from the river's origins in the mountains to Clyde. But in August 1940, the river roared from the mountains, first on the 13th and again on the 30th, cutting wide swaths of heavy damage to a more populated area. It did so again in 1949, when the river crested at 15.44 feet, 5.3 feet under 1940's August 30th crest.

These last three are the floods we remember, and would prefer not to see again.

Images of boaters paddling on Canton's Park Street in front of the Colonial Theater were captured on film. Inside the theater, the seats and carpet were a soggy mess.

Families living in Fibreville below Champion's paper mill fled to higher ground. When the river finally crested, it had reached the eaves of their houses.

Patsy Kelly remembers that her aunt and uncle tired of moving furniture from their Fibreville home and rigged a system with ropes that enabled them to pull up the furnishings and secure them to the ceiling, above the high water mark penciled on the wall.

Her husband Dan once sat on high ground and watched the Fibreville bridge collapse and disappear, tossed apart by the raging water.

In the business section, Canton Laundry shut down with water 6 feet four inches deep in its plant and office; cars in Champion Motor Company rode on a sea of muddy water; Spears Inn, a boarding house, was carpeted with mud; and Smoky Mountain Candy Company lost much of its stock.

Overflow on approaches to Main and Park Street bridges, coupled with water depth on Park, brought traffic to a halt. Train tracks were covered, and trestles shuddered as gallons of water pushed against supporting structures. Power was lost and sewer lines inundated.

The river began rising slowly 6 a.m. on Monday, August 12, and reached the 10-foot stage at 6:30 a.m. on August 13. It didn't stop there. Water continued to rise, more rapidly, at a rate of about 1.3 feet per hour.

The river's bed could no longer contain the water, which streamed over the banks. Crops were heavily damaged in rural areas throughout the Pigeon River basin. East Fork folks watched their bridges wash away, along with a good portion of the highway. Mudslides blocked roads.

Floodwaters on the 30th in 1940 swept Reverend Bill Hampton and his wife on Big Creek, a tributary of West Fork Pigeon River, to their deaths. Mrs. Hampton's body was found miles away, below Lake Logan. Hampton's body was snagged by debris near the mouth of Big Creek.

Champion Paper's lower end flooded and shut down as machines became coated with mud and motors submerged. Over a thousand cords of pulpwood floated away, and coal and other supplies were damaged. Plant employees lost thousands of man-hours.

Over 100 families were driven from their homes.

Clyde didn't fare much better. Water rose to four feet on US 19/23 through town. One bridge washed away and another was damaged, while at least fifteen private homes had flooded basements. Water rather than tourists occupied facilities at Pines Tourist Rooms.

Water was eight feet deep in Canton's National Guard Armory, now Sunburst Fitness Center. In 1949, floodwaters undercut a portion of the town swimming pool and flooded its pump.

Only a child, my memories are of watching the fast-moving, roiling water in horror from a perch on my father's shoulders, a scene replayed later in nightmares. Oft-heard recounts of the devastation, yellowed newspaper clippings, a gathering of memories from among my contemporaries, and a TVA report found in the Canton museum expand the picture.

Hurricane Frances

The Pigeon River, always prominent in Haywood County annals, wrote another chapter; hurricane Frances.

Normally placid, the river showed its alter ego with a massive flood cresting at 20.7 feet during the morning hours of September 7, 2004. Fueled by heavy rain sent to Western North Carolina by hurricane Frances, the river raged from its east and west forks through Cruso, Bethel, Canton, and Clyde, destroying most everything in its path.

A column published June 27, 2004 chronicled "wet and wild floods" in Haywood County's past, using information garnered from old newspapers, a TVA report, hazy childhood memories, and a few first-hand recollections. Little did I know.

Experiencing the river's rampage up close and personal is a different matter.

Following a wet summer, heavy rains from the storm pounding Florida fell on saturated soil and fed the river at its headwaters. Muddy water, overflowing the banks at an alarming rate and depth, tumbled boulders as big as cars downstream, stripped slabs of pavement from roads, cleared fields of crops, undermined foundations, and swept away houses. Flooding left hundreds of county residents without homes, food, water, clothing, and family mementos; hurting, tearful, and dazed.

"I would call this a 100-year flood," said Bill Holbrook, a farmer on NC 215. His 27 acres of crops are gone, his tomatoes and peppers among those plastering buckled chain-link fences and littering the streets of Canton. His ancestors and immediate family have lived here since the 1800s. "I have not seen or heard of the river crossing this road, even when it was a railroad." The railroad was built in 1905.

Joe and Frances Baxley's house sits high above the adjacent river. Nine family members and an elderly neighbor were gathered there, having fled their low-lying houses nearby. A boat appeared at around 11 p.m. Monday evening, manned by volunteers, and all were evacuated. The Baxley house survived undamaged.

Troy Mason's garage apartment sits below Baxley's house with the east fork of the Pigeon River on one side and the west fork, across NC 110, on the other. He heard the roar of the east fork as it topped its banks, and rushed from his house in time to escape before the west fork joined the flood. He believed he could save his house, but his neighbors weren't so lucky. At least half a dozen houses and mobile homes were uninhabitable, unsafe in this area called Arc Park.

East Fork appears to have been the primary culprit, leaving many rural areas and residents pondering an uncertain future, looking at damage that took everything they had.

Canton's Recreation Park and Pisgah High's adjoining ball fields were devastated. Water overflowed two concrete bridges in downtown Canton, and flooded Park Street past Adams and Pace streets, ravaging businesses in its wake. Watermarks on walls showed depths of 8 to 10 feet. Six feet of water occupied the Canton Police Department and lapped at the stage in a newly refurbished Colonial Theater. The town reeked of diesel fuel, kerosene and raw sewage. A propane tank floated on South Main Street. Substation Road was evacuated, threatened by propane tanks at the World Gym, in the old armory building.

Blue Ridge Paper mill was idled, invaded by six feet of mud and water that covered motors, generators, and computers. The sewage treatment plant that serves both the mill and Canton was totally disabled. Blue Ridge Paper Mill was still selling paper from its inventory, though.

The town of Clyde looked like a lake. Buddy Glance owns the Old Grouch's Military Surplus, an army surplus store. He found a mobile home deposited on Broad Street, one of more than eighty homes lost. His store was spared, but he lost a warehouse full of merchandise. Doris Powell mopped water instead of styling hair. Central Haywood High School was forced to relocate temporarily. Canton was off limits, surrounded by police tape, and curfews were imposed there and in Clyde. Schools were closed. Thankfully, no deaths were reported.

Vignettes, only vignettes of widespread damage, devastation, bewildered families and business owners.

Bright rays emanating from the generosity and compassion of people punctuated the bleakness. Friends, neighbors, emergency personnel, even strangers arrived unexpectedly to offer help. Vans from Macedonia Baptist Church in Lincolnton, parked on Max Thompson Road, carried North Carolina Baptist Men, good Samaritans from distant locales like Kinston and Washington, who were emptying houses of muddied belongings.

Salvation Army vehicles in the parking lot of Canton's First Baptist Church were dispensing grab and go meals, containers of emergency cleaning supplies, and words of encouragement. Inside the church, women from area churches served hot meals. A vehicle labeled Greensboro Fire and Rescue, big as a bus, was seen traveling up NC 110.

Many individuals went looking for people to help. Lowe's retiree Neal Lipham of Canton used his time, equipment, and expertise to assist two hard-struck businesses, and also responded to requests for pumping basements. Others offered to wash someone's laundry or provide the use of their showers.

Governor Jim Easley and U.S. Senator Elizabeth Dole flew in to view the damage. Vice Presidential hopeful John Edwards appeared in Canton First Baptist Church on Sunday. The federal government declared fifteen Western North Carolina counties a disaster area.

The sun was shining after Frances, but powerful hurricane Ivan was mimicking Frances' path.

No. Surely not.

Ivan

Frances was a home wrecker, but Ivan was that and more. Ivan was a killer.

Raw, painful wounds scar Haywood County, created by so-called remnants of the two hurricanes. Frances ripped and tore through on September 7. Eight days later, vicious Ivan poured salt into open wounds and created more.

Ivan swept Doris Crawford Baxter of Bethel to her death with raging waters that topped Frances' flood level by 4 feet, measured by high water marks on Canton buildings, including Blue Ridge Paper Company. At least ten other people died in Western North Carolina.

Ferocious waters from the Pigeon River account for the majority of damages. However, the second time around, some creeks normally only a couple of feet wide joined in the fray, showing unexpected authority by turning into torrents as wide as a river. Among those were Crawford, Hungry, Allen's, and Harley creeks, to name a few.

The Pigeon River washed out bridges and carved chunks from roads and streets, even I-40. A concrete bridge on US 276 near the intersection of NC 110 and Lovejoy Road fell victim to a three-bedroom mobile home, which knocked out center pilings as current forced the structure down river. Cruso and Lake Logan areas, nearer the river's origins, are painful to see.

The most obvious damage, what one might call the major stories, has been recorded. But every account represents a major impact in someone's life.

Burnette Cove residents drove their cars over a bridge showing indications of instability, parked them along US 276, and then walked back home across the bridge. A house was deposited on the road, up Pisgah Creek. Houses moved from oft-flooded Fibreville to Penland Street in Canton were a jumbled mass. The river got them after all. Sections of Canton and Clyde are forever changed. Some washed out families say they don't want to live by the river anymore, even If their homes were habitable.

Frightened residents on Rhoda Street off Pisgah Drive in Canton were evacuated to North Canton School when a sliver of a creek rampaged in and around houses, and undermined one lane of the street.

Two men, swift water rescue personnel from Center Pigeon who were checking houses on Meadowbrook Drive, were dumped from their boat and had to be rescued. After the creek passed under Pisgah Drive, it evicted two families and all their possessions.

Blue Ridge Paper's waste treatment plant, which also handles Canton's waste, was shut down for the second time. The mill's first priority was to get the treatment facility up and running, according to company spokesman Bob Williams, before turning its attention to repairs and cleanup inside its buildings.

Reports of flood experiences, big and small, continued to pour in (no pun intended) and more were sure to come. Recovery, financially and emotionally, would require months, maybe years.

But Haywood County folks don't give up easily. Nelson Dillinger, captain of Shelby Fire Department, took note of this trait. "These are amazing people." Dillinger said. "They are so used to taking care of themselves that we have to push them away to let us help. They want to take care of us. They are strong people."

Nelson and his crew, along with another from Greensboro, were positioned at Center Pigeon Fire Department. They were but two of many North Carolina groups who came to help. Those who provided meals, cleaning supplies, manual labor, heavy equipment, child care, and moral support, some unknown and others too numerous to mention, are another story in themselves.

A Clyde couple with three small children at home accepted a friend's offer and moved into a summer cottage at Lake Junaluska. The husband said, "We do have a place to stay...the one positive thing that has come out of all this is that you realize how many really good friends you have in a community like this. I can't begin to list all the people who have already helped us in so many ways, and a lot of the people who've helped tons have been total strangers. The pulling together with others is definitely a good thing."

And so, Ivan wrote another chapter in Haywood's history, one of devastation.

After the storm took its rain and headed north, a welcome sun dawned and the sky became a cloudless, bright blue. A magnolia tree, its blossoming season well over, opened one lone bloom. Nearby, an azalea topped a branch with one magenta flower. Hope?

Tornado or Not, Storm Inflicted Severe Damage

" We heard the noise, but we didn't know what was happening. It was dark and our power went off," said Mary Haynes White, eighty-one, of Canton.

A tin roof lifting from their garage and crimping around power lines, a large oak tree toppling, a shed blowing away, and heavy rain and wind were part of the sounds she and her three small children heard. "We never knew where that shed went," she said.

The storm that night in 1957 wasn't officially designated a tornado, but the bizarre scenes it left behind seem a bit much for merely high winds.

"We had an old Hudson car in the garage and it wasn't damaged," White said, "but concrete blocks (forming) one side of the garage were lying neatly on the ground, unbroken and unseparated."

"We shined a flashlight out the windows and could see some of the damage. I called my husband and told him he needed to come home," she said. Active in the Canton Rescue Squad, he replied that since she and the children were safe, he would continue to help cover gaping holes in a nursing home roof on Beaverdam Street, since he was needed there more.

Jimmy Rhea, who lived across the road from the Whites, lost his basketball goal. "I remember that all the leaves were blown off the trees," he said. "I was fourteen that year."

David and Eva Jane Ashe remember the night the storm hop-scotched its way east along North Canton Road to Beaverdam, then veered slightly to the North Hominy community. An entire herd of cattle in their pasture ran loose after wind blew the pasture gate down. A car hit one cow, said David Ashe. They got out of the cattle business after that harrowing experience.

Others reported damaged or missing roofs and downed trees, including one huge oak in Dick Clontz's parents' yard. Joyce Owen's car was found in a field downhill, behind his rock home and beside Plains United Methodist Church.

The most bizarre scene, however, was on North Hominy Road, just off of Newfound Road.

The storm targeted a small, frame church, clutched it within its swirling winds, and dismantled it piece by piece, scattering the remains around the grounds. Roof, steeple, walls, and furnishings were gone, but an intact piano sat all alone on the floor of the building, said Edna Broyles, who lives nearby.

A block building behind the church lost its roof and one row of blocks was separated from its walls and deposited in one piece on the ground. Yes, Harmony Grove Baptist Church took the biggest blow that night, but its congregation rebuilt and flourishes.

A sense of security blew away that night, too, in the false belief that surrounding mountains protected us from the threat of tornadoes, or storms that bore such a strong resemblance to one.

Dogwood Winter

Dogwoods were in full bloom, tulip poplars were blossoming and "sarvice" trees (serviceberry trees) were dotted with white. Trillium carpeted the forest floor. And nighttime temperatures dropped into the '30s.

Dogwood winter. Never known it to fail.

Most likely, another cold snap is in our future. When tangles of blackberry bushes begin disappearing under a dusting of white blossoms, get ready. Blackberry winter is certain to follow.

Only then can we begin to feel that spring and summer are on their way.

Remember the opening day of trout season in April? Winter usually gives another nasty squeeze on that date. Catching that elusive fish must be some kind of thrill, to justify enduring the cold rain and falling temperatures (or worse) that usually accompany that ritual of spring.

Look for dog days toward the end of summer, when foliage is thick and dark green, the temperature rises, and the air feels heavy.

An eerie quiet, a greenish cast to the sky, and the smell of sulfur in the air is a tornado warning. The only time I experienced those conditions; high winds suddenly twisted the tops out of four pine trees in my yard and flung them to the ground.

I am no meteorologist. Don't pretend to be. But weather predictions from my grandparents and other old-timers are firmly rooted in my mind.

A ring around the moon means falling weather; either rain or snow, depending on the temperature. When wind blows poplar tree leaves inside out, showing their lighter underside, look for rain. Cows lie down before a storm. Rain before seven means clear weather before eleven. Fog in the morning means a sunny day.

My grandfather was right more often than he was wrong.

Keep bedding plants inside and don't display hanging baskets until May 15th to avoid losing them to frost. Some say Mother's Day. Neither is absolutely fool proof.

Old-timers had an uncanny ability to predict the weather without the aid of television forecasters and sophisticated Doppler technology. They closely observed the signs provided by nature and animals. If they had one, the Old Farmer's Almanac might be a weather reference.

Some believed that the equinox, when day and night are of equal hours, predicts the weather pattern for the following season. In spring, rain from the north that day meant a dry summer. Equinox occurs around March 21 and September 23.

Another weather predictor was the shape of the moon. A crescent moon that would "hold water" indicated dry weather ahead. If water could leak from a crescent moon, rain was coming.

Lightning in the north during summer meant rain in three days.

Some believed that in dry weather, all signs failed.

"Evening red and morning gray are sure signs of a sunny day. Evening gray and morning red put on your hat or you'll wet your head." There are several adaptations of this old proverb. Jesus in Matthew 16:2–3 (ESV) said, "When it is evening, you say, 'It will be fair weather for the sky is red.' And in the morning, 'It will be stormy today, for the sky is red and threatening'."

Crows sitting in a row on telephone wires means rain is coming, as does the retreat of spiders from their webs. Spiders are also said to enlarge and repair their webs before the onset of bad weather.

Weather forecasters, searching for logic in old weather beliefs, say a drop in barometric pressure may account for claims that approaching wet weather makes joints ache. Their explanation is that the decreasing pressure allows tissues in our bodies to expand, affecting the nerve endings.

Some old adages ring with truth, so much so that professional meteorologists have studied them extensively.

One last word. If rain falls while the sun is out, the devil is beating his wife.

Balmy Winters

Winters around here are like the old gray mare. They "ain't what they used to be."

I've been told that years ago Pigeon River froze over with ice so thick that a horse and wagon could be driven across. It has frozen during my lifetime, but with only a thin skimming of ice, nothing to walk on. Weather records provided by National Climactic Data Center in Asheville show that 18 inches of snow fell on March 17, 1936; 16 inches on February 16, 1969; 11 inches on April 3, 1987; and on December 3, 1971, 17 inches fell. Snow that deep means that Haywood County is all but immobilized. An ice storm on February 2, 1996 caused $50 million in damages.

We sometimes had snow on the ground for long periods of time. My grandmother always said that lingering snow was waiting for more to fall. And it did.

Where is all the snow now?

During my childhood, our mothers sent us out to play in ugly rubber galoshes pulled over heavy socks and shoes. It was a wasted effort. The snow was so deep that it topped our protective footwear, converting them to reservoirs of packed snow.

As an adult, my family and three others parked at a locked gate on the Blue Ridge Parkway at Beech Gap and trudged on an unreliable crust of snow, so deep that only tops of signposts were showing, to Devil's Courthouse parking lot. When we reached the lot, we picnicked, and our children cut blocks of snow to build an igloo.

Talking about weather in Haywood County, though, is relative. Crabtree may have 4 inches of snow while a few ridges over, Waynesville's streets are clear.

Mountain Research Center (MRC) has records dating back to 1966 that show significant snowfalls in January 1966 and 1977. Bill Upton, retired Haywood County Schools' superintendent, remembers 1977, when schools were open only two days in January, but an average temperature of five below zero was the culprit as much as the snow. "The freeze line was so deep that pipes were frozen," he said.

Brenda Smathers at the MRC, who perused their records, especially remembers the March "Blizzard of '93" when 18 inches of snow fell. The National Climatic Data Center (NCDC) lists it as "Storm of the Century." "I went to a local grocery store the night before snow fell, and was told I had missed all the excitement. Two women had fought on the floor over the only loaf of bread on the shelf. Needless to say, I got no bread," she said.

Eighteen inches of snow were measured during the month of February in 1979 and seventeen for January 1989, with a big snow on January 28, 1989. Heavy snows also occurred on January 3, February 12 and 16 of 1994, on March 8 and 20 of 1996, January 28 and March 11 of 1998, and March 3 and 26 of 1999.

On December 1886, a snow 3 feet in depth fell in Buncombe and adjoining counties, according to John P. Arthur in *Western North Carolina: A History (From 1730 to 1913)._*

As an interesting postscript: "The greatest single snowfall ever recorded in North Carolina fell at Newfound Gap in the Smokies between April 2 and 6, 1987: 60 inches," is reported in *The Western North Carolina Almanac and Book of Lists.*

Is Spring Really Here?

Sun warmed the yellow petals of scattered forsythia blooms and added sheen to the rich purple crocus bursting from my neighbor's yard on the first day of spring, 2010. Robins pecked busily in the grass, seeking food, while brave daffodils nodded their fluted heads in approval. The new season received an appropriate welcome.

So why does it all feel as if an uneasy truce has been called between a relentless winter and a struggling spring? The nip in the air seems to signify that an unusually cold and snowy winter isn't done with us yet.

Weather is a frequent topic of discussion these days, and I am not alone in doubting that spring warmth and sunshine are here, uninterrupted, for the duration. Folks remember some significant late spring snows.

The blizzard of 1993 was a landmark weather event in Western North Carolina history. Walloping the mountains on March 13–14, that storm dumped 18 inches of snow, according to Weather Service records. It was billed as the Storm of the Century by National Climactic Data Center in Asheville.

The latest spring snow recorded in Asheville, leaving only a trace of the white stuff, was May 7, 1992.

On April 3, 1987, another spring snow dropped 11.5 inches on this area. NCDC weather records show that 18 inches of snow fell on March 17, 1936.

Heavy snows also occurred on March 8 and 20, 1966, and on March 3 and 26, 1999.

"The greatest single snowfall ever recorded in North Carolina fell at Newfound Gap in the Smokies between April 2 and 6, 1987: 60 inches is recorded in The Western North Carolina Almanac and Book of Lists," said Robert Beverley. "Fueling doubt that spring has truly arrived are all too vivid images of the worst winter seen in these parts in over 10 years. Snow, ice and frigid temperatures that began on December 18, persisting throughout January, February, and March, have left some of us feeling shell shocked."

That first storm in December left over 60,000 in Western North Carolina without power, some for days. Clyde reported 12 inches of snow, and Cataloochee Ski Resort proclaimed 18 inches. Snow is usually characterized by deep quietness, but not this time. Trees burdened by heavy snow popped and cracked as branches fell or thudded to the ground, leaving extensive root systems exposed.

And so it went, on and on. By the end of January, almost 24 inches of snow had fallen; the heaviest total recorded since 1902.

Wind blew incessantly in mighty gusts while temperatures below freezing endured for days. The snow remained, preserved by the arctic-like temperatures. Old-timers claim that lingering snow is waiting for more to fall.

Constant reminders in the shape of fallen trees, freshly cut stumps and deep potholes in pavement keep memories of this unusual winter alive.

And as I began writing this column on March 22, a glance out the window revealed yet another snow shower, falling on blooming daffodils.

Spring is here? We shall see. Both April and May have brought snow in the past.

THE LENOIR
PLANTATION

Lenoir Creek Farm

C aptain Thomas Isaac Lenoir and others in his family had significant roles in the development of both Haywood County and the state of North Carolina during their extensive and intriguing history.

This was a family whose men served in the Civil War, placed high priority on college education for both men and women, loved the land, and were involved in county, state, and national politics at one time or another.

Thomas Isaac was responsible for the vast family holdings in Haywood, and lived on the farm located on Lenoir Creek in Cruso.

Lenoir/Michal family members tend to scoff at the description, but their property on the east fork of the Pigeon River was once called a plantation. The vast acreage was there and the slaves, but the antebellum home and grand social events usually associated with historic plantation life were missing.

The story begins when Waightstill Avery, who never lived in Haywood County, acquired the first 1,000 or more acres of an eventual holding of 2,571 acres as a state land grant between 1794 and 1805. An influential attorney and politician who moved to Charlotte, his biography is mind-boggling.

He was, among other things, attorney general for the Crown in 1772 until he became an advocate for independence, signing the Mecklenburg Declaration of Independence, and helping draft the Mecklenburg Resolves.

He was the state's first attorney general, later resigning to lead the Jones County militia as a colonel during the Revolutionary War.

Avery County is named in his honor. He also had property in Buncombe and Burke counties, choosing to live in Burke on a plantation named Swan Ponds.

Acquisition of more land grants coupled with more real estate purchases left him owning a significant spread of land on Pigeon River's east fork, all of which he deeded to his daughter, Selina Louisa Lenoir, wife of Colonel Thomas Lenoir, by June 1808.

The couple was the first to live on the property, in a log cabin that stood behind the still-existing springhouse along Lenoir Creek. Thomas wrote one of his brothers that Louisa wanted to go to the east fork of the Pigeon, so he thought he had better go with her.

"You could see traces of the cabin foundation at one time, if you knew where to look," said the late Emily Michal Terrell of Cruso, whose research of her family's genealogy was an ongoing pursuit. "A two-story white frame house, called Little Lonesome, was built later on a knoll overlooking the valley." A lone brick chimney marks its site.

After Haywood County was established in December 1808, Thomas Lenoir, along with Felix Walker and John McFarland, were given the responsibility of "erecting public buildings of said county." He was also elected to the North Carolina House of Representatives, along with Thomas Love in 1809. He was twenty-nine years old then.

Colonel Thomas Lenoir was in the militia, and served in the War of 1812. "It seems he, along with Major William Cathey, took a regiment from Haywood County to Wadesboro on January 25th, 1815, remaining there until they were mustered out of service some time in May," Terrell said.

Unhappy with their isolation and lack of social life, Thomas and Louisa moved to Fort Defiance, a plantation outside Lenoir in an area called Happy Valley, belonging to his father, General William Lenoir. He continued to oversee operation of the farm.

Colonel Thomas Lenoir had added some 2,000 additional acres to those given to him and his wife in Haywood County through state land grants and property purchase.

After his death in 1861, his son Thomas Isaac inherited 2,222 acres and son Walter received the remainder of the property, called Crab Orchard, where Springdale Country Club is located now.

The future of the farm ended up in Thomas Isaac's hands.

Thomas Isaac Lenoir

Thomas Isaac Lenoir, already involved in managing the family farm on the east fork of the Pigeon, moved there in the 1840s when his parents, Thomas and Louisa, left Haywood County to live on a family plantation near Lenoir. He had plans, apparently, for increasing the scope of the property's use.

A student at the University of North Carolina, he was a bachelor when he left school at his father's call for help and took up residence on what we know as Lenoir Creek Farms. In old letters, he referred to his farm as "Bachelor's Retreat," but his sisters and female cousins teasingly called it the "The Den."

Devon cattle, the same breed raised there today by Charlie and Martha Trantham, were introduced to this area when Thomas and his slaves brought the first herd of Devons from Pennsylvania to Western North Carolina in 1845. He settled in to tend his cattle and continue to develop the farm.

He must have known his business; the agricultural census for 1850 indicates that he had 119 cattle, including 25 mulch cows, and 4 oxen, 9 horses, 11 asses and mules, 81 swine, and 109 sheep. He had grown many bushels of wheat, rye, corn, oats, potatoes, barley, and buckwheat, sheared 108 lbs. of wool, reaped 6 tons of hay, 10 lbs. of flax, and had on hand 400 lbs. of butter and 166 lbs. each of beeswax and honey.

Thomas Isaac Lenoir had eighteen slaves and four slave cabins, according to the Slave Population Census of 1860. Buildings included a granary, spring house, smokehouse, the "Broyhill House," various barns, and a "lodge" across the river that eventually became the family's residence, said Dr. Mary Michal, a Johnson City, Tennessee pediatrician and one of two current owners. Ernest Bumgarner remembers his father telling him that Broyhill Furniture owned property adjacent to the farm that they logged, moving the logs down the mountain over Lenoir property.

Colonel Thomas Lenoir had a black smithy, and Thomas Isaac likely had one as well. A gristmill was built on Lenoir's Creek but, unfortunately, the only time it was functional was when Lenoir's Creek was almost at flood stage. Joe Michal, father of the present owners, turned the millpond into a trout pond.

On the 18th of July in 1861, Thomas Isaac left for nine months to serve in the Confederate Army as captain of the Haywood Highlanders, a company he had raised primarily from men of the east fork of the Pigeon. They became Company F of the 25th Regiment of the North Carolina Volunteers. In April of 1862, he resigned because of poor health and age. Reading from his journal, Emily Michal Terrell said he acknowledged he was "a lot stricter than his mountain boys really wanted in a leader," so he decided he had better go home and let someone near their own age lead them.

During the war years, Kirk's Raiders came through the valley, looting and pillaging, leaving gunshots in a corner cupboard that the family still has, and taking all the horses. The cattle were grazing on high mountain pasture and escaped detection. A donkey named Jack ran away from the raiders and made his way home, announcing his arrival with a very loud bray. Legend has it that he was Captain Thomas' favorite animal.

After leaving his company, Thomas Isaac stopped at Fort Defiance in Happy Valley, near Lenoir, to borrow $1,000 from his mother and to pick up his wife, Mary Elizabeth (Lizzie) Garrett. They married June 13, 1861. She was eighteen and he was forty-three.

Thomas Isaac and his brother W.W. Lenoir, who inherited part of the Lenoir acres, were among those who made a formal application to the Episcopal Diocese of North Carolina for the establishment of a Parish in Waynesville in 1866.

Thomas and Lizzie had three daughters; Mary, Laura, and Sarah. After the death of her parents Mary, an artist, graduated from Salem Academy, then moved to Rutherfordton, North Carolina. There she met and married John McDowell Michal, in 1889. The Michals moved to the farm in 1900, where John continued to raise the Devon cattle. The land had been divided among the three girls with Mary, the oldest, getting the home place.

They were the parents of Joseph (Joe) Michal, who married Dr. Mary B. Harris. Because of her medical practice, they bought a second home in Waynesville. He commuted during the winter, and spent summers on the farm. Their children are Joe Michal Jr., who lives in Greer, South Carolina, and Dr. Mary Michal. They are the present owners.

The farm is leased to the Tranthams, who adhere to tradition, playing a prominent role in American Devon Cattle Association.

Gwyn and Crab Orchard

"My grandmother named it Springdale," said Pat Gwyn Woltz, of Mount Airy and Waynesville.

James MacFayden and Amelia Harper Foster Gwyn's Springdale was likely the last sizable piece of land to be sold from the vast Lenoir/ Michal holdings in Little East Fork that once included thousands of acres.

Gwyn bought the 1,500 acres in 1875 from his uncle Walter Lenoir, who had inherited the land called Crab Orchard from his father, Colonel Thomas Lenoir. A bachelor, Lenoir lost a leg during the Civil War and realized that alone, he was unable to manage a huge cattle farm like that of his brother Thomas Isaac, a few miles down the road.

Gwyn's farm, where he raised and sold cattle, fruit, and vegetables flourished. "He was an organic farmer, a man ahead of his time," Woltz said. A graduate of the University of Virginia, he had a degree in chemistry. His cattle business was so lucrative that a railway spur was added for shipping the animals, she said. (Pat Woltz is no longer living so I hesitate to question her words. However, no records have been found of a railroad in that area.)

"He excels for he has made a study and reduced each (raising cattle and farming) to a science," reads an old publication. "He is interested in education and welfare, anything to help people. His farm is self-sustaining with a waterwheel and a Delco system (for electrical power). He has never bought any feed and never used any commercial fertilizer." Gwyn was appointed postmaster at Springdale in 1876, served as a Haywood County Commissioner, and as Justice of Peace for his township.

"I don't know how much he paid for the land," Woltz said, "but he sold stock in the family blanket company (later Chatham Blankets) to buy it."

Gwyn died suddenly in 1913 after his brother, an Asheville attorney, told him all the family money had been invested in Florida real estate, land that was all under water and worthless. The shock of learning his farm was his only source of income, much of which was needed to educate seven children, was too much for him, Woltz said.

His son, Woltz's father Thomas Lenoir Gwyn, left University of North Carolina's medical school at Chapel Hill to return home to help his mother run the farm and educate his siblings. He and wife Kathryn Mackay of Raleigh built a house beside that of his mother, but she died soon after. He later married Hilda Way of Waynesville, Woltz's mother. Fred and Elizabeth "Tish" Peden moved in with his grandmother.

"My mother worried about schools so a house was bought in Waynesville in 1926," Woltz said, a house she still owns. "I spent five or six summers on the farm and really loved it, as did my parents," she said.

The Depression forced lease of the farm to Columbia University as the site for a school called New College, which introduced New York students to hands on life on a farm. "It was a wonderful thing," Woltz said. The farm was sold to the school. Finally, the late Fred Tingle of New York bought the land and built a golf course.

James Gwyn's big house is now a private residence and listed on the National Registry of Historic Homes. Thomas Gwyn's house is also a private residence, and the golf course remains under Tingle ownership.

New College

Vesper Hill is now a parking lot. Tennis courts, riding ring, a barn, and a science lab have given way to golf course fairways. Golf clubs have replaced textbooks. And Springdale School is a memory.

In the 1930s New College, the rural campus of New York City's Columbia University Teachers College, occupied much of what we know now as Springdale Country Club and its golf course.

The late R. Thomas Alexander Sr. was a faculty member on Columbia's New York City campus when the New College undergraduate program was conceived.

Education majors would be required to complete a five-year program designed to broaden experiences, including study abroad as well as in a rural setting, according to Richard "Dick" Thomas Alexander Jr. of Cruso, the senior Alexander's son.

Alexander Sr., who had friends in both Tennessee and North Carolina, came south looking for a farm.

His scouting trip in 1932 included visits to Pinehurst and Lake Junaluska Methodist Assembly before he got word of the Lenoir Gwyn farm in Cruso.

The Gwyn property was maintained as a working farm, although the family no longer lived on the premises. It was for sale. Alexander had found what he was looking for.

The first students and faculty members, numbering around 150, traveled from New York and began classes there during the summer of 1933, Alexander said.

The large Gwyn home place, now owned by Paul and Rene Henson, was the main office of the school. Called the Delco house, it was the only structure with lights, and those were battery powered.

A smaller Gwyn house nearby was the kitchen, dining hall, and infirmary.

A far cry from any typical campus, during its early years New College students and teachers lived in tents, cabins, and bungalows, or boarded in nearby homes.

No dorms, no electricity, and no bathing facilities, other than the nearby Pigeon River.

Improvements came later. One wonders how former students, children of David Rockefeller, noted author A. J. Cronin, actor Frederic March, and New York Times executive Max Frankel, along with other well-known figures, reacted to the rustic environment.

Ed Schoen, seventy-nine, who retired to Flat Rock after fifty years in the publishing business in New York City, was one of those students. He had come from Chicago to the school.

He described Springdale school as "one of the first progressive education schools."

His memories are good ones.

"It was a fun thing for a youngster," Schoen said. "We felt independent. We milked cows, curried horses, and got to know who was who on campus."

He recalls classes and specific teachers, as well as being involved in the community, which included singing lead tenor in a local Methodist church choir.

The facilities may have been rustic, but the education wasn't. Math, English, history, and science were supplemented with enrichment classes, such as the school's music and art programs. Outdoor biology classes were an effective way to learn.

Responsibilities for work related to the farm, caring for animals, raising and harvesting crops, chopping wood and such, were in themselves an education.

It wasn't all work, Alexander said.

Students dammed the river temporarily to create swimming holes, hiked, rode horses, met local young people invited to Springdale for dances in the pavilion, and sang in local churches and schools.

In 1934, a summer camp, High Valley Camp, became part of the New College community. Springdale School, a high school program for boys and girls, was added.

Columbia's New College closed in 1939, but Springdale and High Valley Camp endured until the 1960s, when the property was sold to the late Jonathan Woody and the late Aaron Prevost, both of Waynesville, who had visions of a golf course on the land.

Work began on the course but Woody and Prevost sold the property before the course was completed. Later, it eventually went into receivership, according to the late Fred Tingle, Springdale County Club owner, who had tried to buy the site earlier.

Tingle's daughters Susan and Jane were campers at High Valley in 1963 and 1964. He came down from New York City to visit them.

"That is how I got impressed with the place," he said.

One of their counselors was Richard Thomas Alexander III, who would later be named Haywood County's sheriff.

Gus Ringwald, a close friend whose wife worked at Columbia for Alexander Sr. and who had directed the camp for several summers, called Tingle and told him of the status of the property.

By 1968, Tingle and a partner, Ralph Pierson, had assumed ownership of Springdale. Pierson later sold his share to Tingle, who lived in Springdale with wife Eunice until his death. Mrs. Tingle continues to live in Springdale.

I-40 THROUGH
HAYWOOD COUNTY

Building and
Maintaining I-40

During the late 50s and early sixties, North Carolina highway engineers, contractors, heavy road building equipment, and a swarm of workers (many were locals who knew their way around in the mountains) descended upon Haywood County, blasting rocks and gouging at the mountains to shape the first section of I-40 in the entire nation.

Although the Walters Dam/Fines Creek/Harmon Den area received the first and probably the most attention, the first section of I-40 completed in Haywood County was between Clyde and Buncombe County, according to Verlin Edwards of Maggie Valley, retired division engineer for the North Carolina Department of Transportation (NCDOT); the last was though Crabtree and Coleman Gap to Tennessee.

The expressway that traverses the length of North Carolina and ends in Barstow, California, was authorized by President Dwight D. Eisenhower in 1956. When he penned his signature on the Federal Aid Highway Act, he toppled a row of dominoes that would heavily impact this county.

Heavily traveled I-40 snakes its way across Haywood County through mountainous terrain, following, in part, the route of the Pigeon River. The drive bypasses county municipalities and bisects rural communities on its way to the Tennessee State line.

The circuitous route through the Pigeon River Gorge can arguably be called the most scenic drive on the entire expressway. Few would argue, though, that the twenty-two miles through the Gorge was the most difficult to build and is the most difficult to maintain on I-40's journey.

Frequent fog, speeding cars and tractor-trailers, some hauling potentially dangerous cargos, can turn that segment of the highway into a drive as deadly as the countless rattlesnakes and copperheads evicted from their dens during construction of the highway.

Robert Pless of North Wilkesboro, retired DOT engineer, said, "In the early '60s, survey work began on the section of I-40 from the Tennessee State line to Cold Springs Creek, about a six mile section. A two-lane road had been rough-graded earlier, and the entire area had returned to wilderness, infested with bees and snakes. Trees and rockslides covered the old roadbed, severely limiting travel through the project by vehicle. Access to the east end of the project was through Harmon Den Game Refuge, and to the west end of the project, through Cataloochee."

From an engineer's viewpoint, he marvels that the road was built without today's more sophisticated equipment. "We had no computers, total-station surveying instruments, or even electronic calculators. Horizontal and vertical angles had to be turned with a decades-old transit. Distances were measured with steel and cloth tapes. Crews of four or five men set slope stakes (marking where cuts or fills would begin on original ground) using tapes, hand levels, level rods, and bush axes. Moving measured distances and elevations from centerline to slope stake most often meant climbing rock cliffs and cutting dense brush," he said.

"Snakes came to the top of the old cut slope in search of a way to the river and had to be dealt with, avoided if possible. Survey work had to be done at times in snow, while the note-keeper, working without gloves, was balancing on a rock cliff and near frostbite. Rock cliffs had to be cross-sectioned for excavation volumes by a ball and chain tied to a cloth tape."

Roadway alignment was indicated by stakes and bottle caps on trees in the woods, and reestablished continuously, he said.

"The twenty miles between Fines Creek and the Tennessee line was a real bargain," said Edwards. "The cost was a million dollars a mile, even with all the blasting. If it had to be built now, it would cost many times that amount." Since that area of the road runs through national forest lands, the property did not have to be purchased; another money saver.

Getting to the work site was the most difficult part of working on the road for Edwards. "It was a long drive and a long walk to get to work. We usually drove through Max Patch or Fines Creek to Cold Springs and walked in, chopping our way through the woods, climbing banks and carrying our equipment. But we had no traffic to contend with. A lot of good people worked down there, both state employees and contractors."

High cuts through steep mountainsides often create unstable slopes prone to rock slides. A major problem was the geological fault encountered at Walters Dam. "The two plates along the fault line "floated," moved up and down. We checked it everyday, but never figured it (fluctuations) out. We cored (drilled) back in the mountain and pumped concrete grout into the drilled holes," Edwards said. Finally, in the 1980s, a retaining wall had to be built above Walters Dam.

Three tunnels, the only ones on the entire interstate, help keep the roadway as level as a mountain road can be; carving through a mountain is easier than moving one. One is a single tunnel, and the other a double; one for eastbound traffic, and the other for westbound.

Millions of cubic yards of rock were blasted, then crushed, to gravel the road, Edwards said. "We blasted rock from one side of the road and put it on the other side."

The Pigeon River Gorge segment was complete in 1968, but additional stretches throughout the county had to be built to connect those that had been finished. Jonathan Creek was among the roadways dubbed "temporary I-40" for a time.

"Beginning with the section from Buncombe into Canton, completion of I-40 proceeded in stages in a westerly direction," said Jonathan Woodard, NCDOT district engineer, based in Bryson City. "Preliminary work was underway in other sections at the same time."

Missing links in Haywood County's thirty-six miles of Interstate 40 were completed in the 1970s and our share of North Carolina's 420 miles of I-40 became part of the 2,554 miles of highway connecting Wilmington, North Carolina with Barstow, California.

Traffic ran smoothly for a time, but ancient rock had been disturbed; rock that had been twisted into folds, fractured, faulted, and compressed for more than a billion years, a part of the oldest continental crust in the Eastern United States.

"Each phase of the highway was built to the state-of-the-art' at that time, (but) mass wasting (in geological terms) will occur due to gravity, freezing, and natural decay of rocks and the seams holding them together. Efforts were made to re-route water away from critical areas, provide catchment areas for the falling rock and provide stable foundations for embankments by benching and sub drains," said Pless.

Rocks and boulders, minus part of their eons-old foundation, did what they normally do. Freezing and thawing resulted in their contracting, expanding and shifting. Heavy rains affected their stability. Eventually, tons of rock cascaded down the mountains and blocked the highway. Some were minor events; others were major.

In 1985, a severe rockslide collapsed the westbound entrance to one of two adjacent tunnels under the weight of large boulders. Westbound traffic was shifted to the eastbound tunnel, and a temporary viaduct built to carry traffic heading east. I-40 was moved farther away from the mountain, creating a fallout basin between mountainsides and road. Woven-wire fabric drapes much of the rocky cliffs in the Gorge, in an attempt to catch tumbling rocks.

On July 1, 1997, 250 feet of highway about three-tenths of a mile from the state line at Big Creek lay under boulders, according to a statement released by the NCDOT at the time. Crews trying to stabilize the 500-foot slope began working around the clock on August 20th. It would be November before all four lanes were open. In 1998, part of the fill beneath Interstate 40 near Canton gave way. The road was rebuilt, and a new retaining wall was constructed while traffic shared the westbound lanes. Later, a third hill-climb lane was added to existing westbound lanes, and an electric fog alert system was installed in this area in an attempt to avert further pileups.

The road was fully or partially closed in the Gorge due to rockslides in 2009 and 2012.

Vehicle crashes are not uncommon, especially in the narrow, twisty run through the Gorge, despite efforts to slow the speeding traffic. In 2002 and 2003 two state troopers were killed in two separate accidents by speeding semis that drifted off the road and hit the police officers' cars during traffic stops.

Passing of hazardous materials through the county has dictated training, especially for Haywood's firefighters and rescue personnel, in how to handle accidents involving a hazmat carrier, and further emphasizes the importance of I-40 bypassing heavily populated areas.

Haywood County's rugged, mountainous terrain has created varied experiences for NCDOT and for I-40 travelers, enormously challenging those who built and maintain the road, which is a time-saving route for drivers, a fearsome journey in certain conditions, and a scenic drive with beautiful vistas.

VARIOUS AND SUNDRY STORIES

Nance Dude

Nance Dude's story is not a pretty one.

Born of poverty-driven desperation, the murder of her own grandchild marked her life, led to fourteen years imprisonment, and left her to live out her days in harsh, lonely existence.

The Legend of Nance Dude, written by Maurice Stanley, is fictionalized but based on facts garnered from official sources and memories shared by locals. A shroud of mystery obscures all but this scant information. Stanley, a 1962 graduate of Canton High School, told me, "I sometimes had bad dreams (when writing the book) and feared that I was turning loose an evil spirit into the world, but after I was done I had a deep sense of sorrow for Nance and Little Roberta. They were poor and without much hope."

In February 1913, Dude was seen by Stanley's grandmother with two and a half-year-old Bonnie Roberta Ann Putnam walking near Lake Junaluska, he says. She had set out that morning to give the child to some family, or try to leave her at the county home. They were living on the Adtate place on Utah Mountain in an area roughly described as overlooking Queen's Farm on US 19 on one side and Jonathan Creek on the other, not far from Lake Junaluska.

The story goes that Will Putnam proposed to marry Dude's daughter Lizzy, a wedding contingent upon the condition that Roberta live elsewhere. Dude was to find another home for the little girl.

She returned alone that day, delivering varying accounts in her stoic manner of Roberta's whereabouts. After a few weeks Deputy Jack Carver jailed Dude, Lizzy, and Will Putnam since Roberta could not be found. After Lizzy gave birth to Putnam's son in the jail, she and Putnam were released and later married.

In April, search parties combed the area for days before sixteen-year-old Frank Jane's dog led him to a small cave on the Adtate Knob of Utah Mountain, a crevice sealed with hand-piled rocks. Roberta's decaying body, clad in layers of dresses, was inside. The cave, on private property, still draws visitors.

An impartial jury could not be seated in Haywood County. The judge decided to move the trial to Bryson City in Swain County, but almost lost the defendant to an angry mob determined to lynch her. And there was speculation among locals that Lizzy, not Dude, put Roberta in the cave.

Pleading guilty to second-degree murder, Dude was sentenced to thirty years of hard labor and incarcerated in the women's division of Central Prison in Raleigh on March 6, 1914. Paroled after fifteen years, she left prison May 21, 1929. She was eighty years old. She lived alone another twenty-four years in a shack on Conley's Creek near Bryson City, dying at age 104 in 1952.

Dude was born Nancy Ann Conard in 1848. Following the Civil War, she married Howard Kerley and had a son, but left them to "take up" with Dude Hannah. Hannah was believed to have fathered Lizzy, but abandoned them. Homeless and destitute, they moved in with Joe and Jane Putnam and their son, Will, who became attracted to Lizzy. Putnam would later deny paternity of Roberta, born in the Putnam house.

The truth died with Dude, or perhaps with Will or Lizzy.

Roberta's grave is in Dellwood Cemetery, and Dude's is near Bryson City. Will and Lizzy died in 1955 and 1969, respectively.

Author's note: During research, I interviewed a young woman who led horseback rides on mountain trails that passed by the cave where Roberta was found.

Intrigued, she vowed to learn all she could about the incident and the people involved. Her research ended abruptly after a nighttime visit from an apparition she believed to be Nance Dude. "I woke in the night and saw the figure of a woman at the foot of my bed. She was speaking to me in anger, telling me to stop meddling in her business. I ducked under the covers, covering my head, but when I peeked out she was still standing there, threatening me. I can't explain it. If it was a dream, it was very real, and convinced me to end my 'meddling.'"

Her reaction and that of Stanley ended my search, as well, although the story still haunts me.

Pulpit Crashers and Other Tales

Ted Reese of Hendersonville wants his grandchildren "to know him better and to be remembered in years to come," so he has written *Boogum Tree Stories* about his growing up in Canton in the 1930s.

Reading of the shenanigans he and his friends managed to survive, I hope his grandchildren are advised "don't try this at home."

Paraphrasing Reese, with his permission, his "Paw's wooden ladder" was a makeshift sled. Reese lived on aptly named High Street, roughly paralleling North Main Street below, with the two connected by a series of steep streets. "We ran the ladder sled at night to keep Paw from putting a quietus on the use of the ladder," he said.

One bright, starry night, Reese "borrowed" the ladder to ride down Holden Hill where they had earlier cleared a fifty-foot section at the bottom so pavement would stop their slide. "We loaded the ladder to maximum capacity and the Ladder Master (the rear sledder, who guided the ladder by shifting his weight), pushed off. "Boy, were we flying!" he said. "We forgot one very important fact. Holden Hill was a southern exposure...during the day some snow had melted, run down our sled run, and after sundown had frozen." At the bottom, across North Main Street, was a store converted into a church and services were being held that night. "The pastor was yelling, stomping and crying, trying to put the fear of the Devil into the congregation. He couldn't, but we sure could after we hit that ice. We hit those two white wooden doors of that church...the two front paws of that ladder went through. Here we were, eight to ten little urchins, holding on to each other for dear life, and down the center aisle we went...and hit the pulpit with a crash. We ran for home." The church was rebuilt and moved fifty feet up the street, Reese said.

Another time, some older boys built a merry-go-round, using a stump as a base, scrap lumber, and other odds and ends. It worked, but screeched and groaned until Reese borrowed his mother's lard bucket. A hand full of lard applied to the stump where the planks were fastened solved that problem until the lard ran out. The same materials were used to construct a Ferris wheel, powered by human hands. That worked fine too, until the ten feet high, two-seater began to pick up speed. Centrifugal force loosened nails securing the seats occupied by Reese and Canton alderman Ted Woodruff. "About the time that I made my one-man flight, Maw came out to hang clothes on the line... seeing I wasn't dead, she turned her wrath on the building crew and the Ferris wheel came down," he wrote.

Four boys decided to sneak a smoke in their tree house in the oak in Reese's front yard, and caught the burlap sack "privacy wall" on fire; Reese's brother climbed higher in the tree, while the others wisely descended through the trap door. Singed, the brother survived. Another day, ten "white balloons" were borrowed from the dresser drawer of a boarder in a nearby house. After huffing and puffing, the two five-year-olds finally had all ten balloons floating through the neighborhood but couldn't understand why the ladies wouldn't play catch with them. Reese's mother grabbed his ear, pulled him into the kitchen, and beat his rear. The balloons disappeared and the boarder moved.

Reese swam in the creek, gathered chinquapins, smoked rabbit tobacco and grapevine twigs, removed several inches from a pair of his father's pants, fashioned a cape, and played Zorro.

Men and Women
to Match the
Mountains

N.Y. Rector's
Sermon a Time
of Homecoming

T he Reverend Dr. Daniel Paul Matthews, retired rector of the Parish of Trinity Church on Wall Street in Manhattan, came home to deliver a sermon during the Centennial Celebration of Canton Presbyterian Church, his boyhood church.

The morning service must have been an emotional experience for him as he reminisced, seeming to fight tears a time or two, before a congregation that included former classmates and friends. He delivered a sermon eloquently, yet informally, and its dynamic content indicated why he is where he is today. His pleasure in greeting old friends afterwards was enthusiastic and genuine.

This man's leadership has been recognized by four honorary doctorates. He has preached in Canterbury Cathedral in England and Nanjing Seminary in China, had tea with the Queen of England, and was a close friend of recently retired Archbishop of Canterbury. This is a man who, seeing the second plane fly into the south tower of the World Trade Center on September 11, 2001 from his Parish office, evacuated from Manhattan with his staff and parish preschool children and supported the use of his parish chapel, St. Paul's, facing the World Trade Center site, as a 24-hour center of refuge and relief for eight months after the attack. In retirement, he is co-chairing the development committee at the Cathedral of Saint John the Divine, in Manhattan. He and wife Deener built a family retreat on Hemphill off Jonathan Creek that has evolved into a renowned inn called The Swag.

Those in Canton who knew him in earlier times regard him as simply their friend; Dan Matthews, a cute, slender boy with crew cut hair and perpetual smile, nice to everyone and involved in much.

His mother, Martha, was guidance counselor and math teacher. His father Robert was band director at Canton High School. Their musical talents were shared with their church and their boys, Dan and Bob, now deceased, were active in the institution.

He graduated in a class of bright, ambitious, energetic overachievers who became a doctor, company CEOs, college president, union president, a minister, teachers, and nurses among other occupations. Voted the most talented boy in his senior class, he was involved in student council, yearbook staff, marching band, tennis team, and numerous clubs, and was named junior marshal. Many of his classmates remember him as outgoing, fun loving, friendly and involved; a people person. His interests as a youth would be manifested in programs, and areas of focus in his ministry.

Matthews and close friend, Charles H. Duckett of Winston-Salem, retired physician, medical school professor and professor emeritus of East Carolina University School of Medicine, shared many interests.

"Our friendship began in eighth grade," Duckett said. "We played in the band and went to music camp together. Dan was always interested in the arts and theater."

"We put together a tennis team. We organized a band, the Rhythm Rockers, with Dan on the drums, and I played clarinet. Others played trombone, saxophone, trumpet and piano. We played for small dances and other functions, some in Asheville. Dan kept the rhythm rocking," he said.

Matthews remembers the Reverend Robert McCloskey, minister at St. Andrews Episcopal Church in Canton and a jazz pianist, as a powerful influence. "He practiced regularly with the Rhythm Rockers, only one of whom was Episcopalian. He taught us.... configurations and tones of jazz."

Music was always important in his life. His father had been pianist for the late evangelist Billy Sunday and his mother sang in Sunday's choir. "His folks had a player piano, and we gathered at his house often and sang along with the piano. I think back on that as a really splendid, fun activity. It kept us off the streets," Duckett said. The piano now resides at The Swag, and is still used for songfests.

Matthews and Duckett shared an interest in photography, and each had a home darkroom in a closet. "I like to say that we earned our way through high school taking prom pictures," Duckett said.

The late Dr. A. P. Cline, a dentist, influenced Matthews. "He allowed a group of us to spend weekends in his rented cottage at Lake Logan. I admired Sit 'n Whittle (Reuben B. Robertson's log cabin). When we built at The Swag, I tried to build a Sit 'n Whittle," Matthews said.

Matthews and Duckett organized a school tennis team, with Christ School and Asheville School for Boys their only opponents. "I doubt we ever won a game," Duckett said. Dr. Barry Pate of Asheville, now retired, remembers playing on the team.

"I went to Rollins College in Florida to major in theater," Matthews said. "When I found classmates like Tony Perkins, I realized I was little league among big leaguers and majored in business instead. In the summer, I worked as a disc jockey and radio announcer at WWIT radio in Canton." He utilized that background when he saw potential in using radio and television in his ministry.

Appropriate descriptions for Dan Matthews include risk taker, innovator, and astute financier along with unpretentious, humble, creative, and down-to-earth.

Freedlander's Many Legacies to Haywood

Abraham L. Freedlander's legacies will surely reverberate for years and years in Haywood County.

Well-known as the man in charge at Dayton Rubber (Manufacturing) Company, later Dayco Corporation, in Hazelwood and Ohio, his role of importance in the rubber industry, nationally, is a story unto itself, but to Waynesville he was company president and general manager of a plant that provided good jobs, a philanthropist, and much more.

Invited to Waynesville by astute businessmen who learned he was scouting the Charlotte area for a plant site, Freedlander found what he was looking for near the cool waters of Allen's Creek and took root.

The late Curtis Russ, owner and editor of the Mountaineer newspaper, said of him on one occasion "His greatest interest is his deep concern for his fellow man."

The Dayton Rubber plant opened in Hazelwood in 1941 with sixty-five employees, a number that grew, enabling families to enjoy a decent living. "If he were still alive, we would still have a 2,000-employee industry," said Lee Finger, former Dayco plant manager. "He nurtured the company and the people who worked there, and the plant continued to grow under his guidance." An aging Freedlander sold the plant, which eventually closed in the 1980s.

He had in mind to build a YMCA until Canton built a large facility. His attention turned to Haywood Technical College, then an extension of Asheville-Biltmore Tech in Asheville, operating in old schools and other buildings. Having seen the need for vocational training to benefit "citizens (who) are rugged, independent and have natural resourcefulness," he felt the county should have an independent school.

Haywood Community College (HCC) may be his most enduring contribution. Land was acquired in 1969 through Freedlander's contribution of $250,000, seed money to be matched by others, and campus buildings were erected. Freedlander Drive, A. L. Freedlander Learning Center, and a renowned arboretum designed by Doan Ogden testify to his philanthropy. "I would like to join with others...in providing the money for large and modern school. God made it possible for me to make the money, and I believe He wants it passed on," he said.

Turning the first bucket of dirt in 1970 with a gigantic hydraulic backhoe, wearing a borrowed hardhat while operating the machine, he told the crowd later, "This is home, right here in Haywood County, and my plans are to spend more and more time here. I like the people and I like the privilege of contributing. This is my personal money, and mine alone (including A. L. Freedlander Foundation), not from Dayco Corporation." HCC has continued to grow and prosper.

Deeply interested in protecting natural environments, Freedlander stipulated that the property's sizeable oak forest be preserved. He envisioned a campus with a beautiful learning environment. Dahlias were also a passion of his, so a dahlia garden was another stipulation. He had bought property on Allen's Creek and built Freedlander Estate with a lodge to house Dayco guests, as well as a small guesthouse, pool, pond, and a garden, where he grew some 1,000 varieties of dahlias.

He bought two old schools, Cruso and Allen's Creek, then gave them to the communities and outfitted the Tuscola High School band. Other interests included Little League ball teams and the public library.

Finger and Sam Wiggins, another retired plant manager, create a picture of a remarkable man. "He loved the people of Haywood County and wanted young people to have opportunities. He was a strong businessman; tough-minded, exacting and detailed, but with a love for his employees. He expected a hard day's work, while expecting the company to take care of them in return. He took time to be pleasant, to talk to his employees. He didn't get to the top accidentally."

"He recognized the need for people to be appreciated and let them know how much they were appreciated. He also recognized the quality of work ethics Haywood County people had," Finger said, calling Freedlander the paternal leader of Dayco who gave a lot of attention to Haywood people.

Governor Dan Moore

Election night in 1964, forty-four years ago, was an exciting event in the Western North Carolina mountains.

When all the votes were tallied, Daniel Killian Moore of Canton had been elected to lead the state as Democratic governor from 1965 to 1969. It had been eighty-eight years since the mountains had sent a governor, Tod R. Caldwell of Burke County, to Raleigh, and 132 years since David Swain from Buncombe County held that office.

Moore's inauguration ceremonies on January 7-8, 1965, were witnessed by throngs of mountain residents; so many that a long-time Raleigh resident asked a group of mountaineers if anybody was left up in the hills. Moore's friends, neighbors, relatives, and other supporters were so numerous that the inaugural ball was a sellout for the first time in history.

Bob and Bobbie Harpe of Canton, Moore's neighbors when he lived on Pennsylvania Avenue in Canton, shared a collection of *Citizen-Times* newspapers and programs from the inauguration and the inaugural ball that tell part of the story of that weekend.

The Canton to Raleigh fourteen-car, inaugural special train was filled to capacity with people traveling to watch "Dan the Mountain Man," as supporters called him, take the oath to serve as the state's top official. Others traveled by car and plane. Moore had asked that his inauguration have a mountain flavor. According to reports; that it did. Canton High School's marching band led the inaugural parade, and the Champion YMCA Cloggers entertained the crowd.

Moore, fifty-eight, was division counsel and assistant secretary for Champion Papers before leaving that job to run for governor.

He earned undergraduate and law degrees from the University of North Carolina at Chapel Hill and established a law office in Jackson County, where his political career began. After beginning his political career as a precinct worker, Moore was elected state representative for that county in 1941, leaving the position to serve in the U.S. Army in World War II. He was a member of the North Carolina Democratic Executive Committee in 1938. After the war, Governor Gregg Cherry appointed him to a seat on the Superior Court, a position he held from 1948 to 1958.

An Asheville native, Moore had followed family tradition into the practice of law. His father, Fred Moore, was, at age 28, one of the youngest people ever to serve as a superior court judge. From his family came two other superior court judges, a congressman, and a speaker of the House of Representatives.

After completing his term as governor, he went into private practice in Raleigh, but later that year his successor Governor Bob Scott appointed him to fill a vacancy as an associate justice of the North Carolina Supreme Court. He remained in that position until the mandatory retirement age of seventy-two. He died in 1986.

A.J. Hutchins

"You write about everyone else. When are you going to write about your father?" Doris Powell asked me. How can I? How can I not?

A. J. Hutchins was superintendent of Canton City Schools from 1924 to 1953. Under his watch, the school system grew from two buildings to eight, including a new high school and Reynolds School for African-Americans, and a new athletic field was built. A lunchroom was added to each school, and libraries (a pet project) were improved and expanded.

Before Canton Middle School was built, he told a reporter that the system's property evaluation had increased from a total of less than $110,000 to more than $1.9 million.

High school curriculums were expanded to include not only the traditional college prep classes, but also classes in home economics, business, and carpentry, to benefit those who would not be attending college. With the support and cooperation of Reuben B. Robertson of Champion Paper and Fibre Company, welding and machine shops were added to train students for immediate employment at the paper mill and elsewhere.

Canton High School became the only school west of Asheville to earn the distinction of accreditation by the Southern Association of Colleges and Schools.

He physically labored by harvesting rocks and timber from Beaverdam and other locations with the help of students and others to complete Canton High's football stadium, which is still in use. He also built shelves and storage units for the high school library and classrooms.

He was appointed to the state textbook commission and, by a governor, to a state study commission on education in the '30s.

The decision to build Reynolds school was made with Jack Messer, who was then superintendent of Haywood County Schools, to provide a high school for the entire county's African-American students who were having to leave the county to further their education. The county had an elementary school for these students.

The late Mary Gillis, English teacher, wrote, "Without the flow of money which came later, he accomplished great things. He did not just plan and supervise. Mr. Hutchins loaded the rocks and pushed the wheelbarrow." Quoting other teachers, he was "strict but fair," "supportive," and his "faith in youth is steady and unfaltering."

In my biased opinion, he was a man of tremendous foresight, beyond his time; a scholar, with many interests and activities, a genuine caring and concern for people, especially young people, and an abiding love for this mountain area.

Andy, or "Professor," as many called him, developed a small business tying dry flies after retirement, designing several originals. Hazel Creek Special is one of those still in use. After all, he had two children to educate; me to Wake Forest and John to North Carolina State at Raleigh.

I live with furniture he made for dining rooms, living rooms, and bedrooms, most made from solid walnut, and his personal library. He loved woodworking and made boats, among other things—in our basement. Boats we used for fishing and skiing for years.

Graduate of Wake Forest College, he served his alma mater on the board of trustees and the planning committee overseeing the school's move to Winston-Salem. As a student, he set a high jump record, broken years later by my uncle, Gus Hargrove, at Trinity College (Duke). His master's degree was from Teachers College, Columbia University, in New York City.

Civic minded, he was active in the Civitan club, Western North Carolina Associated Communities, and Boy Scouts. At Canton First Baptist Church, he was a deacon and taught Sunday school.

An avid gardener, he also had a grape arbor and kept hives of bees that swarmed every time he left town. He hunted bear with my grandfather and loved to fish. An outdoorsman, he recited the names of every mountain in this area and identified every tree. I wish I had listened more intently. We camped, hiked, boated, and spent hours in the woods.

He was director of Yancey Collegiate Institute, taught summer school at Mars Hill College for Wake Forest and Meredith, and was principal of Asheville High School, where he assisted in coaching basketball, track, and baseball. Harry Blomberg (Harry's Cadillac) remembered my father telling him he was wasting time in school, and suggested he get a job, since he was interested only in cars.

I am aware that money for things I craved was spent, instead, on school supplies and to help fund college for others, both local and abroad. That is okay now. We were not rich in material things, but what he gave my mother, brother and me, the intangibles, are priceless.

"Uncle" Albert

The foxhounds are gone from Albert Burnette's house in a secluded area of Dutch Cove, as are his infectious laugh, his tall tales, his energy, his genuine spirit, and his spontaneity.

When he died in April at age ninety-two, we lost another true mountain man. We also lost a master storyteller and foxhunter, a legend in our area.

Uncle "Hoss" Burnette, or Uncle Albert, was known far and wide.

Remnants of a crude shack on a hilltop on NC 215 are a silent reminder of the times Burnette and Walt Hargrove, my uncle, sat by the light of a fire, drinking coffee and listening to a chorus of hounds chasing a fox. They could identify individual dogs by the sounds of their voices.

Shelves in his house are heavy with trophies he won showing his dogs, and more are packed away; over 100 of them. "That is what he liked to do," said his wife Gennell, "show his dogs. He also liked to put on a red coat and ride a horse to judge fox hounds, following them in the chase." A handsome man, he must have cut a fine figure in his red garb astride a horse.

Walker fox hounds chase fox and bay loudly and endlessly, in the procession, but are bred not to kill them, she said.

"He loved people and loved telling tales," Gennell said. "If he didn't know the answer to a question, he made one up."

He served his country at Normandy on D-Day, Battle of the Bulge, Omaha Beach, during WWII and liked to say he came home without a scratch. One of his commanding officers said, "He was the best soldier in my command and I had thousands." He came home, worked at Champion Papers for forty-three years, married a "pretty woman named Gennell", and had two children David and Mary.

"Sit back and let big daddy show you how to do it," and "How do you like me now?" were two of his favorite expressions, according to Norm Medford, his son-in-law. He called himself the richest man in the world. "My family lives above and below me. How can you get any richer than that?" he said.

Nephew Richard Hurley calls him his hero, this man with whom he spent much of his childhood. "He was kind, caring, loving, genuine, always there for you, and loved every moment of his life. He had a big heart," Hurley said.

Hurley wrote a song about his uncle that includes these words, "Load up your jeep with your brown haversack, turn the dogs loose on a fresh fox track, call up the hounds and run a red fox, he'll be there when the Good Lord knocks...lay on the mountain and cook a little meat, make a cup of coffee that can't be beat...as long as hunters go in rapid pursuit of the red-back fox the legacy and spirit of Uncle Hoss will live forever."

Troy Mann allowed the foxes in Haywood County are resting easier since Uncle Albert passed on.

At his funeral, so many people wanted to recount their memories of this man that one finally said, "We better stop so we can bury Uncle Albert before dark."

Marc Pruett of Canton and others have captured some of the essence of Uncle Albert in an hour-long documentary titled *Spirit of the Mountains: The Stories of Uncle Albert Burnette.*

Garrett Smathers

G arrett A. Smathers, Ph.D., was an uncommon man.
One of us, he was born into a respected local family, grew up in Canton, and was educated in Canton City Schools. He became regarded as a learned man, a scholar, and as an accomplished scientist in biology and ecology, whose expertise was sought by many high-profile people throughout his career.

Each conversation with this fascinating man left me in awe. In time, I began to call him a national treasure, much like the many national parks where he had worked: Hawaii Volcanoes National Park, Haleakala National Park, Yosemite National Park, Olympic and North Cascades National Parks, and Big Thicket in Texas, as well as the Blue Ridge Parkway and Lava Beds National Monument in California.

Research he conducted for the National Park Service covered a myriad of topics: plant ecology, acid rain/acid fog, plant recovery on volcanic eruption sites, and natural history of the Appalachians in North Carolina, to name a few.

After his retirement, he returned home rather than remain in some of the more exotic locales he had known. Haywood County has been the beneficiary of his vast store of knowledge.

As environmental consultant for Canton, Smathers completed and published a study in 2004 based on findings uncovered by scientific, archaeological methods as exacting as the boundaries of archaeological research allow. Canton Mayor Pat Smathers called the report "an integral part of an effort to compile a comprehensive history of Canton." While pointing out the significance of the industrialization of a small town, the report also traced other aspects of the town's history, including early inhabitants, the Cherokee and their predecessors.

Smathers described the evolution of this area's physical characteristics, its weather and climactic changes, a progression of changes that began millions of years ago and defined the Pigeon River Valley and surrounding areas. This evolution, he said, explains why the Southern Appalachians are one of the most biologically diversified regions on the North American continent. He went on to relate information gathered by the excavation of three mounds built by the people who would later become Cherokee, in the Garden Creek area along NC 110, 2 miles upstream from Canton. Fascinating reading.

His love for teaching and coaching started at Bethel High School in the early 1950s. "Those were some of the happiest days of my professional career. The students were superb," he said. So was the teacher, I suspect. After retirement he taught for a while at Enka and Owen High schools, in Buncombe County. He was a teacher throughout his career, conducting seminars, writing papers, and doing some public speaking.

When the Beaverdam community was under consideration for a high-level nuclear waste dump, called the DOE Crystalline Repository Project, Smathers› research confirmed that rock in the repository area was not as stable as the DOE believed. The project would have buried 70,000 tons of extremely radioactive nuclear fuel in a geologic formation underlying Madison, Haywood and Buncombe counties. In 1987, Congress eliminated Western North Carolina from the priority list of potential sites.

The proposed site included Canton's Rough Creek Watershed, an 870-acre tract once used as the town's source of water, an area on which Smathers had done an in-depth study for the town. The watershed, also known as the Glades, is protected from development and logging by an easement owned jointly by The Southern Appalachian Highlands Conservancy (SAHC) and the Clean Water Management Trust Fund (CWMTF). Smathers was credited with achieving the protection by the SAHC. "Much of the credit for the easement arrangement goes to Garrett Smathers, who also provided data and was the champion behind protection from the start," a SAHC official said. The Glades is a haven for wildlife that also includes rare plants and a pristine water source.

As a six-year-old, he watched as drilling progressed for the Devil's Courthouse tunnel. Fifty years later as senior research scientist for the Blue Ridge Parkway/Great Smoky Mountains National Park, he was involved with placing and composing descriptive signs at various points of interest on the Parkway, including Devil's Courthouse.

"My great uncle, Garrett Smathers, had the blessing of mixing extensive intelligence with the common touch," Zeb Smathers said. "That is why he was such a great teacher."

"Garrett had vast knowledge of the parkway, its ecosystem, and natural history," Zeb continued. "He wanted to educate the public about one of our most amazing assets. He could look at a forest and see a million things, while most see only the trees. He wanted visitors to see more than what met the eye, more than the beautiful landscape. He wanted them to understand more in depth and then share what they learned with other people."

I have merely scratched the surface in relating his many contributions and accomplishments. His resume, including employment, grants, awards, and in-depth studies, covers thirteen pages. Most of all, he was a valued friend, always eager to share his expertise. Without fail, he would agree to being quoted but without "aggrandizement."

Mary Cornwell

When considering Haywood County's strongest leaders, those who have served this county and its people and left it a better place in which to live, Mary Cornwell's name rises to the top.

As a county extension agent, her influence reached to the remotest coves and lingers among us still.

Simply speaking, she changed many lives for the better. The recipient of numerous prestigious awards, she would tell you her legacy lives not in plaques on the wall but in people.

One of those awards was Western Carolina University's 1989 Mountain Heritage Award, given to individuals or institutions dedicated to preserving and interpreting the history and culture of Western North Carolina. The award honored her for her roles as creator of the Village of Yesteryear at the North Carolina State Fair, and founder of the Museum of North Carolina Handicrafts in Waynesville.

"She was the most influential woman in this county, perhaps in the state," believes Jim Trantham, who worked alongside Cornwell for almost forty years. "She made a mark not equaled by any other that I know."

She is remembered for her emphasis on teaching homemaking skills through a network of Home Demonstration Clubs throughout the county. Proper handling of food and the art of preserving various fruits and vegetables was a favorite topic. Recipes from some of the county's best cooks were recorded in several editions of Home Demonstration Club cookbooks. The late Curtis Russ of Waynesville, editor of *The Mountaineer*, was quoted as saying "Thousands have a better way of life due to Mary Cornwell's leadership..."

Cornwell said she believed her greatest accomplishment was the growth and development of homemakers throughout the county, pointing to the education programs provided by the extension service.

Becoming aware that many Western North Carolina craftspeople were selling handmade objects for little more than the cost of materials, she was incensed. As a Haywood County Community College Board of Trustees member, she insisted that HCC open a professional crafts program and used her political clout in Raleigh to help get necessary funding. The crafts program was opened in 1977, and is still a valuable asset.

She was asked to create an educational division of The North Carolina State Fair in 1951 where craftspeople could demonstrate their skills and sell their handiwork. The Village of Yesteryear began with fourteen craftsmen working in a small building. Today it is located in a permanent brick structure, and more than 100 master crafters from across the Southeast participate. She continued directing the Village for forty years.

The late Jim Graham, North Carolina Commissioner of Agriculture, became a close friend and ally, calling her a "gentle George Patton," according to Trantham.

Cornwell was named chairman of the board for a proposed permanent exhibit in Raleigh, of the state's best crafts. When the project met numerous stumbling blocks, she told the board to "Forget it. We will do it ourselves, but not in Raleigh," Trantham said.

Fortuitously, the stately Shelton House became available and was viewed as the perfect site for a museum. Assisted in fundraising to buy the house by her Home Demonstration clubs' members, she saw the dream come to fruition. The North Carolina Museum of Handicrafts lives in the house on Shelton Street in Waynesville. "The museum was her baby," Trantham said.

Obscure Haywood Inventor's Vision

If Calvin Filmore Christopher had come along in a later era, his name might have been written in history books. He had a calculating mind; some called him a genius. Some of his inventions affect our lives even today, yet he is buried in obscurity in Bethel Community Cemetery.

Some of his creations are displayed in the Canton Area Historical Museum, including a gasoline price computing scale labeled Christopher Computing (patented in 1928); the Lumber Lightening Calculator, another scale; a diagram of a railway switch device, patented June 2, 1908, which enabled streetcars to switch tracks; and a tabletop scale. All were ideas born of necessity.

L.A. Coman, Jr., has one of his gasoline scales. Joe Worley has one of the unique dinner pails, patented April 14, 1914 and manufactured for a time in Canton, as does Mike Cairnes, who bought it at a flea market in another state.

Most of the information about Christopher, in old newspaper clippings, was supplied by his friend the late Way Abel and by the late Haywood County historian W. Clark Medford.

Christopher was born in 1859, coming to this area when his family moved from Pittsburgh, Pennsylvania, around 1862. They lived in a white frame house along Pigeon River in an area called "Ark Park," now Max Thompson Road, off NC 110.

Christopher kept to himself, typical of his kind, probably because his mind was churning with ideas. His income was from his patents. He organized the Independent Scale Company in Washington, D.C. in 1900, later sold it, and opened a factory in Western North Carolina to manufacture a new type of scale.

Abel apparently knew him best. "He had inside vision...knew what things would be possible," Abel said.

He is also credited with developing a boxcar locking device, a cradle registered with the U.S. Patent and Trademark Office in 1917 (which rocked for thirty minutes after being set in motion), an automatic churn, an automatic monkey wrench, and a machine that dug a ditch 4 feet wide and 2 feet deep in one minute, purchased by the French government during World War I. Patent office records are said to indicate that he developed a light bulb that emitted light without connection to a power source.

After buying some racehorses, he built a racetrack in Ark Park, bought a turbine, and built an electric plant that powered both the racetrack and his nearby county home.

Medford said Christopher sold his more than 100 patents before his death in 1940, for a lump sum of $87,000.

He told a cousin about electricity years before its development, saying that eventually a box would be built to store energy (transformer). Many scoffed at him and called him "Crazy Miller" when, in 1890, he foretold that man would build a flying machine that would be faster than a train.

Those who have ideas that transcend their time often suffer such labels. After all, Orville and Wilbur Wright were ridiculed for their vision of an airplane.

C. C. Poindexter Prepared Young Men for War, and Life

Teenage boys in the early '40s had more concerns than jobs, cars, girls, or which college to attend. When they became eighteen years old they had to register for the draft. The United States was at war, having been drawn into the battle raging in Europe when the Japanese bombed Pearl Harbor.

The late coach C. C. Poindexter had an immediate concern. His worry was the well being of the young men he taught at Canton High School and their ability to face the demands of active combat, but he had a plan.

He could design his physical education class to mimic the military's basic training for new recruits, and prepare the young men under his watch to better handle the rigors they would endure. "He went to an army base and studied their program," Garrett Smathers said.

"There is no doubt in my mind that he saved lives," said Bob Robeson of Arden. Smathers agreed, saying "He received letters from soldiers thanking him for what he did, one of whom served in the South Pacific, I recall."

In the process, Poindexter may have organized the first cross-country marathon race in Haywood County, although that was not his aim.

In 1943, Robeson, Smathers, and Canton Alderman Bill Edwards were among thirteen boys who ran a 25-mile marathon with Poindexter, leaving from the school at 7 a.m., running over Newfound Mountain, through the Leicester community, and arriving at the *Citizen-Times* building in Asheville at 11:30 a.m. as part of their fitness training.

"A radio announcer asked me if I was tired," Edwards said. "Sure, we were tired and our feet were sore, but we were elated that we had done it. We didn't have a car escorting us, but there wasn't much traffic back then, anyway, and we were mostly on a gravel road. It was quite a feat for that time."

"Poindexter was tough, and he made us tough," Edwards said. "The crazy thing is that he was around forty-five years old and we were young, but we ran together."

A photo in the Asheville paper showed the runners that day, dressed in their street clothing and tennis shoes. "We did not have professional marathon clothing and gear," Smathers said. He did buy a new pair of $1.00 canvas tennis shoes for the run, later suffering from a number of blisters. They carried chocolate candy bars for energy, and lemons to quench their thirst.

After leaving the newspaper office, all met at Asheville's Pack Square, then ate at Tingle's Restaurant before riding home on a Trailways bus. Once home some had to go to work, while two had a baseball game to play.

Poindexter's class was the first one of the day, beginning with a 1.8-mile loop run up the backside of the river. "He timed each of us," Robeson said. "We kept running straight to the obstacle course," Smathers said, "and jumped hurdles, climbed over walls, hand-walked horizontal bars, crawled through barrels, and ran up and down the football stadium steps." Calisthenics were part of the rigorous routine, too.

"We could pull ourselves up a rope fastened to the gym ceiling without using our feet," Robeson said, an accomplishment that stands out in the minds of the three men.

The local National Guard drilled the high schoolers as well, and pronounced them "ready to go."

"I was only thirteen in 1943 and it (World War II) was over when I turned eighteen, but he (Poindexter) instilled in me the importance of being physically fit. I am seventy-eight years old, and spent part of the summer climbing mountains in Colorado," Robeson said. "He made me tough."

Smathers was so proficient on the training course at the U.S. Army's Fort Hood in Texas that his drill sergeant used him as an assistant trainer. "When I came back from Europe, I was assigned instructor duty," he said.

Other class members, many of whom are deceased, were: Reuben Murr, Howell Pless, Bill Morris, Wilburn Rhea, Jay Broyles, Ray Brown, Joe Roberts, Ted Whitted, James Bentley, and Nick Woodruff.

Autumn's Fashion Show

Autumn's fashion show is ending. Mother Nature's dazzling coat of many colors lies scattered over the runway, but the pattern from which it was fashioned is preserved, certain to show up again next fall with some minor variations.

When designers put away the chlorophyll green that dominated the summer showing, a rainbow of colors emerged, delighting observers. A profusion of bright yellows, bronzes, reds, russets, oranges, even a faint tinge of purples, covered the palette.

Perhaps no other designer is as closely associated with fall as maple. Attracting much attention, maple's line-up used many variations of yellow, especially attractive when highlighted by sunlight. Hints of green and orange enhanced the garb. The occasional blazing red received rave reviews.

Poplar, birch, beech and sycamore showed predominately shades of yellow and orange. Hickory's color scheme is best described as golden bronze, a true gold rather than yellow, as is that of beech. Beech used a supporting color of lovely silvery gray. Tulip poplar is an amazing gold. Dogwood added purple to red for variety.

Mountain ash, when red and used in clusters, was especially popular when viewed in contrast to its customary yellow background. Oak, sourwood, some sweetgum, persimmon, and sassafras chose red, as well. Black gum always likes red ornamented with blue.

A bevy of gorgeous redheads in close proximity by maple inspired oohs and aahs.

Accessories didn't offer as much variety, but one could depend upon seeing blue aster, goldenrod, orange and red hearts-a-bustin', lavender Joe-Pye weed and, infrequently, the deep pink of thistle. For bright scarlet, burning bush is almost unequaled.

Some designers refused to depart from their shades of chlorophyll green and they do add a welcome contrast, particularly pine, fir and the dark, almost black, balsam.

Many use tints of brown and tans for late fall and winter. Winter white seems to be used sparingly these days, as opposed to widespread use several years ago.

Nature's fall fashion shows abound, in Cataloochee and Maggie Valley, in Crabtree and Iron Duff, in Beaverdam and North Hominy, in Bethel and Cruso and points in between. Those most in demand include the Great Smoky Mountains from any vantage point, the Blue Ridge Parkway, and Pisgah National Forest.

Seats for viewing the shows were plentiful, reservations were not required, and no admission was charged.

POPCORN SUTTON, MOUNTAIN MOONSHINER

Legendary
Popcorn Sutton

Popcorn Sutton is an original, a self-proclaimed mountain moon-shiner who has spent most of his life tending stills in the mountains of Western North Carolina and Tennessee and running whiskey.

He and his craft have garnered fame, creating a local living legend who has appeared in videos about Western North Carolina, on numerous television programs, subject of his self-written book *Me and My Likker the true story of a mountain moonshiner*, invited to appear at events showcasing old-time mountain culture.

"I have been famous for years," he says, "in all the wrong ways, but I am honest and I have good credit." He seems to revel in his notoriety.

"Likker put me in the spotlight. My likker has been in every state and to England, Scotland, France, places like that. People bought it here and took it back with them," he says.

Popcorn's usual garb is overalls, plaid flannel shirt, and felt hat drawn low over his eyes; those piercing blue eyes, alert and watchful. Thin and wiry with a full, graying beard, he often drives an old A-Model truck with a still mounted on the bed.

Popcorn fits the timeworn image of an old-time, illegal whiskey brewer in his appearance. He enjoys his notoriety and promotes it in every way he can. In the process, he also draws a good number of tourists to Maggie Valley.

He answers only to Popcorn, a name acquired after an altercation with a popcorn machine that gave him neither popcorn nor his money back. The machine lost.

His back is worn out, he says, from carrying 100-pound bags of sugar up steep mountainsides to remote sites, wherever his still was located, and pains him all the time.

His language, profane at best, could spark a fire. This is the way he expresses himself, and is a part of his persona.

He says that he uses only one match a day as he chain smokes through the hours, no doubt contributing to the pain in his gut.

Ernestine Edwards Upchurch, whose roots run deep in Maggie Valley, says Popcorn approached her, asking for her assistance. "I want to write a book," he declared. "I told him that I would not write it, but I would interview him, ask questions, and record his answers," she said.

Upchurch, actively involved in Haywood County Genealogical Society and spending hours researching and writing about her own heritage, understood his need to preserve his history. "It was refreshing to meet someone with absolutely no pretense, and I was intrigued by his use of archaic language," Upchurch said.

Sutton's book was published in 1999, and he has some notes for a second. In 2002, he hired Neal Hutcheson of North Carolina State University (NCSU) to film a video entitled *The Last One*. Hutcheson spent a week in Maggie Valley filming Popcorn and some friends making a run of "likker."

When Hutcheson teamed with NCSU linguist Walt Wolfram, Gary Carden of Sylva and others to produce *Mountain Talk*, a video on mountain linguistics that aired on public television, he included clips of Popcorn.

Interviews with Popcorn have aired on television stations in North and South Carolina, and on Country Music Television. His antique store is mentioned in Roger Bansemer's *Mountains In The Mist*, and he has appeared by invitation at the annual Moonshiners Jamboree in Climax, Virginia, at the Mountain Moonshine Fest in Dawsonville, Georgia, and at the Old Mill in Pigeon Forge, Tennessee, where he makes home brew and hands out tiny samples in paper cups.

Popcorn grew up on Hemphill near Maggie Valley, where his grandfather "Little" Mitch Sutton and his father Vader were both moonshiners. He was only six, he says, when he began sneaking sips of the potent beverage from jars hidden by men gathering at his house on Saturday nights to "make music."

"I went to Rock Hill School—Rock Hill Academy—but I was no good in school and quit in about the seventh grade," he said, "but I guarantee I could come up with a college education if someone wants to talk to me, if I haven't burned my brain cells out drinking likker."

He left home at age sixteen to work for a furniture manufacturer in Hickory, lasting four years before answering the call of the mountains. He tried pumping gas for a living before hiring on as night watchman, guarding equipment for contractors working on I-40. He entertained himself at times, taking joyrides on the unfinished road in a dump truck, he says.

"I made likker in different places, on Hemphill and on Snowbird over in Tennessee," he said. "I moved to Upper Cosby, Tennessee, where I found out what sugar was made for," he said. It was then he turned to his life's work—building copper stills and making moonshine whiskey. "The law was not too bad on you down in Tennessee, but up here, back when Fred Campbell (former sheriff) was in there, they was rough on you."

This is what he knows best. He had been exposed to the art of making moonshine, but he says that he taught himself. "That is the only way to learn anything."

"I didn't make bad likker," he said with pride. He explained that he used only lead-free solder to make stills. "I didn't want the lead to get into the whiskey and kill somebody."

Caught running whiskey in 1974 around Newport, Tennessee, he related, "I was on probation, and they like to have drove me crazy checking on me. They busted up my still, but I made a new one and put it in the same place. I didn't figure they would think I would put one in the same place. They checked on me every day but Saturday and Sunday, so I made likker on the weekends." He was caught three more times, in Maggie Valley and Tennessee, but managed to escape charges.

He opened a cluttered antique shop on the road to Soco Mountain and ran it for fifteen years, making pithy, hand-written signs on cardboard that he nailed to the walls. As often as not, the signs would be stolen. One read, "Helping ugly people have sex for 20 years."

Talking by a wood burning stove inside a cabin that he and friends built, he became pensive at times, thinking intensely about something unspoken. Then he stood on the porch to smoke, lighting one cigarette off another. Stove wood was piled high on the porch and under a shed. "You judge a man by the woodpile he keeps for his woman," he says.

This man is tough, has had to be to survive years of making and running whiskey. But underneath that carefully maintained, crusty exterior, he can't completely conceal a different facet of Popcorn. He tells it like it is in no uncertain terms, but inadvertently drops crumbs that lead to a man who is loyal to his friends, capable of deep affection, and generous in ways he won't reveal.

Popcorn Sutton

Popcorn Sutton must have lost his proverbial lucky rabbit foot. And Haywood County may have lost a living legend.

After revenuers destroyed six 1,000-gallon stills and seized hundreds of gallons of "likker" in less than a year's time, Popcorn was arrested and jailed without bond. The second of two raids took place only a few days ago.

An ailing, frail-looking man of small stature managing to produce that many stills and that much white corn liquor in a few months? Though he is tough as a pine knot, he must have had plenty of help. Medical bills totaling at least $33,000, I was told, were his motivation for a sharp increase in production of the potent beverage. He has no insurance and isn't old enough for Medicare.

Popcorn has two personas, it seems. One is the moonshiner who lives the way mountaineers and flatlanders alike once lived, plying the only trade they knew that would provide ready cash; call it a survival tactic. That persona believes he has the right to make whiskey, regardless of the law. "God made wine out of water. I make likker out of it," he says. He is contemptuous of those who use makeshift stills, especially those that incorporate vehicle radiators, and cut corners to make inferior whiskey, the kind that makes people sick, even kills. Rotgut, I've heard it called. Popcorn takes pride in the care with which he constructs stills and the superior quality of his likker, its pureness. "I don't make bad likker," he says. He abhors those who traffic in illegal drugs, especially those who target young children, he said. A young child in Maggie Valley recently asked his father, "Why are they (federal agents) picking on Popcorn when they know where the meth labs are?"

The Popcorn Sutton I know perpetuates a way of life he learned as a young boy living on Hemphill, a way of life documented by historians of a long ago time when merely surviving was difficult and men turned to making liquor to feed their large families. He seems to have one foot rooted in the past and the other firmly planted in the present.

Then there is the other persona, the person who quietly paid the property taxes of an elderly person in immediate danger of losing her home. This Popcorn walks through the valley leaving collection jars at businesses to help raise money for someone in need. "Honesty and integrity and love for his fellow man are outstanding virtues of a man we call Popcorn Sutton. He is generous to a fault," Peter Hession of Maggie Valley said.

Popcorn lives by his own code. Any device I know can't take his measure with accuracy.

Popcorn has had many brushes with the law, but none quite like this latest one. Perhaps there is a third persona who lives in a dark, inhospitable place, a place I don't know.

I don't condone breaking the law. Nevertheless, I like Popcorn and am saddened by the possibility of his losing his freedom.

Author's Note: Legendary Marvin "Popcorn" Sutton spent his adult life making and selling moonshine whiskey, a craft he said he learned from both his father and grandfather. He was quite a character and an enigma to me, a throwback to earlier times. He had gained wide-spread notoriety before we met, having authored Me and My Likker and been filmed in documentaries about making liquor and about mountain talk. Both films are still shown, at times, on public television.

Arrested in March 2008 by federal and state agents in Tennessee, he was charged with making untaxed whiskey and possession of a firearm by a felon. He had been in and out of prison before, but this time he was looking at a lengthy incarceration in federal prison. Already ill, some said with cancer, he apparently could not endure such a future and took his own life. He was 62.

People like him don't come along every day. Neither does the opportunity to glimpse into a disappearing mountain culture.

MOONSHINE STILL

MOUNTAIN BORN
AND BRED

Nat the Cat once had Western North Carolina Jivin'

"**I**t's five past five and time to jive with Nat the Cat, your host who loves you the most. We're going to be around for the next fifty-five with some of the best rhythm and blues."

Wafting over the airways from Canton radio station WWIT, the words meant it was time to climb aboard the "A Train" with Nathaniel Lowery and listen to the latest musical hits interspersed with his inimitable chatter.

"All aboard, all you daddy-os and mommy-os, time to jive...to keep all you tigers alive. So let's cut the chatter and dig some of these cool platters, so let's rock, doc."

Lowery can still roll the familiar words, only a bit more slowly. "I tried to please everybody, black and white and red and green," he says. Ever mindful of his youthful audiences, he chose his words with care. As his popularity grew, so did his sense of responsibility for projecting a positive image.

Song requests and dedications, by mail or phone, poured into the station. "We never used last names. We didn't want to get people in trouble."

Listeners became acquainted with musicians like The Platters, The Four Tops, Jackie Wilson, The Temptations, Laverne Baker, James Brown, and Elvis Presley. Radio was the primary source for music and news. Television sets were few; boom boxes and sophisticated stereo systems were yet to be. No CDs. No musical tapes. A 45-rpm record player was a treasure.

A fan told him once that when his program came on the air, she would sometimes stop her car, get out, and dance. "I told her she should be careful," he said.

Some thirty years later, Leanna Kilpatrick repeats without hesitation "It's time to jive with Nat the Booted Cat for all you heartbreakers, hip-shakers, and men-takers."

Lowery was manning the mic at a Reynolds High School football game when someone from WWIT recognized his talent and recruited him as a deejay. The A Train program was already in place, targeting the black community, but Nat the Cat carried it to new heights. Some of his coworkers over the years included the late Wiley Carpenter, formerly of WWNC, Richard Hurley, Square D human resources director, and Bob Caldwell of WLOS TV.

Lowery's job as mail clerk at Champion Papers was interrupted by two years in the U.S. Army, but he returned to his job, eventually retiring with forty-six years to his credit. He dispatched mail throughout the paper mill until shortly before 5 p.m., when he folded his mail bag and hurried to the station on Radio Hill, where he assumed his other identity.

He learned to talk into the mic and found the words flowing easily. He refused offers from other radio stations, preferring to live in Canton, enjoying his job at Champion. On some Saturdays, kids were allowed into the studio to see a live program and talk to him. On Sundays, he played gospel music. He refereed Reynolds High School basketball and played league baseball for the Canton Eagles, calling on friends in the white community like Sam Powell and Joe Rhinehart to fill in when the roster was short.

He became a link, an emissary, between the black and white communities. In a time when racial unrest was just beginning to stir, that was important.

Lowery gathered friends throughout the paper mill, through his radio program, and in athletics; friends in many locales, friends who keep in touch. His once teenage listeners recognize him and stop to talk about the old times and the music.

Does he miss what he called his "social job?" He smiles and says he had three children to raise and educate, all of whom are doing well.

His communication and contact with others within his community and beyond continue, even though his radio stint ended after ten years when the station was sold and a new owner changed its format.

He is on the board of directors of Haywood's Habitat for Humanity and does his share in building houses. Lowery is also a board member and chaplain with the Lawndale Elk Lodge in Asheville, and involved with Man to Man, a cancer support group at Haywood Regional Medical Center.

He worked with Junior Achievement programs in the school system.

He is a familiar figure at MARC, Mountain Area Resource Center, where he helps out with Senior Games.

As coordinator for Haywood County's AARP chapter, he travels a bit with wife Alice, whom he calls his travel companion and soulmate.

His radio personality is a pleasant memory, but his influence continues in a different realm.

"The clock on the wall says we got to crawl, but jump on the A-Train tomorrow."

Georgia McAfee's Memoirs of a Black Community

A glimpse into the past is Georgia McAfee's legacy for her family and, ultimately, for her community. Her memoirs and interviews with students attempting to preserve historical facts give a personal touch to bits of history.

Her original, hand-written book, filled with invaluable photos, has disappeared. Its whereabouts are unknown. A real loss, but copies of her writings are being preserved.

She remembered the first black school in Canton. Known as Frog Level School, it was built by Turner Sharp, Canton businessman and civic leader, so black children could have an education. A white, frame building located near present Champion Credit Union, it had one room for some fifty to sixty youngsters. A dipper hung on the wall over an outside faucet, and everyone drank from the one dipper. Restroom facilities with running water were apparently in a separate structure.

McAfee walked through an alleyway beside Imperial Hotel to reach the school. "It had a big, black, pot-bellied stove, and in the wintertime we would hover around it to keep warm." School was from 9 a.m. to 3 p.m. Pupils sat in desks, divided by grades, and carried their own lunches; sometimes jelly biscuits. Mornings always began with scripture reading, singing, and prayer.

Sometimes students brought along younger brothers or sisters to baby-sit, she wrote. "I had to take care of my baby sister when Mother went to work, and that meant taking her with me when I started school."

McAfee had a picture, faded with age, of a teacher dressed in a long, black skirt and white blouse, standing in front of the building with some children.

Her own teaching career is mentioned very little in her memoirs, but she talked to student interviewers about teaching school in Sunburst, the logging community, after her family moved there in 1915.

"I guess we had about twenty students. "We taught first through seventh grade. We bought our own textbooks. We had to go to the white school to get library books, you know. You see, the schools weren't integrated....."

Those who wanted to go to high school had to attend boarding school in Asheville. Very few were able to go because of the cost. "Unless you made A's you didn't go to high school. You had to get in there and dig to do those things. And, you had to have someone to help you to do it. They didn't have the opportunity like they do now. Anybody that wants an education now, they can get it," she said.

"We didn't have to get a degree (to teach) at that time. Professor Madison (from Western Carolina Teachers' College) gave us our exams at the courthouse in Sylvia [sic]. That's where we got our teaching certificates." She was sixteen.

"I did very well with my schooling in Canton (and was) very happy when I was asked to take the teachers' examination. I stayed overnight at Grandpa's in Addie. The next morning I got up early and walked from Grandpa's house to Sylvia [sic] where the teachers' examination was administered," she wrote.

She and two others took the exam. One did not pass, another was assigned to Sylva, and McAfee was sent to Andrews, where she taught half a school year. At Christmas, she came home and found her mother ill; she stayed home to help her and didn't return to Andrews.

Her well-written, descriptive memoirs tour a part of downtown Canton in the early 1900s, mentioning names, businesses, and locations, and detailing the growth of the black community. And she left her family a sense of their history.

McAfee died in March 1980. She was seventy-seven years old.

Scotty Rhodarmer

S cotty Rhodarmer shared morning coffee with more people than he can count during his fifty years at the microphone at Asheville radio station WWNC.

As host of the morning show on "Radio Ranch", his melodious voice began the day for folks sitting at the breakfast table or driving to work, along with the familiar lyrics of "Nothing could be finer than to be in Carolina in the morning."

Listening to Scotty as he talked about country music and musicians, read the news from the day's *Asheville Citizen-Times*, or made conversation was like spending time with a good friend.

Hired by the station in 1954 after graduating from UNC Chapel Hill, he had, at one point, the "largest share of audience of any station in the nation," according to *Asheville Citizen-Times* reporter Tony Kiss.

He was born and raised in Canton, where he continues to live.

Richard Hurley, another Canton native and former human resources manager at Square D. Company, was a radio announcer at WPTL in Canton and became friends with Rhodarmer.

"Scotty was the standard we all tried to emulate," Hurley said. When Rhodarmer retired in 2004, Hurley, a songwriter and musician whose original "Ballad of Old Fort" gained regional prominence, penned a tribute to his long-time friend, joined him at the station during his final shift, and read it on the air to station listeners.

He called it *A Tribute to Scotty Rhodarmer*. The lengthy essay reads, in part, like this:

A native of Canton was destined for fame;
His heritage from Haywood—Scotty Rhodarmer was his name.
With roots in Dutch Cove and Morning Star Church,
He left our great mountains—his fortune to search!

Chapel Hill beckoned and he headed for college;
A bright, gifted student—he hungered for knowledge.
Down at "The Hill", a different world he would see,
Where he worked hard and studied, and earned a degree!

With a God-given talent and a voice rich in tone,
He returned to his mountains—the place he called home.
"The Pioneer Voice of Western N. C."
Gave Scotty a job doing station breaks, you see!

The morning man, Reed Wilson, a legend for years,
Retired one day—he had no known peers.
No one could replace him! The sponsors would stray!
But Scotty was chosen for his sincere, down home way!

For fifty years now, Scotty's been at this station,
And he's known as a legend across our great nation.
A key to the city and the old Long Leaf Pine,
Are honors bestowed on this good friend of mine!

The keys to success, I've heard him exclaim,
"Just be yourself and treat all people the same.
Give it your best and see what prevails!"
With an outlook like that, there was no way he could fail!

"Nothing Could Be Finer", will echo no more.
A legend is leaving; he's closing the door.
But another will open as retirement begins;
You'll pass on the mic, bid farewell to your friends!

But the lives you have touched and the mark you have made,
Will not be forgotten—those memories won't fade.
Your career has been stellar; to yourself you've been true,
And that's why we've written this tribute to you!

The entire tribute, printed and framed, hangs in a prominent spot in the Rhodarmers' Canton home.

Dred Blalock

Etheldred "Dred" Blalock is remembered as an excellent builder, a master craftsman.

Although he died in 1896 at age seventy-nine, three buildings he constructed remain in the Pigeon River Valley. One is an occupied house. The other two are a barn and a springhouse on the former Thomas Lenoir farm.

A 693-page volume entitled *The Dred Blalock Families of Haywood County, North Carolina*, published in November of 2000, is in the possession of Tom and Doris Cathey. They live in the oldest house remaining in the Pigeon Valley, the Cathey House, completed in 1864 by Dred and Willis Blalock for Joseph Turner Cathey.

The structure has been in constant use as a residence since it was built. The Tom Cathey family represents the fifth generation of the Catheys to reside there.

Its foundation and framework are twelve-inch square locust beams, mortised and pegged at every joint. Hand-cut nails were used. The front section of the house was built and occupied before the Civil War. When the war ended, a kitchen and dining room were added to replace a log cabin where meals had been prepared, giving the building a T-shape. Certain interior details are cited as being the best examples of Greek revival in Haywood County. The fact that the home is still standing and in use after more than 143 years is testimony to the excellence of Blalock's craftsmanship.

Two additional farm buildings, can be seen at Lenoir's Creek beside US 276, at the Joseph Michal farm. One is a springhouse built in 1853. Blalock is said to have hewn the logs from which it is constructed by hand. The logs and dovetail joints at the corners are amazingly smooth. White oak shingles on the roof have been replaced two times; once by Blalock and the second time by his son, Thomas. The spring still flows through the time- and weather-grayed building.

A barn at the same location was designed and built by Blalock. A central passageway made to allow a wagon to be pulled into the barn and unloaded is flanked by two corncribs, each of which can hold six hundred bushels. Chestnut logs were used for the sills, and chestnut boards six inches thick floor the structure. It was completed in 1864, a year after the springhouse.

The three-story mill that Blalock erected for Colonel Joseph Cathey must have been a work of art. Wheat was milled on the first floor, corn on the second, and buckwheat on the third, according to the tome about Dred Blalock's family. Machinery, all constructed of wood with exception of stone mill rocks, "was placed on each separate floor so that the grain being ground on one floor would not sift through into what was being ground on the floor below."

The hand-carved machinery was designed "so that there was only one belt in it...all the rest were cog wheels." Blalock designed the wheels and their operation, and then took the designs to Colonel Cathey, who worked out the needed mathematical calculations.

The mill water wheel was an undershoot. Blalock favored this design because the wheel buckets would fill evenly and the machinery would work smoothly without jerky, uneven motions. Unfortunately, the mill was destroyed by fire.

Demand for the skills of Blalock, who was also a stonemason and a millwright, left him little time for farming. He had many children; sons and grandsons followed his example, becoming accomplished builders and masons.

Most of his 1800s buildings are no longer standing. Some were destroyed by fire; others, replaced with more modern buildings.

This master craftsman built and designed remarkable structures without the modern tools and detailed, computer-generated blueprints of today, and did so with remarkable success.

Signs of Spring

S pring in the mountains is capricious, indecisive, and sometimes cruel as the season darts in and out behind waning winter. It's snow showers one day, sunny and warm the next.

Brave crocuses and daffodils show their pretty faces, one waving its yellow trumpets that whisper of a new season, and the other snuggling its purple blooms close to the earth amid dry leaves for more reliable warmth. Yellow bells, known also as forsythia, are more cautious, keeping blooms tightly folded. Not yet, they seem to say.

Creamy white flowers decorate mountainsides as "sarvice" trees contrast with bare, brown limbs still gathering chlorophyll to produce leaves. They are dependable trees that were nature's only florist available for early spring weddings or funeral services for old-timers.

North-facing rock faces still wear their icy winter coats, flaunting their icicles, but their attire is showing signs of wear as droplets of water fall to the ground. Melting ice is heard in noisy streams that dance and sparkle with the infusion of fresh water.

On creek banks, pussy willows are showing their gray, fuzzy decorative offering amid their dense growth of limbs. Tulips are poking their heads above the ground.

An internal alarm clock sounds among the robins in their winter homes, telling them to pack their bags. They arrive all together one morning, scurrying around with cocked heads to decide if their breakfast of earthworms is moving underground. A flash of bright red says that the cardinals are arriving as well. Bird song is spring's orchestral offering.

Deep in the mountains, bears are stirring, awakening in their dens, hungry after winter's hibernation. Their new cubs emerge to survey new surroundings, new life in the wild. Squirrels shake off their sluggishness, and the woods are alive as they bound from limb to limb, play a game of chase around a tree trunk.

Rustling from the forest floor indicates that snakes are moving again, searching for a rock in the sun. In the valleys, rectangles of freshly plowed fields reveal dark brown; rich soil awaiting seeds, tobacco slips, and tender plants to nourish. Hand-cut poles lie nearby, ready for insertion in the ground where they will provide support for climbing tomato plants and beans. Before fertilizing, the soil emits a fresh pungent odor, adding its contribution to spring's perfume.

The green field over yonder is "creases," waving for attention, calling for harvesting. Old-timers regarded a mess of creases as an essential spring tonic, swearing that the greens made one symbolically shed his skin, throwing off a cold winter spent indoors by the fire.

Signs of spring are everywhere for the observant. The time is coming, but don't get too comfortable too soon. Remember the chill that accompanies dogwood winter, blackberry winter, and the opening day of trout season.

MORE MEANDERINGS...

County Football
Rivalry

"What it was, was football," in the words of actor Andy Griffith. Sounds of colliding helmets and leather shoulder pads foretell fall's impending arrival, as surely as the harvesting of crops, the beginning of the annual leaf show, and the subtle change in the air.

Football season! Living in Haywood County without awareness of the fierce rivalry between Tuscola High School's Mountaineers and Pisgah High School's Black Bears is nigh unto impossible! Diehard football lovers see the annual clash as the highlight of the year, the night that gives one school bragging rights for twelve months.

Canton High School and Waynesville Township High School, predecessors of Pisgah and Tuscola, lit the fire that has fueled the intense rivalry and steadfastly fanned the flames.

The annual contest assumed a new perspective when Garrett Smathers of Waynesville handed me a May 30, 1974 clipping from the old *Enterprise* newspaper in Canton. The newspaper's account offers insight into the origin of the rivalry and two football coaches who fostered and encouraged the competition.

The late C. E. Weatherby of Waynesville and the late C. C. Poindexter of Canton were coaches and individuals of the sort often called "larger than life." Weatherby coached the Mountaineers, and Poindexter coached the Bears. On the football field they appeared gruff, the worst of enemies, but in reality, they were good friends who respected each other.

Following the untimely death of Poindexter in 1959, Weatherby spoke at the dedication of a new Bethel School field house to the memory of his old friend and the clipping recorded his remarks, which revealed much about the county rivalry and their friendship.

"Weatherby's remarks recalled the era when the small towns of Canton and Waynesville, struggling to raise spirits after first a depression and then a world war, pitched themselves into the keenest high school football rivalry witnessed until that time in Western North Carolina. And if the football players were the soldiers of that battle, the generals were Poindexter and Weatherby, men in ways very much alike and very different," the clipping reads.

"'While the teams were competing, the communities were vying with one another, and it was healthy,' said Weatherby. 'Some people think the competition was bad,' he continued, 'that if old Weatherby and a few others would die, it would all pass away.'"

He recounted the time when one town acquired a stadium and the other town quickly followed suit. "'I remember Canton put lights in their stadium one year, so we had to get lights in ours the next year,'" he said.

"'The competition never means that you should think less of the other man but more of him for making you improve yourself,' said Weatherby, 'and the only people who got bitter about it were not the athletes but the poor sports, those who never played athletics.'"

The reporter, Tim Reid, continued. "The best years for the two teams were those after World War II. Coach Poindexter had returned to Canton High, and the return of GIs meant squads of forty or fifty active players. Champion Papers would sponsor the Paper Bowl, attracting between 5,000 and 10,000 people to the annual event.'

Surely neither of the two coaches would be surprised that the competition continues as fiercely as it ever did.

This homegrown contest is now one of the best-known and fiercest rivalries in the southeastern United States. *USA Today* has also named it the best high school rivalry in the state of North Carolina, typically drawing between 10,000 and 15,000 fans each year.

Haywood's Paper Bowl

Haywood County once had its own football bowl called, appropriately, the Paper Bowl.

A game program from 1950 discovered during a search for class reunion memorabilia prompted a question. What happened to the Paper Bowl? Finding the answer was difficult. Reaching a conclusion involved reading more than fifty copies of *The Log*, tweaking memories of former Canton High football players, questioning Champion Papers retirees, recruiting Mary Louise Miller, wife of the late German "Nazi" Miller, who went through four thick notebooks of YMCA sports records.

The first game was December 4, 1948. It paired Waynesville Township High School, the year's Blue Ridge Conference champions, with Marion High School of Newberry, South Carolina. Waynesville walked away with the win. About 3,500 people gathered in Canton Memorial Stadium to watch the battle.

The Waynesville Mountaineers took the field again in 1949, losing a hard fought game to the Monroe High School Pythons on November 30th. The score was 13–0.

"Although a stronger Monroe defeated the powerful Waynesville 13 to 0, more than 4,000 jubilant fans witnessed one of the most outstanding football games ever staged in Canton Memorial Stadium," reported *The Log*, a Champion Paper and Fibre Company publication. At halftime, Waynesville head coach Carlton Weatherby received the Conference Trophy.

Yellowed newspaper clippings chronicle the 1950 Paper Bowl when Canton's Black Bears crushed the Blue Devils from Erwin, Tennessee, 38–13. The Bears had also won the Blue Ridge Conference.

"Coach Don Hipps' Bears celebrated their debut to their hometown postseason classic by turning in the most lopsided triumph on the Bowl's three year record," reported the *Asheville Citizen-Times*.

The late Boyd Allen was Hipps' assistant.

Team captain Charles Poindexter, Neil Rhymer, and the late Bobby "Snake" Moore were credited with outstanding performances. Poindexter, Moore, and teammates Jim Morgan and Larue Amos were named to the All Blue Ridge Conference football team that year, along with Bill Sutton, Bobby Setzer, Alden McCracken, and J. C. Deweese of Waynesville.

When the Champion Y's Men's Club announced the formation of the Paper Bowl in 1948, the group said a strong team from another conference would be invited to furnish competition for the winner of each year's Blue Ridge Conference.

The Blue Ridge Conference, according to *The Log*, endorsed the postseason game.

Don Randolph, seventy-eight, of Waynesville was employed at the paper mill and involved in the Y's Men's Club. "The idea was conceived by Ralph Goforth (deceased), who was president of the Y's Men's Club," he said. "I had responsibility for the game program, and drew a cover design that included a pine tree."

Each year the two teams, their coaches, and guests gathered at the YMCA following the afternoon game for trophy presentations and a banquet. Randolph was in charge of dinner arrangements, and Goforth headed the event for a second year in 1949.

Added attractions at the first game were All American Charlie "Choo Choo" Justice, brother of the YMCA's Jack Justice, and All Southern Hosea Rodgers, in town to referee a game between Justice's Gray-Y Bears and Brevard, and attend the bowl game.

Adrienne Smathers of Canton, a black-haired beauty, was crowned Paper Bowl Queen in 1950. Her court included Freda Grey Hipps of Clyde, Birdell Gorrell of Bethel, Lois McCracken, Crabtree-Iron Duff, and Rose Marie Leatherwood from Waynesville.

The customary banquet in the YMCA gym preceded a dance in Canton's Armory honoring the queen and her court. The late George Howard Trostel, the Y's Men's Club president, was chairman of Paper Bowl arrangements that year.

Miller's search indicates the Paper Bowl was relegated to the YMCA Mites and Midgets. "Pug" Parker, 1950 CHS team member, speculated the game's demise was because of conference realignment. Dewayne Milner, younger CHS team member, opines that the Thanksgiving

Day game between fierce rivals WTHS and CHS, a second yearly tussle between the two that ended the season, replaced the Paper Bowl.

Howard Sellars of Canton, 93, vaguely remembers Goforth mentioning a conflict between the Blue Ridge Conference and the North Carolina Athletic Conference ended the bowl game. Sellars remembers clearly, though, the year that a snowstorm threatened to cancel the game until he and other Y's Men manually shoveled snow from the playing field.

Canton's Former "Boys of Summer"

The glory days of Canton's "boys of summer", in the 1950s and '60s, are etched in the record books.

Champion YMCA's fast-pitch softball team climbed from a small town, industrial league competitor to one that dominated North Carolina, then the South Atlantic Region, and finally took its place as a major presence at the World Championship level. Talented players and strong support from Champion Paper Company, town merchants and professionals, and others backed their ascent on the softball ladder.

An image of weekend game nights would show a small town gripped with excitement, glowing with ball field lights, roaring with sounds that only a crowd of vociferous fans can create. The cacophony would be punctuated with the unmistakable sounds of balls slapping against leather, the crack of bats striking balls, and loyal fan Charlie Fullam's booming voice. Tall, wooden bleachers arc around the green and brown of the diamond, with a backdrop of lights and steam from Canton's paper mill.

German "Nazi" Miller, generally considered the force behind the team, was an outstanding pitcher credited with twenty-one no-hitters during a career that began in the mid '40s and endured until 1965. He assumed the role of manager following Flossie Deweese. Director of

Athletics for the YMCA, he positively influenced the lives of innumerable youth who passed through his strong youth sports programs. His many hats—manager, pitcher, youth leader, YMCA employee—included North Carolina Commissioner of Softball, worn from 1969 until his death in 1975. In 1969, he was honored as the most outstanding state commissioner in the nation, a year that saw registered softball teams in the state jump from ninety-nine to 683.

"He kept things going when the team began as a mill league," former pitcher David Anderson of Canton, said. "He was the organizer. It all started with Nazi."

Twelve players were inducted into the North Carolina Softball Hall of Fame: Miller, Wade Garrett, Bob Holcombe, Dave Anderson, Clyde Miller, George Price, Bobby "Snake" Moore, Charlie Poindexter, George "Speedy" Stamey, Gus Colagerakis, and Nazi's two sons, Eddie and Tim. These names evoke memories of strong, talented players, fast pitches, home runs, and dusty slides into home base. Jim Rhea would have joined them, but his personal records had been lost, according to Juanita Dixon, who was also named a hall of famer for meritorious service to the team. After Miller's death, she became business manager for the team. "The team, under Miller's direction, began the domination (of softball)," she said, "but the young men who followed the initial groups continued the domination."

Yearly records of wins and losses were lost in a fire, but a certificate found in Anderson's scrapbook, complete with players' photos, verifies that the first state title came in 1949, initiating a five-year string of North Carolina State Amateur Softball championship trophies, 1949–1953. The title was lost in '54 but regained in '55, the same year the Southern Regional Softball Championship was added to their accomplishments. Former player and assistant manager Bobby Green of Lake Junaluska confirms they won the Regional tournament in '55, '57, '59, '60, and '62, at the very least. Champion advanced to the World Championships at least three times, finishing third in 1960 and fifth in 1963.

"We had a strong nucleus of pitchers," Anderson said, "and when you have that, a team will work properly. I was fortunate to get to play with them. The experience helped me grow as a person."

Players, although primarily Canton residents, were recruited throughout the county and at times from other North Carolina towns and other states. The Champion Y team was a "pied piper" of sorts, attracting a large crowd of diehard fans who followed them up and down the East coast, into the Midwest, and to places like Birmingham and Chattanooga. One particularly popular destination was Florida, where eventual victories over the Clearwater Bombers left players and fans ecstatic.

Various circumstances, including nationwide decline of company sponsorship for softball teams, ended the reign of the team known as Champion YMCA, although Canton teams playing under different team names and with different sponsors continued to capture outstanding players and win trophies.

But for nearly two decades Champion YMCA teams were the highlight of summer in Canton.

Haywood County War Memorials

Haywood County has sent many soldiers to war, even before its official existence as a county. Monuments of all shapes and sizes testify that soldiers from at least eight wars lie beneath our county's soil.

These various memorials are reminders of the families whose lives abruptly changed course because of death or physical impairment to a serviceman. One is poignantly enhanced by a pair of bronzed boots. One is a helicopter mounted at VFW Post 5202 in Waynesville; another is a naval antiaircraft/antisubmarine gun in Clyde. Regardless of their appearance, they are more than physical structures. They are people and their families.

"Bravely they sacrificed, gratefully we remember," words engraved on the Korean War commemorative in Waynesville, summarize the message of each, along with expressions of honor for those who served and survived.

Among the more obvious are individual tributes on Waynesville's courthouse lawn to Revolutionary War soldiers buried in Haywood

County, to Confederate Veterans, to those who died or served in the Republic of South Vietnam and in Korea, and another for all veterans who served in defense of the United States of America.

Handsome markers on Canton Area Museum's lawn are dedicated to the men and women of Haywood County who served in WWII, and pay tribute to two Canton Medal of Honor recipients, Max Thompson and William Halyburton Jr., two of 464 nationwide. Another is located at Pisgah Memorial Stadium accompanied by twenty-three timeworn markers lining the end zone, naming Canton High School graduates who died in WWII. One bears the name of my uncle.

Naming every monument in this county and recounting the touching stories behind them would fill pages. They are found in cemeteries, at volunteer fire departments, at veteran organizations, at schools, and at other sites scattered around this county. Jim Howell of Canton rescued a roadside marker near Waynesville, but he couldn't save the seventeen large pin oaks planted by Waynesville Woman's Club to commemorate WWI veterans, hewn to make room for a widened road, he said.

These memorials reflect the sacrifices of ancestors, friends, strangers, neighbors, and families within our boundaries.

Stadium War Memorials

Twenty-three monuments dedicated to former Canton High School students who died during World War II stand at attention in the end zone at Pisgah Memorial Stadium in Canton, having survived years of exposure to the elements, the building of a new stadium, and two devastating floods that twisted and uprooted most everything around them.

Bells began tolling silently for these young men, symbolically speaking, at 8 a.m. on December 7, 1941, when Japanese bombs began raining on Pearl Harbor, an act of aggression that drew the United States into World War II. By 1945, all had been killed in action. They had voluntarily clad themselves in uniforms and left homes and families to defend their country, unaware that their days on this earth were numbered.

Patriotism was alive and well during that war. American soldiers were respected, regarded with pride, and strongly supported back home in the states. Efforts to honor those who died were equally prevalent. Monuments in memory of those who did not come home were erected throughout the nation.

Canton's monuments were formed and poured by young students and their teachers at the high school shortly after the war ended. The surname of each soldier was chiseled in the concrete. Bronze plaques listing the name and rank of each man, the years he attended CHS, and his enlistment date as well as the date of his death were also attached to the monuments. Pine trees were planted behind them.

They served in the Army, Navy, Air Force, and Marines. Details about the monuments, precisely when they were built, dedicated, and the person(s) who had the idea to erect them, are uncertain. Consensus among those with whom I have spoken is that A. J. Hutchins, Superintendent of Canton City Schools, is largely responsible for their being built.

Their existence seemed threatened when new bleachers were erected on the home side of the field. During stadium construction, the monuments, stretching from the ticket booth to the river, were removed, according to Danny Miller, Pisgah High School principal. Unexpectedly, foundations were imbedded two to three feet in the soil, he said, and government regulations pertaining to the removal of military monuments had to be followed. The concrete columns were reset with careful attention to alignment and height, and situated in an area that allowed better visibility and more protection. Devastation to the memorials' surroundings, caused by the floods, is a sad story. But Miller, students, and community people worked together to save the stadium and playing fields, and to give the memorials proper attention.

"The precious monuments that speak of great personal sacrifices made for our country and our freedom were moved to protect them from damage, and to provide positions of better visibility. Many pains were taken to see this done in an appropriate manner," Miller said.

"They have always been part of that stadium, and the stadium has always been part of this community." When they were reassembled in what Miller calls a memorial garden setting, disease-resistant cedar trees were planted as a backdrop.

"With every disaster comes opportunity, and we used that opportunity to our best advantage. It was a labor of love by the community," he said.

Apple Cider

Apple cider tastes better when the minutes-old beverage is sipped from a glass clutched between grubby hands on a sunny fall day in an orchard. Air heavy with the aroma of apples, abuzz with pesky bees, and rhythmic with sounds of a hand-turned cider press added something extra to the flavor.

Pure, clear cider with no additives is smooth and silky to the palate.

The cider press with which I was acquainted was not large or fancy, nor was it powered by a noisy, humming motor. Its weathered gray frame was sturdy, and its gears and wheels were black cast iron. Normally stored in the second floor of the wood and stucco apple house, it was carried outside and thoroughly cleaned when the surrounding trees were weighted with ripe fruit.

Apples were picked from the drooping limbs, some of which were accessible only with the assistance of a ladder, and washed. Paring knives and sharp pocketknives flashed as the fruit was relieved of stems, soft brown spots or other blemishes, and chopped up.

Prepared apples were dropped, faintly thudding, into the hopper, a funnel-like wooden container that topped the mill.

Turning the wheel with its curved spokes to begin the process of crushing the apples looked like such fun. Being allowed an attempt to rotate the wheel made one feel so important, but that feeling quickly dissipated with the realization that the opportunity was actually hard work. The hopper held about a peck of apples.

The side wheel activated a gear beneath the hopper that turned two rollers in different directions, squashing apples between them.

The crushed apples, skin and all, fell from the hopper into a wooden tub made with vertical slats with spaces between them. I have been told that the mixture is properly called "pomace," but it looked like supper for the hogs to me.

When the tub was full, the wooden, grooved bed on which it sat was pulled forward from beneath the grinder. A wooden lid was placed atop the ground up apples and a mechanism that resembled a large screw was lowered until it rested on the lid. The square-threaded rod was turned by another wheel that had four vertical handles. The handles had a purpose. Exerting enough pressure on the lid that covered the pomace was not easy, and a lack of sufficient pressure would mean that juice would be wasted. The answer was to insert a board through the handles, giving a sturdy, flat surface to push against to turn the big wheel and get more squeeze.

At this point the juice or cider was literally squeezed out into a pan underneath the slatted tub, then poured into gallon jars. Since the only refrigeration available was a well house, through which cold water ran continuously, large amounts of cider were not produced at one time. A few gallon glass jars were filled for drinking and for making jelly. The remainder would ferment until it was undrinkable, for use as vinegar.

Cider-making time seemed to be a special event, as were making molasses in the furnace down by the Pigeon River and stirring up apple butter on the spot where the old home place had stood before the newer house was built. The family always gathered for the fun of being together and to lend willing hands for tasks involved.

The old apple house? While the upper section was generally used for storage, apples were wintered in the cool space below. It still stands, partially bermed, on a slight rise overlooking the Pigeon River, no longer shaded by an orchard. I call it beautiful.

Memories of Molasses Get-togethers

Sugarcane, in bottomland by the river, marched in rows with tasseled topknots stirring in the breeze, ready for harvesting. It was fall and time to make molasses!

Time to chop down the cane, top and strip it, leaving only the bare cane pole.

The molasses furnace waited under a shed on the riverbank for its annual revival. Wood was stacked, ready for the fire. The pan, 3'x8' with a copper bottom, was scoured, as well as buckets for collecting the syrup.

A one-mule power mill sat above the shed, because the process depended on gravity. A wooden barrel stood ready to catch the syrup, with a spigot at the bottom for releasing liquid into the pan.

Making molasses was surely an art for old-timers, as fire to heat the pan had to maintain the right temperature consistently and someone had to judge when the molasses were done. Experience substituted for thermometers or any newfangled gadgets that might simplify the process.

Methods and equipment differed from farmer to farmer, but the process was basically the same. Familiar to me is that of my grandfather, Joe Hargrove.

For us, the fun started when the mule began circling endlessly, wearing a path in the ground, as cane poles were fed into the mill, where it was ground until the juice began flowing.

The mule trudged along as sap flowed and bubbled in the pan. Froth was continuously skimmed from the surface. My grandfather would dip the strainer into the syrup and test it, much like making candy. He just knew when it was ready.

Two strong men would lift the pan from the furnace and set it aside. Molasses were dipped from the pan into metal buckets, and the pan was returned to its place on the furnace, ready for another run. When the pan was lifted, everyone backed off; a spill of boiling molasses could burn severely.

My aunt Cora Lee Devlin loved placing chestnuts, gathered from the woods above the house, in the fire. Mmm. Real roasted chestnuts. She also liked to sit on her father's lap and feed cane into the mill.

This went on for a week, with the cookers working in shifts. My grandmother Mary cooked pots of food to feed them.

Word went out to friends and family before the last cook off. It was a special time—party time—as the cook off continued into the evening. Air was nippy as the sun set and dark surrounded the glow from furnace and lanterns.

Shadowy figures materialized in the shed and on the perimeter as people drove up from town. You peered through the dark, squinting a little, to see who else had come. Faces were illuminated, then shadowed as the fire flickered and the lanterns hissed. Familiar voices were identified.

The work, and work it was, was transformed into a social gathering of sorts.

Cane poles were cut into sopping sticks with a diagonal slice on one end for gathering syrup.

Voices grew louder and laughter rang as the crowd told tales and joked through the evening. Children, especially the boys, ran and tumbled as children will do, and slipped off to play in the river. Once, my brother and cousins found a nest of snake eggs below the shed, cracked them, and released tiny, agitated snakes. The boys laughed and ran from their parents, while the girls screamed.

Your body heated from the fire and your face burned. You turned around to warm your backside, or stepped away to be cooled quickly by the chilly air.

When the last panful of molasses was lifted from the fire and emptied, children and adults alike eagerly grabbed the cane sticks. Molasses were scraped from the pan and licked from the canes. Chewing on the cane filled your mouth with a taste of syrup and a sweet tang from the cane itself

The pan was sopped clean and the crowd gradually diminished, reluctant to leave, as one last tale was told in an attempt to prolong the evening

It was over for another year. Molasses waited though, to be spread on fat biscuits slathered with home-churned butter, throughout the winter.

Molasses are still made by a few here and there and the taste is good. But it isn't quite the same as those molasses flavored by childhood memories.

Signs and Colors of Autumn

I n the unexpected chill of an early September morning, shortly after sunrise, fall was observed gently but persistently nudging summer aside.

In the distance, mountaintops were all but obscured by puffy blankets of fog hugging the peaks and snuggling in the valleys.

Nearby four chipmunks, nervously scurrying and bounding, vied with a squirrel for fallen chestnuts (sadly, the Chinese variety). Their interest was confined to prickly burrs that had split, revealing the nuts inside.

Overhead, hummingbirds uncharacteristically paused for long sips of nectar, unlike their normal hovering for quick gulps. A long journey to warmer climes awaits them.

The lush green foliage of August is interrupted by a rusty red tinging to the dogwood leaves. Breezes weaving among the trees send brown, curling leaves to litter the ground.

In the porch corner a small spider builds an ambitious web, rappelling on an invisible strand before quickly retracing the path of his descent, endlessly repeating the exercise at varying angles.

Fall brings with it a variety of creatures, particularly tobacco-spitting grasshoppers, woolly worms, and writing spiders. Walking through a field lined with dried cornstalks requires constant vigilance, lest you find yourself eye to eye with a large yellow and black arachnid that decorates its webs with indecipherable scribblings. Their bodies can measure as much as two inches long, not including legs.

Down the road, hayfields have had their seasonal shearing and nutritious grass that waved its way through the growing season is bound in rolls, lying in clusters around field perimeters. Rabbits can live in peace without the threat of mower blades for a bit, while cattle grazing in adjacent pastures are assured of winter food.

Colorful weeds and wildflowers adorn roadsides, playing their role to usher in the fall season. An abundant display includes touches of blue and white as asters and chicory proliferate, goldenrod waves its yellow head, jewelweed blows its orange bugles, and leggier Joe-Pye weed and thistles oversee all with their pink and purple heads. In an earlier time, "granny women" would be harvesting jewelweed for a salve to treat encounters with poison ivy, replenishing their store of nature's remedies.

A few pumpkins lie in a small heap, first evidence of an essential fall crop. Native Americans used pumpkin as a staple in their diets centuries before the pilgrims landed. When white settlers arrived, the Indigenous Peoples introduced them to the fruit, believed to have originated in North America. They showed the settlers how to grow pumpkins and how to use them for food.

These signs and more indicate that Western North Carolina is readying itself for transition into one of four distinct seasons that make our home so appealing.

Baptizin'

"Shall we gather at the river...the beautiful, the beautiful river..." Lyrics from this old hymn rang out from the banks of the Pigeon River in Cruso recently, sung by the Oak Grove Baptist Church choir.

In a scene reminiscent of an earlier time, Reverend Bruce Cayton, pastor of the Thickety church, waded into the chilly, gently flowing waters of the Pigeon, and stood there waist deep, awaiting the men, women and children who had asked that their baptism be in the river.

They came one by one, stepping carefully on the rock-strewn riverbank and into the water, each guided by a reassuring arm offered by Chris Stevens, who was assisting Cayton.

With one hand raised as he spoke appropriative words and called each by name, Cayton baptized nine people, each with a quick immersion. Some exited the pool gasping from the shock of the cold water, while others appeared exhilarated after their dip. Shivering in wet clothing clinging to their bodies, each was met by family or friends and wrapped quickly in a thick towel or blanket.

Tree limbs heavy with thick foliage stretched over the quiet pool and the gently sloping riverbank. Upstream, water frothed noisily over and around boulders before calming and quieting in the deeper riverbed, creating a lovely setting for the baptisms.

That Sunday afternoon was reminiscent of other customs, as well. The congregation gathered on the expansive lawn of Charlie and Martha Trantham's Cruso home for lunch, called "dinner on the grounds." Long tables were crowded with home-cooked dishes of all descriptions, including plenty of cakes and pies.

After the dishes were emptied and the crowd had eaten its fill, Reverend Bill Terrell brought out his guitar and the singing began.

Before the advent of today's modernized churches with baptismal pools incorporated inside sanctuaries, river baptisms were commonplace in the Pigeon. Although no longer the norm, the symbolic river cleansing still isn't too unusual in Haywood County. Cayton's church partners with four others on Memorial Day, gathering at the Canton Recreation Park, situated beside the river, for a picnic, gospel singing and baptisms.

Baptisms have also been conducted in creeks and ponds. Oak Grove and other churches used Haynes' pond on Thickety for years, Cayton said. Some churches dammed creeks temporarily in order to create a pool deep enough for immersions, he added.

Large, elongated metal tubs continue to be used by some churches, particularly those who meet in unconventional church buildings such as barns, according to Cayton.

The word baptism originated from a Greek word, *baptizo*. Greeks used the word to describe the method of dyeing cloth, the immersing or dipping of fabric in tinted water.

Interestingly, the founders of three different denominations made specific comments on the practice of immersion.

Martin Luther (Lutheran Church) said, "I would have those who are to be baptized to be entirely immersed, as the word imports and the mystery signifies."

"The word 'baptize' signifies to immerse. It is certain that immersion was the practice of the ancient church," a quote attributed to John Calvin (Presbyterian Church).

And John Wesley (Methodist Church) is credited with saying, "Buried with Him, alluding to baptizing by Immersion according to the custom of the first church."

Once-a-week Bathing

In these days of modern plumbing, the notion of bathing only once a week, of taking a "Saturday night bath," may seem unthinkable to us. It was a reality, though, for Charles Fletcher, eighty-six years old, when he was growing up in the Thickety area of Haywood County in the 1930s, as well as for many others.

"This was not as simple as you may think," he says. "There was quite a bit of planning and lots of work in this weekly ritual, and it involved the whole family that is except for Dad. He usually did his bathing at the paper mill, where he worked. There were modern bathrooms at the mill, complete with a shower room."

"First a galvanized wash tub was brought into the kitchen. The next thing needed was the water. Here again it took some manual labor to fill the tub with water for the bath. This usually was the job for T. P., my younger brother, and me. Some places that we lived at had a spring. This meant that there were many trips from the house to the spring with our ten quart water buckets. In our younger days this was quite a task, because we were not strong enough to carry a full bucket of water and had to make a lot of trips to the spring."

At other places the Fletchers lived, a hand-dug well was available, with a well box and a windlass with a rope and a water bucket. The water bucket, tied to one end of the rope, could be raised and lowered by cranking the windlass. "We would unwind the rope until the water bucket was sunk below the top of the water in the well. Next we would crank the windlass until the bucket with the water was near the top, where we could grab hold and empty it into the tub. We would only fill the tub about halfway full. We would fill several large cooking pots and set them on our old wood-burning stove. When the water began to boil, we poured it in the tub of cold water until it was warm enough to bathe in."

The first bather was always the oldest person, Fletcher said, and continued down the line according to age. Sometimes the water was a bit dirty for the last bather, depending on how many children were in the family. He surmises this routine inspired the old saying, "Don't throw the baby out with the water."

Soap was always used for bathing, according to Fletcher, but they did not always have store-bought soap. "We had to use the soap that Mom had made from the excess fat from the hogs that were slaughtered at hog killing." However, this soap was very strong since lye was added to the fat. The family had to use caution, as it could blister the skin.

"My oldest son, Gary, asked me how an adult could bathe in such a small place as the washtub. I explained that first you would sit in the tub with your legs hanging on the outside. You washed the part of your body that was in the tub, then stood up in the tub and finished washing your legs and feet," he said.

"This was no problem for us children. We could sit in the tub with our feet inside. We were mountain people, and were taught by our elders the way to survive and do the many things that had to be done without any outside help. After all, we didn't have the many things that we have today to make life a lot easier with our daily tasks."

During the summer, he and his brother often bathed in a nearby creek.

"We did survive, we kept our body clean, and we had our Saturday night bath in the 1930s," Fletcher concluded.

Charles C. Fletcher lives in Tennessee, but grew up and spent his earlier years in Western North Carolina. He considers himself a storyteller rather than a writer. His brother T. P. still lives in the Thickety community.

Fletcher tells the story of once-a-week baths in *The Panther on Cold Mountain and Other Stories*, the second of two books he has penned and published.

Plott Hounds, Legendary Hunting Dogs

When sixteen-year-old Johannes Plott immigrated to the United States from Germany in 1750, he couldn't have known that he would establish a canine dynasty that endures 254 years later.

The Plott hound, North Carolina's state dog, is descended from dogs journeying with him, believed to be Hannoversche Bluthunde (Hanover bloodhounds). Bred to hunt boar, the dogs were fierce hunters of enormous stamina, characteristics that led to their reputation as bear dogs without equal.

Johannes landed in Philadelphia on September 12, 1750, according to a Plott genealogy compiled by Grace Plott, his great-, great-granddaughter, and made his way to New Bern before settling in Cabarrus County.

The first Plott to live in Haywood County was Henry, second son of Johannes. He traveled with his wife Lydia to a spot on the Pigeon River near present-day Canton in the 1800s, before moving further west to establish his home on the waters of Richland and Dick's Creeks.

The Plotts and their hounds, now legendary figures, had arrived to run Western North Carolina mountainsides for more than 200 years through six generations.

Henry's seventh son, John, then John's son Montraville, carried on the tradition of hunting and breeding the dogs. Von or Vaughn, depending upon who did the spelling, was next in line, hunting, breeding, and caring for the hounds with passion. His love and knowledge of Plott hounds was passed to his son William M. "Bill" Plott, who died in March 2000 at the age of seventy-eight.

Somewhere along the way, the family property became known as Plott Creek. Then in 1989, the Plott hound received the state dog designation.

It appears, for now, that maintaining the legendary breed lies in the hands of hunters other than Plotts. Dr. Mark Plott, a veterinarian in Concord, is not aware of any immediate family members actively engaged in breeding or selling the dogs, although he knows that hunters in Haywood County own them. He remembers going on bear hunts as a youngster, and describes the Plotts as being better suited for hunting big game. "There is something in their makeup that enables them to take on large game, even though their size is no bigger than other hounds," he said.

Craig Rogers of Cruso affirms that Plott hounds are still hunting bear in Haywood County. He has one. "The old-timers called them Plott curs," he said.

A National Plott Hound Association yearbook records 1944 as the year the United Kennel Club, Inc. registered the first Plotts. Most full-blooded Plotts are a deep, brownish brindle, or "saddled" with a large black mantle and brindle only on the legs, according to the yearbook, with an occasional golden brindle or rare smokey blue brindle. Some cross breeding was inevitable, with the most successful occurring around 1875. Mont Plott loaned a stud dog to a North Georgia bear hunter who owned bear dogs, known then as leopard dogs. Dogs from this breeding possessed the bluish brindle color with scattered darker spots.

Reputation of Plott hounds began grapevining around the country. Judging by the number of web sites, the dogs are alive and well from coast to coast, although one wonders if Henry Plott would approve of all the strains.

Vaughn is no longer around to talk about his beloved hounds, but a 1978 edition of *Foxfire*, published by students at Rabun County High School in Clayton, Georgia, records an interview.

"I train my dogs when they're three or four months old—take them to the woods and let 'em know what their nose is for. It's up to the dogs. They train themselves. It's instinct," Vaughn told his interviewers. "They just keep on (on a hunt). They got no quit in 'em. That's why the Plotts are better. They've got more guts and they're gamer. I've used 'em all my life."

"I breed pure Plotts—don't mix 'em with anything else. Mine are pure bred just like my daddy left 'em to me," Vaughn said.

"The Plotts are as popular as they ever were," said Junior Frisbee of Waynesville who has eight Plotts and hunts in all terrains and climates in various states. "They perform well, regardless of the conditions." And he sees Plott hounds wherever he goes. New Mexico, Idaho, Maine, Wisconsin, and North Carolina, from mountains to coast, are among his hunting sites.

In addition to their aggressive hunting and never-give-up attitude, he likes the dogs because their coarse, thick hair protects them from briars and other brush, the pads on their feet are tougher, and their voices are deep and clear. He prefers dark-colored Plotts, because bears with their poor eyesight can't see them as well. "They can get in close contact with bear, especially in swampy areas. I see more and more hunters turning to them," he said.

He believes that most Plotts all across the United States can be traced back to Haywood County.

A large, wooden sign erected by the United States Department of the Interior's National Park Service, on the Blue Ridge Parkway overlooking Plott Balsam Range, pays tribute to Henry Plott and his Plott bear hounds.

PLOTT HOUND

Mount Lyn Lowery

A highly visible cross atop a mountain peak illuminates nighttime in the Balsam area of Haywood County.

The lighted cross shines brightly against the dark sky, an ever-present symbol that has topped Mount Lyn Lowry for forty-five years. Painted white, it is equally as visible against daytime's blue sky.

A story lies behind the erection of the 60-foot-tall structure, a story of a family's love for their daughter and their wish to memorialize her too-brief life.

When the memorial was officially dedicated to Ivilyn "Lyn" Ingram Lowry on August 9, 1965, evangelist Dr. Billy Graham stood at the foot of the cross and spoke the words of dedication.

The story began when Lyn was born on August 27, 1947 to General Sumter L. Lowry, U.S. Army (ret.) and his wife Ivilyn of Tampa, Florida. The Lowrys, who had family in Waynesville, spent what must have been a very enjoyable summer vacation in the mountains. Captivated by this mountainous region, the couple, in partnership with other investors, purchased land that included what was then known as Jones' Knob, and built a summer home. An account written by General Lowry tells that their daughter had a special love for the mountain where she roamed and played as she grew up.

The heartbreaking chapter in the story was written when Lyn did not survive a bout with leukemia and died almost a month after her fifteenth birthday.

The grieving parents discussed a number of projects that would perpetuate her memory while bringing joy to others. The result of their soul-searching was the giant cross crowning the mountain their daughter loved. The couple saw the cross, reached by a strenuous climb, as a "religious shrine where religious-minded people" could come to meditate and to pray.

Several chapters involved the momentous task of building the 60-foot cross on a 6,280-foot mountain near the Blue Ridge Parkway. A road had to be graded, power lines had to be extended, and part of the mountaintop, a natural table forty feet wide and 500 feet long, blasted to make way for the huge foundation. The project occupied more than a year's time.

The 50,000 pound cross was built in six sections in Jacksonville, FL, segments of rustproof steel (Cor-Ten) that had to be shipped to Western North Carolina, trucked up the mountain and assembled. The half-inch steel was shaped into tubing 3.5 feet in diameter. Eight mercury vapor lamps were installed on each side for illumination. The cross and its massive base were built to withstand 100-mph winds.

The monument is visible thirty to forty miles in all directions.

General Lowry believed he was "led by God" to the building of the cross in the form of three miracles. First, in 1940 he purchased a steel-fabricating factory in Jacksonville. "I had no possible use for a steel plant, but I had a strong feeling I ought to buy the plant, anyway," he wrote. "A steel mill was the most necessary ingredient in building the cross..." Second, the Lowrys made a trip to Waynesville and fell in love—especially daughter Lyn—with the mountains of Western North Carolina. When an acquaintance offered to sell a mountain to him, Lowry accepted the offer. In *I Believe in Miracles*, Lowry wrote, "This turned out to be the present location of the cross...at that time, I did not understand why I took this action, as I certainly did not need a mountain." The third miracle occurred, he relates, when choosing the exact location of the cross. A construction worker driving a stake into the ground struck a rusted horseshoe. The general considered the horseshoe a sign that they had picked the right spot for the cross.

The Lowrys established a foundation to perpetuate the care and maintenance of the cross and surrounding area. Jones' Knob officially became Mount Lyn Lowery in 1967 due to legislative action by the State of North Carolina, and the US Department of Interior recognized the change by placing the name Mt. Lyn Lowry on published maps.

The Lowrys are all dead now, but their vision memorializing their daughter shines on.

Memories, Remnants of Bomber Crash Remain

C old Mountain was wrapped in a dense coat of fog the morning of Friday,

September 13, 1946 as rain fell, wind blew, and streaks of lightning split the sky. Not a good day to be on the mountain.

Around 11:30 that morning, tragedy, in the form of a B-25 bomber carrying five World War II Air Force officers, struck the north face of the peak a little below the summit. The crash killed the five men, scarred the mountain with impact and fire, and scarred the lives of many people in other ways.

O. C. Chambers Jr., seventy-four, was fourteen years old at the time. He and three others skipped school on Monday, after the plane had been found, walked up Lenoir's Creek, then picked out a trail up the mountain. "The Air Force (personnel) had been there to carry off the bodies, but we found small body parts they missed. Engines, fuselage and wings were still there. We rolled one of the tires down the mountain and hid it, and one of the boys went back with a horse and sled to get it," Chambers said. The tire is mounted on a support behind his house on US 276, aligned with the crash site.

A few are said to have seen the plane and thought it was flying too low. Others reported hearing a loud crash, likened to a huge clap of thunder or a dynamite explosion. The aircraft had left Detroit, Michigan that morning, heading for Tampa, Florida.

A recovery crew, assembled at Donaldson Air Force Base near Greenville, South Carolina, surely had no conception of difficulties they would face. There is no easy way to reach the summit of Cold Mountain, and they would descend emotionally spent, laden with an unpleasant cargo. Local folks who helped them, some of which were atop the mountain when they arrived, eased their job.

Robert "Bob" Fisher of Asheville, retired attorney, climbed the mountain by way of Crawford's Creek with some friends on Sunday,

362

following the crash. He was fourteen, and lived in Canton. "I was glad to get off there," Fisher said. "It was the first time I had been around a place where people had died. I recognized some bones and the smell of burned flesh was strong. The ground and trees were still smoking and I could feel the heat." He and his buddies rolled the other tire, bouncing and careening, to the foot of the mountain.

Those who died had survived military action during World War II, distinguishing themselves along the way for bravery and leadership. The pilot was a forty-year-old major general, and the co-pilot was a lieutenant colonel. Another lieutenant colonel, also a pilot, a master sergeant, and a staff sergeant rounded out the crew.

Parts of the plane are still around, collected as souvenirs: the tire at Chambers', a tire rim in which flowers are grown, a piece of metal carried in a hunter's pocket, and various and sundry other items gathered from the wreckage. A propeller blade occupies a spot in Canton Area Historical Museum.

Cold Mountain had made national news long before Charles Frazier penned his civil war novel named for the 6,030 feet high summit.

Two Generations, Two Ghosts Occupy Old Cathey House

The oldest remaining house in Pigeon Valley stands alongside Pisgah Drive/NC 110, occupied by fourth and fifth generation Catheys and two resident ghosts, a warm and inviting house despite its age of 141 years.

Before the Civil War, construction was begun on the white frame home of Joseph Turner Cathey and his wife Martha Ann Iva Killian Cathey, but he, one of Captain Isaac Lenoir's "Sons of the Pigeon," died serving in the war and did not see its completion in 1864. The front section was finished first, containing two rooms with fireplaces and a hallway on first and second floors, attic, cellar, and porch across the front, and portico opening from the second level. The kitchen, a log cabin, was a separate structure behind the house. After the war, Martha Cathey added a kitchen and dining room wing, giving the house its current T shape. A bathroom was added even later.

Doris and Tom Cathey, who live there now with their two children, are determined to maintain the house with its original features, Doris said, as she led me through the rooms.

Tom was raised in the house by Turner and Aurelia Cathey, both educators, along with brother Ashley and sisters Bush and Ann.

"After stripping faded wallpaper from the first floor bedroom, we found original tongue and groove paneling," she said. Hand-cut nails are seen in the walls along with handmade brick in the fireplace.

The house abounds with interesting details: front doors of walnut on both levels, finely-crafted walnut bannisters put together with pegs lining three levels of stairs that unusually, face the rear of the house, three-dimensional panels topping the downstairs rooms and hallway, walnut bedroom mantels, and Greek Revival details said to be some of the county's best. Family heirlooms furnish each room, such as an old handmade dollhouse, and a collection of cowbells from the days when cattle ranged free and were summered on Cold Mountain.

"I pulled off Formica, then linoleum (exposing original walls and counter tops in the kitchen)," Doris said, "and rubbed the wood with oil."

Twelve-inch square locust beams in the cellar, mortised and pegged, form a solid foundation, attesting to the craftsmanship of Dred and Willis Blaylock, who built the house. Green shutters are hand-hewn, pegged, and affixed with hand-wrought iron. A reverse scallop trim edges the roof.

And the ghosts? Three generations of family, along with some guests, report hearing the squeak of Augusta Cathey's leather sidesaddle, as well as faint hoofbeats and whinnying of a horse in the attic. She lived in the house in the late 1800s. They believe, collectively, that shaking tables, the clatter of an old adding machine, a sense of someone passing by, scattered objects, firm footsteps in the "piney-knotty" passageway above the dining room, even a touch, are the presence of cousin John Boone, who spent summers in the house for many years.

Ghosts or not, the house is a fine example of early farmhouses in this area and the Cathey name is listed prominently among those who contributed to Haywood County's growth.

Entertainment Dinosaur

"Drive-in theaters are a dying dinosaur," Troy Mann of Canton told me. "Entertainment is changing too much. Families can rent several movies and watch them at home for the price of one outing to a drive-in."

The subject was on his mind and mine, because his father, Tom Mann, ninety-five, was buried this past Sunday.

Tom Mann, who was dedicated to caring for his farm, leased three of his twenty-six acres along NC 110 in the '50s and '60s for use as Canton Drive-in Theater, the one and only drive-in theater in this end of the county.

Homer West and Clayton Mehaffey, co-owners of Waynesville Drive-In Theater, approached Tom Mann in 1948, proposing to lease the land. Before he agreed, the two had to demonstrate to him that application of gravel for parking cars would not hurt the soil and that his farmland, his livelihood, would revert to its original productivity. "They must have been good salesmen, because he let them have a five-year lease with an option for five more," Troy Mann said. Tom Mann wasn't easily persuaded, his son said, but he contributed to the fun and enjoyment of Canton people by his willingness to lease those three acres. "I feel he provided a service to his community."

Going to the drive-in was a real treat. Families loved it. Bill Churm would take his wife, two young sons clad in their pajamas, and plenty of snacks to the drive-in, hook the speaker to the car window and enjoy the movie with his wife while their boys, at some point, went to sleep.

"As a young mother and daddy, my husband and I would take the kids and fill the back seat with blankets and pillows for the kids, while we sat in the front in peace eating popcorn. It was the only place we had to go until they were in school...then we still went anyway. Good memories..." said Nancy Garrett.

Teenagers loved it; something new and different to do. Jenny Thomason Morin, who wasn't allowed to go to a drive-in on a date, remembers going there in Lynn Vance's father's station wagon, full of kids, most of who were hiding under blankets in the back until they got in. "Then we all got out and sat on the hood of the car," she said.

"I can remember one time when several folks hid in the trunk so we wouldn't have to pay as much to get in. This was a group of girls. I remember being afraid of getting caught, but I don't think we did," Judy Stinnett Fuqua admitted.

Troy used to help his mother in the concession stand, where you could get a box of popcorn and a drink for thirty cents, and remembers hearing that a car came in with four kids hidden in the trunk. When the driver tried to unlock the trunk, he broke the key and had to call Buck Rogers, a locksmith. Rogers was in the projection booth at the theater, operating the projector. He opened the trunk and freed the four.

And let's admit it: In the fall, when weather was chilly, heavily frosted windows were an indication that someone wasn't watching the movie.

The drive-in opened in 1949 or '50 and accommodated 200 cars, Mann said, and closed around 1963. Regular moviegoers were buying television sets and staying home to watch TV, and that contributed to its demise. The screen was torn down when the road was widened, around 1976.

West and Mehaffey were right. Grass has grown around the gravel and the land, once again, is devoted to agricultural use. And the old concession stand is filled with hay, feeding cattle instead of people.

Old Hatchery a Destination

The old North Carolina Wildlife fish hatchery near Balsam was a favorite destination on Sunday afternoons, when families gathered a picnic lunch and piled in their cars for a drive. Parents visited, children played, and then everyone headed to look at the fish.

Raceways and pools teeming with rainbow trout in various sizes were the attraction. Childish hands itched to plunge into the water and touch the slippery fish. Adults surely had the same urge. In fact, it is reported that some concocted ingenious ways to catch a fish, like the young boy who rigged a fishing line in a pants leg, dangled a red worm in a raceway, and pulled a fat trout up his leg. His twitching leg gave him away, and a hatchery employee relieved him of his catch.

The 12-acre site was purchased from J. R. Morgan in 1919 for $1,200; the hatchery was built in the 1920s, named the Morrison Hatchery after North Carolina Governor Cameron Morrison, who served from 1921 to 1924. Once called a "rearing station," it was one of several built during the '20s and '30s.

Wild animals were an attraction in the beginning, as were the fish. Two monkeys named Herbert and Joe, deer, snakes, a mountain lion, a black bear cub, and prairie dogs shared the site with the fish. Prairie dogs were fun to watch, popping their heads in and out of their holes. The atmosphere was one of a small zoo.

The water was cold, with several springs as the original water source. Construction of round, concrete ponds and raceways was a 1930s project of the Works Projects Administration (WPA). These New Deal workers also dug a water supply by hand, gravity-fed water from Winchester Creek, and laid the lines, some of which were as much as twelve feet deep.

In the absence of factory-produced trout feed used now, a mixture of grain and ground, raw meet was used to feed the hungry fish.

The first superintendent of the hatchery was Leo Reiger, followed by his son Leo Jr. Johnny Byrd took the position in 1963. Then Jerry

Hodge assumed responsibility, managing the hatchery until it was closed in 1983.

The Fisheries Commission Board, which preceded the Wildlife Commission, built the facility. The hatchery closed in 1983, when the U.S. Fish and Wildlife Service turned over operation of the Pisgah hatchery to the state. The site now houses offices and depots for Inland Fisheries, Wildlife Management, Engineering Services, and the Enforcement divisions.

Snake Bites, Related Death Made News

Several stories about Haywood County have headlined in the national news, but none were as bizarre as the year the sheriff was bitten by a Florida canebrake rattlesnake.

The year was 1985 and the incident involved former sheriff Jack Arrington and the late Charles Prince, preacher and snake handler.

Prince bought and sold night crawlers for fish bait in a business outside Canton, but his calling to preach the gospel and handle poisonous snakes during church services brought about a confrontation with former sheriff Arrington.

"There were really two confrontations," said Sheriff Tom Alexander, "but not everyone knows that. At the first service, Jack took the snakes to milk them to see if they were poisonous and took the bottle of strychnine to have it tested." The snakes were poisonous and the strychnine the real thing, although diluted.

Arrington's son Joe recalls what his dad told him. "Prince was advertising church meetings and the public was invited. Dad got word that snakes and strychnine would be involved, so he called Prince and said, 'Don't do that. You are endangering the public and my job is to see that they are safe.'"

Lieutenant Dean Henline was one of four deputies who accompanied Arrington to the second service. "We couldn't find the snakes," he said, "but when Prince went to the podium to preach, he started pulling out the snakes. They were inside the podium in a secure box, where we didn't think to look."

"We confronted him," Henline said. "He had a snake in each hand and wouldn't turn them over to us. Jack grabbed one snake with his left hand, but didn't get it close enough to its head and it bit him below his thumb. He threw it to the ground and pinned its head with a walking stick and told me to step on it. I had one foot just behind its head and the other near its tail and was holding the box of snakes. All his people were screaming at me to give back their snakes."

"A state trooper took Jack to the hospital and I made an emergency run to Asheville for the serum. My car quit running in Asheville, and a Buncombe County deputy took me and the serum to Haywood County hospital," he said.

The incident took place outside a rock building on Newfound Road, just outside Canton city limits.

"Jack was going blind on the way to the hospital," said his wife Lillian, "but (Dr.) Fred Wenzel saved his arm and his life. He completely recovered from that snake bite."

"The sheriff in Buncombe County, Tom Morrissey, was so nice. He called me and told me that he would gladly send his men to help in case of trouble, and offered to relay the anti-venom to the Haywood County line," she said. There was none available in Haywood. Former deputy Grady McCarter, who was not on duty that night, remembers that Arrington was in serious condition for a time.

Prince wasn't so fortunate.

"'A man who was free on bond after being charged in North Carolina with illegally handling snakes died today of a rattlesnake bite on the thumb,' authorities said," according to an AP story in August, 1985. "'Charles Prince, 45 years old, was bitten here Saturday at the Apostolic Church of God and refused treatment,' said Sheriff Gail Colyer of Greene County (Tennessee). Mr. Prince had vowed to defy laws against the religious practice of snake handling."

Arrington had been bitten about two weeks earlier.

Prince was said to be a widely known and well-liked evangelist in the Holiness Church who crisscrossed the South delivering sermons. He took Bible verse Mark 16:17–18 literally, and was said to have no fear.

Arrington survived the snakebite and resumed his work, dying years later from an unrelated condition.

Electric Lighting

White Sulphur Springs Hotel guests, clad in their finest, were enjoying music and dancing in the hotel's grand ballroom on a balmy summer evening in 1904. The extravagant social event was brightly illuminated with new incandescent light bulbs, rather than candles or oil lamps used in previous events. The newfangled luxury of electric lights had come to Waynesville.

A nearby mill whistle sounded and the lights dimmed; time to light the oil lamps for an intermission. Guests likely strolled the grounds and engaged in conversation for a half hour or so, while the band took a break.

Unfortunately, intermissions were not scheduled. They were timed instead by a steam boiler at Killian Woolen Mill, across Richland Creek from the hotel. Daniel Marcus Killian, owner of the mill, had contracted with the town of Waynesville to bring 60 kilowatts of electric power to a new town distribution system. The generator Killian installed beside his mill, driven by a water-powered turbine, could provide only enough power for a few streetlights, homes, stores and hotels wired for electricity, on an unpredictable schedule.

According to Carolina Power & Light records, Benjamin J. Sloan, who owned the hotel, took over Killian's contract and built a steam plant to supplement water power. This system also became overloaded and could not meet Waynesville's rising demand for power.

Sloan, Dr. Thomas Stringfield and Sam Welch organized Haywood Electric Power Company (HEPCO). Property they acquired included Leatherwood Shoals in Haywood's White Oak Township where a larger power plant and reservoir were built.

Champion Paper Company, in the process of building its paper mill, was one of the first customers when the power plant began production in July 1905.

In 1918, with power consumption growing in Haywood County, A. C. Springs of Charlotte and Sloan organized Great Smoky Mountain Power Company and acquired options from Waterville to the mouth of Cove Creek and up to Crabtree Creek, according to local historian W. C. Allen. Their plan was to construct a major hydroelectric power dam below the mouth of Cataloochee Creek.

Sloan died in 1922 without seeing his dreams completed, but he had laid the groundwork. Three years later, with HEPCO's plant needing repair and its reservoir filling with silt, Sloan's son, Hugh, gained power rights from Lake Junaluska, installing a generator to supplement power generated by the Pigeon River. Seven years later, Carolina Power & Light Company, foreseeing future needs for hydroelectric dams and plants across the state and already leasing property in the area of Waterville, entered the picture.

Sloan's son Hugh and his partners sold portions of their property needed for the construction of Walters Reservoir as well as their distribution system to CP&L in 1929. Waterville Lake would eventually be impounded and the current Walters Power Plant would be constructed.

When the Pigeon River flooded in 1940, high waters washed out the HEPCO dam and the last vestiges of Sloan's electricity-producing enterprise floated away.

Early Days of the Telephone

P hone bills in Waynesville in the early 1900's were inexpensive, with a "party line" (several customers sharing one phone line) costing $1.50 a month and a private line costing $2.00 a month. Service was as limited, though, as the cost.

Motivated by White Sulphur Springs guests' frequent calls for their horses and carriages, housed at J. P. Swift's stables in an old warehouse at the corner of Depot and Haywood streets in Waynesville, Swift installed a magneto-type system in his livery stable in 1894 and connected it to the hotel.

In 1900, S. C. Sattethwaite, owner of Eagle's Nest Hotel, another tourist resort atop a mountain and reached by a long, winding road, R. D. Gilmer of the Suyeta Hotel, Swift, and W. H. Cole, a Hazelwood lumberman, were granted a franchise by the town of Waynesville, allowing them to install additional lines and telephones.

Jerry Davis was contracted to install lines and a 100-line switchboard was ordered. When it arrived at the depot, Swift, afraid the day's heavy rains might damage the equipment, left it there overnight. During the night, Waynesville experienced one of its worst fires, and flames devoured the depot and all its contents. Another switchboard was ordered and installed.

The late Fay Toy, a switchboard operator, worked for the phone company for almost forty years, and compiled its early history before her death.

The fledgling system was above McCracken Clothing Store, later Curtis Drug Store. Among the first subscribers were the courthouse, Waynesville Pharmacy, Kenmore Hotel, Clyde Ray's store, and attorney J. R. Morgan. Service was local only, and two digit numbers were used. The telephone directory was a cardboard sheet, about 8.5"x11", usually tacked to the wall behind the telephone. An operator's salary was $20 a month.

About 1904, lines were installed to the Turnpike Hotel, a longtime drover's stop just across the Buncombe County line, Eagle's Nest

Hotel, Knight's Store in Balsam, and Fish's Store in Clyde. Rural lines went to Messer's Store in Cove Creek, Haywood Electric Power Company, Retreat (a boarding house on the old Sunburst Road), Dellwood, and Jonathan's Creek.

In 1908, Southern Bell installed two long distance lines—both pay stations—at Reeve's Drug Store and Waynesville Pharmacy. "They collected silver dollars, fifty-cent pieces, quarters, dimes and nickels," Toy said.

Asheville Telephone Company bought the business in 1916; a larger switchboard, more phones, and personnel were added. Toy moved to the business office.

Southern Bell purchased the Asheville Telephone Company in 1923, and Toy began work for "Ma Bell."

Demand for phone lines continued to grow throughout the county, to Maggie Valley, Canton, Crabtree, and beyond. "In June 1953, we 'cut to dial'," Toy wrote.

The Chamber of Commerce collected phone bills, but because of steady growth, a business office was added in Canton.

In August 1958, with phone service apparently extended to all areas of Haywood County, she wrote, "We feel that our county is now one of the best 'telephoned' counties in Southern Bell."

Little Privacy with Party Lines

"Eight people were on our party line" said Mary Rogers, eighty-two, ""but they were later reduced to four. You could listen to anyone talking on the phone."

In this age of instant communication with cell phones, caller ID, computers, and hand-held messaging tools, the idea of sharing your telephone line with seven other families is alien, unheard of by some generations.

These early phone systems had no dial system. Brainard Burrus, who was too young to make calls at the time, remembers his uncle picking up the phone and saying, "Central, give me number..." He was talking to the operator who made the connection. "I grew up with party lines," Burrus said. "Phones hung on the wall like that pencil sharpener over there, and had a crank just like it does."

Bernie Mock of Waynesville came to Haywood in 1957, as manager of the county's Southern Bell office.

"At that time, we had many two, four, and eight party-line users, with the eight-party lines in the far-reaching corners of the county. We tried to reduce as many eight-party (lines) to four party as we could, and then later, to two. It was all a matter of economics," he said. "Party lines were all we had to offer to some. Private lines were expensive; not only for the customer, but for us as well, with the expense of labor and equipment.

"The very few who had private lines were mostly businesses, but there weren't many of those," Mock said. "Maggie Valley had limited phone service. The few motels there at the time wanted private lines, but we couldn't furnish them. Haywood County had party lines even in the 1970s."

"The phone was a gossip line. You could get all the news by listening in," said Rogers. "You could hear the phone picked up during your conversation. Some yelled, 'Get off of there,' or 'Quit listening in,' or some banged the phone in your ear over and over to tell you to get off the line." Every home's phone had its own distinctive ring so customers knew when they were being 'rung up.'"

"Lots of eavesdropping went on," Burrus said. "Even the operator could listen to your phone calls."

Rogers said in a low voice, "One man on our line in Stamey Cove was being unfaithful to his wife. He made late night phone calls, between nine p.m. and ten p.m., to the other woman, thinking everyone would be in bed and not hear, but that wasn't the case. By the next morning, the news had spread throughout the cove."

Bonnie Hibbs remembers standing on a chair to use her grandmother's phone. "I turned the crank to ring for the operator. She would say, 'Number please.'"

Jean Powell, who grew up at Sunburst, also used hand-rung telephones "with sometimes annoying" party lines as a child.

"We were one step away from the crank," Rogers said. "We had a dial on our phone. Older people who had nothing to do listened in on everyone. And when they called their friends, they wanted to talk a long time. The phone was their entertainment."

Wall-mounted phones, with bells clearly visible, were usually black. Those constructed of golden-hued wood, usually oak, are highly collectible today. Another style was called the candlestick phone. It could be held by one hand, much like a microphone, with the other hand pressing the receiver to the ear.

These devices were probably a thing of beauty to those with no way to communicate other than by traveling from place to place, but they look strange to us now.

Rabbit Tobacco

"You had to be careful, smoking that rabbit tobacco," said eighty-one-year-old Glenn Norris of Waynesville. "You had to draw real easy, or you would pull the fire into your mouth."

"It's been about seventy-three years since I did that, me and some neighbor boys," he said. "It was way years ago, as a boy growing up."

For the uninitiated, the makeshift cigarettes weren't sold in packs or cartons. And rabbit tobacco, a small, gray weed, was no cash crop. The plants grow wild in clear areas, such as a pasture.

"We would be playing a little ball in the pasture and see the weeds. We were just looking for something to do," Norris said. "There wasn't much to do then like there is now."

"We cut the stalks and put them somewhere to dry for awhile. Then we stripped off the leaves and crushed them up a little. We didn't have any cigarette paper. We used an old brown paper poke that we tore into strips." Norris said. "That's why you had to be careful not to pull the fire into your mouth. We couldn't pack the leaves tight enough or roll them tight enough. And they tasted awful."

Did he ever use corn silks in lieu of rabbit tobacco or smoke a grape vine? "I did all that, too," he said with a laugh. "The grape vine piece had to be dead and dry and the bark stripped off. You didn't smoke them green."

Addiction to the "smokes" was no problem. Those who tried them say the taste is terrible.

"We would go behind the barn or a corncrib to smoke," Norris said. "Any place out of sight of the house."

Emulating their fathers and other adults with chews of tobacco in their jaw, young boys would also pack the rabbit tobacco into wads, chew on them, and spit. Spitting contests to see who could propel the liquid the furthest were part of the fun, for children and adults alike.

The weed or herb is also called lasting, everlasting, sweet balsam, white balsam, feather-weed, and sweet cudweed, with the scientific name of Gnaphalium obtusifolium. Growing to a height of 1 to 3 feet, its leaves are long and slender and its small, white flowers bloom in late summer or fall. This common native plant of eastern United States grows in fields, pastures, or cleared areas.

The Cherokee are said to have given the plant its name because they believed rabbits tended it.

Included in lists of old-time remedies, it was thought to be beneficial primarily for respiratory problems. Rabbit tobacco is available today from herbalists who sell it as a tea, a compound to be chewed, or as a nicotine-free tobacco.

Waterdogs

Waterdogs, otherwise called salamanders or hellbenders, were once plentiful in the Pigeon River, but are currently on North Carolina's list of species to be protected. Finding one now is a rare occurrence.

WATER DOG

Despite their ugly, somewhat prehistoric countenance, they are harmless. When mature, their size ranges from 11 inches or so to 2 feet long, their heads are blunt, and undulating through the water, they do resemble snakes. Their diet is varied, but does not include humans. Convincing those of us who, as youngsters, swam or fished in the Pigeon of that fact was nigh on to impossible.

Sam Warren grew up on the west fork of the Pigeon and he has a quick, emphatic reaction to waterdogs. "I was scared to death of them. They were the ugliest things that I ever saw," he said. "When my brothers and I were fishing and reeled one in, we took a rock and bashed in its big, flat head. They were terribly ugly."

"My brothers and I were talking about them recently, and none of us has seen one in years," Warren said.

Swimming in the Pigeon River was one of the highlights of summer for many of us, and probably a necessity for some of those who came before, who wanted to wash away a cold winter's grime.

Some risk was inherent, as our parents preached. Stepping off a ledge into a deep hole, the force of the current, no lifeguards, hidden rocks, and submerged trees were just some of the dangers we faced, according to those intent on discouraging swimming in the river. They were right, of course.

There were other considerations not for the faint of heart. Playing in the river meant sharing space with all manner of creatures that live in or near water, such as fish that brushed against or nibbled at legs, turtles that might grab a toe and not let go, an occasional snake that was sure to be poisonous, and, topping the list, that ugliest of critters, the waterdog.

Sighting one led to a hasty exodus, a scramble for the bank and safety; those escapes were frequent.

So frequent, in fact, that my cousins named a fishing hole by my grandfather's farm the "Waterdog Hole." If one took their bait, and swallowed it hook and all, arguments ensued since not one of those boys wanted to touch them.

These salamanders are apparently disappearing from the waters of the Pigeon and other rivers and streams. We didn't know we were observing and needlessly killing an aquatic species that may well be extinct in our lifetime.

But at that time, our parents could have voiced a more effective deterrent to swimming in the river by reminding us that the dreaded salamanders populated the waters.

Obviously, these are the recollections of young children whose first introduction to aquatic life was provided by the Pigeon River, or one of many swift-flowing creeks in this county.

As for the waterdogs, we weren't the primary threat to their existence. Too many people and too much development along the river have hastened their demise by polluting the pure, clean water they require.

Cruso Sign Creates a Stir

Twenty-eight years ago, the Cruso Community on US 276 was the victim of a practical joke that became a local mystery for years, creating a bit of anger and lots of laughter.

Cruso Community Club had erected a sign reading "Cruso, 9 Miles of Friendly People." During the summer of 1979, drivers were surprised to see an amendment to the original sign. Someone, apparently having decided that more spice was needed, had hung a small plaque under the larger one that added the words "Plus One Old Crab."

The new addition disappeared frequently, but the late George Sharp would quickly replace it.

Most thought it was hilarious and rushed to claim the title. Visitors were intrigued. However, two community residents, each convinced he was targeted by the sign, were highly incensed, to put it mildly. Loudly and frequently protesting, their displeasure may have been responsible for the sign's frequent disappearances, as an expression of their anger, said Pat Sharp (who lives on Hunger Creek).

The community embraced the idea, eventually erecting a new sign that incorporated the new slogan. Capitalizing on an attention-grabbing idea, Cruso's Volunteer Fire Department commissioned brightly-colored yellow and green license plates imprinted with the slogan to be sold as a fundraiser, according to Ann Crawford, Cruso Community Center president. The tags began appearing on cars of those who live there—and some who don't.

Pat Sharp and husband Mike were vacationing in Cody, Wyoming when they found a tour bus full of North Carolinians in the motel parking lot one morning, delaying their departure to learn who owned the vehicle with both North Carolina and Cruso tags attached. They wanted to know the story behind the Cruso tag.

Ending years of speculation, two fun-loving pranksters, both summer residents who were very fond of Cruso and their neighbors there, confessed collaboration with two locals in altering the sign. "It was all done in fun," Crawford said.

The culprits were John Harrell of Atlanta and Cruso, now ninety-one, and Earl Hazelton, now deceased. They had enlisted the help of Mike Sharp, who was building a home for Harrell, and his father George, two more fun-loving pranksters who had built the original Cruso Community sign. The idea was that of Harrell and Hazelton, who needed assistance from the Sharps to execute their plan, Crawford said.

The sign, having been permanently adopted by the community, is the inspiration for Cruso Community Center's yearly Old Crab contest, which includes food and music accompanying the naming of the year's Old Crab.

Camp Daniel Boone

Camp Daniel Boone on Little East Fork of the Pigeon River is a favored destination for Boy Scouts across the nation, even from foreign countries. Edged by Pisgah National Forest, Shining Rock and Middle Prong Wilderness areas, the camp is shadowed by mountain peaks with familiar names like Shining Rock, Cold Mountain, and Sam's Knob.

The upper section of the camp, where tents are pitched, seems an extension of the wilderness until you discover separate clusters of tent pads here and there, surrounded by twisted laurels, tall trees, rocks, and the music of rushing water.

A page from the February 6, 1941 *Canton Enterprise* provided by Richard Hurley of Asheville, who has been involved with the camp as a youngster and as an adult, details some of the history.

Camping during those first summers after the Daniel Boone Boy Scout Council took ownership of the site was primitive. In 1941 the first dining hall was a large army surplus tent, with platform and rustic kitchen; the second, in 1943, was an old CCC

Camp building, moved and rebuilt. Water was supplied by springs, pit toilets were used, and forty to fifty Scouts could be housed in eight tents on platforms. Bill Wall was the first camp director, with a small staff of eight to ten people.

With World War II in progress, food and other supplies were hard to get. Equipment and supplies were stored in a warehouse in Asheville and had to be hauled back and forth in a pickup truck, traveling a dusty two hours on an unpaved, crooked country road.

An excavated hole in front of the present campfire circle was the swimming hole for a time. A log crib dam was constructed to impound an acre lake that gradually disappeared as the dam leaked. That problem was solved in 1946, when the leaky dam was replaced with a still-intact earthen dam that enlarged the lake to five acres.

Hurley, a camper in 1957, remembers the archaic mattress on which he slept. He was given a "tick" and told to stuff it with straw stored in bales under the lodge. However, he and innumerable Boy Scouts enjoyed their experiences immensely, generating lifelong supporters of the camp who return in any capacity available.

Haywood County became home to Camp Daniel Boone in January, 1941, when a council-appointed group of dedicated men (including Harry W. Love, Robert Lee Ellis, and Walter Damtoft, a Champion Paper and Fibre Company executive, all deceased) acquired the 700-acre tract and planned construction of the facility. After looking at more than thirty sites, they chose what is now known as the Robert Lee Ellis Scout Reservation. Ellis purchased the land and gave the "Mostly steep mountain-side land to the Daniel Boone Council, Boy Scouts of America."

Walking around the beautiful area, Hurley pointed out numerous additions put in place over the years, such as Ledbetter Lodge, a handsome dining hall; a pavilion with a massive stone fireplace; Robertson Lodge; Chip's Chapel; Lake Allen; and High Adventure Lodge, with its stone climbing wall. Most all were built with donations from individuals and groups. The Rotary Club of Asheville has supported the camp since 1941. "Order of the Arrow" members, Scouting's National Honor Society, which is composed of both youths and adults, have done an immense amount of work on camp improvements.

Camp Daniel Boone can accommodate 500 scouts and leaders each week, and has a 100-strong staff. Reservations must be made well in advance.

MOUNTAIN MUSIC AND DANCE

Square Dancing

S quare dancing is one of the most joyful legacies of our mountain culture.

With rhythmic footwork, dancers move through swirling, twirling figures as directed by the caller. "Do the Georgia rang tang," or "Make the ocean wave," he might call. "Do-se-do," or "Walk the king's highway."

Called the "dancingest man in the land," Sam Queen Sr. of Waynesville is said to have done the most to preserve the mountain square dance. He organized square dances, assembled the band, and called the dances.

And he carried the dance far beyond the mountains in the '30s, with his Soco Gap Dance Team. The team performed in major cities like Chicago, St. Louis, and New York City, dancing at the New York World's Fair and in Carnegie Hall.

The team's claim to fame was the night they performed in the Blue Room of the White House. President Franklin Delano Roosevelt and the first lady, Eleanor Roosevelt, King George VI and Queen Elizabeth of England, and Vice President John Nance Garner had front-row seats. The queen smiled and tapped her foot, according to newspaper accounts.

Bascom Lamar Lunsford and his five-string banjo accompanied the team. Lunsford also deserves huge credit for preserving mountain dance and music, co-founding the Mountain Dance and Folk Festival with Queen in 1928, which is still held "'long about sundown" each year in Asheville. Lunsford, a lawyer and teacher born in Mars Hill in Madison County, traveled widely collecting material on folk music and dance.

Queen and his dancers, and Lunsford, clad in his trademark white shirt and black bowtie, shattered the stereotypical image of hillbillies in their wake.

Mountain square dance shows its roots in English reels, Irish jigs, Scottish flings, and Dutch clog dances. Square dancing is a child born of old traditions mixed with American individuality.

Performed the old way, no two people exhibit exactly the same steps, letting the beat of the music dictate the movement of their feet. And that is the heart of old-time square dancing: individual styles. Stepping high or moving adeptly closer to the floor, dancers show off their personal styles in energetic clog dancing, a more emphatic and individualized performance.

Overall-clad old-timers usually answered the call for someone to do the "buck and wing." Their brief exhibitions were a complicated shuffle ending with a gleeful, heel-clicking jump. My grandfather, if pestered long enough, delighted his grandchildren by shuffling and clicking on the living room floor.

The most pleasing to watch, in my opinion, mimic the Irish step dancers by moving from the waist down while keeping the upper body relatively still; stepping with the beat of the music, staying in rhythm at a consistent pace, and moving smoothly through the various patterns.

"Birdie in the cage and can't get out; birdie out and old crow in."

Long ago, dance was an escape from hard work, whether it was in a barn loft, a yard, or a cleared room. Struggling to establish their existence, these early settlers had little time and opportunity to mingle with others. A dance was their outlet, time for socializing with neighbors, courting, or celebration. Music was played by a fiddler or two, maybe a banjo picker, and later, guitarists.

We danced in Waynesville's armory or on the street in front of the courthouse during summer. We danced in the gym at Canton's old Champion YMCA, as well as in recreation parks, in schools, and at festivals. Along about sundown, we were on the stage at Lunsford's yearly Festival. The taps on our shoes were frequently replaced.

"Ride the wagon wheel."

Joe Sam Queen of Waynesville, who represents the 119th district in the North Carolina House of Representatives, dances in his father's footsteps as he organizes summer street dances and participates in the annual Smoky Mountain Folk Festival at Lake Junaluska, which he founded. A traditional dance caller, he too is infected with the fever of mountain square dancing.

Old Mountain Music

"I fell in love with a pretty little girl. Her name was Barb'ry Ellen." Jim Trantham strums the strings of his handmade dulcimer and sings softly. The words of the mournful ballad are among those collected over half a lifetime by this man, who has performed and researched authentic folk music for years.

Lowland Scots from England and Scotland settled in our mountains, he says. Their material possessions were few but their traditional songs, passed down by word of mouth, were priceless.

"Are you going to Scarborough Fair? Remember me to one who lives there, for once she was a true love of mine."

Isolated and unexposed to any influences that might change their music, they continued to sing the poetic old ballads that reflected the cultured civilization they had left. They sang to relieve the boredom of their lives as they hoed corn, swept the dirt floors of crude cabins, and tended to broods of children.

Mainly about tragedies, the tunes were simply recollections, accounts of unusual events. Unaccompanied by any instruments, the stoic, unadorned music was sung in a straight-faced unemotional manner. Few details of events were mentioned in the recountings. Only the high points were touched upon.

"And there he ended her sweet life on th' bonny, bonny banks of th' Rye-O."

Over time, the ballads subtly changed. "If music is used by real people, it changes," says Trantham.

Local landmarks were substituted for English locations in original songs. Titles, such as dame and lady were replaced with adjectives, like little and pretty.

And so the old songs were modified, reflecting more of the everyday lives of people who dwelled in our valleys and coves.

They also started their own ballads, recounting things happening to them in their new world. The formats of their new songs were basically the same as those of the old, but the tunes were rarely as poetic. Ninety percent of them were tragic, according to Trantham, and in probably 85 percent, women were victims.

"Well, I came home the other night just drunk as I could be. Found a hat on my hat rack where my hat ought to be."

Musical instruments were not used until much later, probably because the church frowned on string instruments. The fiddle was most popular, though some believed a good fiddler had "sold his soul to the devil."

Crude banjos appeared, an African influence from the Deep South, and a few dulcimers, probably the only German influence on mountain music.

There were those who made their way through the mountains collecting and preserving the songs as sung to them by the shy, wary people who could be persuaded to do so.

The song catchers found in these people, along with their music, reflections of their fine, inherited culture. With little formal education, these mountain dwellers, in homemade dresses and "britches" living in cabins often precariously perched on the side of a hill, displayed appropriate social behavior, dignity, pride, intelligent conversation, and a rich musical heritage.

And the old music, still influencing the new, is alive and well today, preserved in meticulously recorded volumes.

"I give my love a cherry without no stone. I give my love a chicken without no bone. I give my love a baby with no cry'n. I told my love a story that has no end."

Panhandle Pete

Panhandle Pete was a one-man band.

Canton's Labor Day celebration, back in the '50s, wouldn't have been the same without him.

His "band," a contraption strapped to his body like a backpack, could be called an engineering feat. It was an intricately designed conglomeration of both traditional and improbable instruments.

Fully clad for performing, he could not have slipped in quietly. When he walked, he jangled and clanged and boomed.

On-stage, the discordant sounds became a "marchable" type of music, according to Joe Sam Queen who, as a young boy, shadowed him in fascination during Labor Day festivities. The background sound seemed appropriate for the old ballads he liked to sing in his raspy old-timer's voice. He called himself the "poor man's philharmonic (orchestra)."

"His performance was active, with plenty of dance-like movements," Queen said. It had to be.

Collective memories reassemble components of his band. An old photo, apparently posed, adds details.

A patting foot beat the drum, leg movements clanged cymbals strapped to the insides of his knees, and moving feet and legs rang attached bells, along with a tambourine on his right foot. Mounted on a bar around his neck were a harmonica and a garden hose that powered his tuba, instruments that sounded as he puffed and blew, moving from one to another. A washboard hung around his neck, to be strummed with thimble-tipped fingers. A cowbell hung behind his back, near the bass drum. A red rubber bulb was squeezed to sound a bicycle horn. Somehow he also played a kazoo, and train and exhaust whistles. Oh, yes, he played a banjo, too.

My mind did not process the sounds I heard as music, strictly speaking, but he was an entertainer and a comedian, fun to watch. "He certainly had rhythm," said C. W. Hardin of Canton. "He was a curiosity."

Panhandle Pete was evidently well-coordinated physically and had a quick mind, first to design his band and then to play it. Said to have weighed 104 pounds, his first one-man-band included fourteen gadgets and instruments.

At times, he would abandon his burden and team with other musicians for music/comedy routines. Another old photo shows him picking a bass fiddle, wearing his traditional slouchy felt hat.

Panhandle Pete became known elsewhere, eventually appearing on the Ed Sullivan television show and performing in at least thirty-three states. A website on country music profiles the performer, and credits him with recording several albums of old-fashioned ballads for the United States Library of Congress.

Always a popular attraction at Ghost Town in the Sky, the old mountain top amusement park in Maggie Valley, his audiences saw him as amusing and amazing; a colorful character. He was hired as director of the park's country music show in 1961, and continued to perform for another ten years. One of his fellow entertainers at Ghost Town was a banjo picker named Raymond Fairchild, then a relative newcomer to the music business.

Born James Howard Nash in Buncombe County in 1913, Panhandle Pete died in 1972 of cancer.

A small man, he grew tired of traveling with his heavy band. He built a miniature of his band for son Eddie, who carried on his father's performance tradition as an adult, taking over his dad's job at Ghost Town when Nash could no longer work. Eddie Nash died almost eight years ago.

Infamous Salty Dog Inspires Song

"I bet you don't know that a hit song was written about a honky tonk in Canton," Hoyt Mason of Cruso, a musician himself, said to me.

He was right. I didn't. But I have heard the song, "Let Me Be Your Salty Dog," and remembered there was a place called The Salty Dog in West Canton.

Zeke and Wiley Morris of Black Mountain, both dead now, had a bluegrass band. Zeke told an interviewer, "I got the idea when we went to a little old honky tonk just outside of Canton, which is in North Carolina. We went to play at a school out beyond Waynesville somewhere and we stopped at this place. They sold beer and had slot machines. At that time, they were legal in North Carolina. I think we hit three or four jackpots. The name of that place was The Salty Dog, and that's where I got the idea for the song," he said. The year was 1935.

"It's considered a standard," Wiley said. "Everybody uses it in the bluegrass field, just about. I reckon that song is known all over the world. That song is even popular in Japan! It's our biggest song 'cause it's a good five-string banjo number, played bluegrass style."

The Morris brothers had different bands, over time, as well as a radio show on WWNC in Asheville. Along the way, they became acquainted with many people in the musical world, including Lester Flatt and Earl Scruggs, who recorded "Let Me Be Your Salty Dog," later shortened to "Salty Dog Blues," in 1951. Don Reno, a musician who lived on Beaverdam, played with Flatt and Scruggs for a short time.

The Morris Brothers version did become a bluegrass standard and was recorded by many, including the late Jerry Garcia of The Grateful Dead. He recorded the song with a band called, ironically, the Black Mountain Boys, in March 1964

Other businesses in and out of North Carolina are or have been called The Salty Dog and various versions of the song have been recorded, but the Morris brothers' version seems to be the one most recorded.

The Salty Dog and surrounding buildings on the curvy road were demolished to make way for US 19/23, shown on some maps as "New Clyde Highway." Collective memories can't recall ownership or exact location of The Salty Dog, but Bill Boyd, eighty-two, said, "I was just a child at the time, but I remember it was a pretty rough place."

The song always reminded me of that infamous business by the same name, but I had no inkling that the two were connected until the conversation with Mason, about music in general.

Now, when The Salty Dog and unrepeatable tales of antics that occurred there are mentioned, I might consider that the rustic old building did have a bit of historical significance.

Uncommon Instrument

My grandfather played an unusual twangy melody when he put his Jew's harp to his mouth, as he danced around the living room with a low-stepping buck and wing. Clad in his overalls and heavy brogans, his image and the quirky sound of the small harp are deeply etched in my mind.

Years later, I found a harp at a craft fair. It resides in a cache that includes a small, brown cloth sack he gave me that even now emits the perfume of an evergreen tree.

The Jew's harp is a small musical instrument held against the teeth or lips and plucked with the fingers. A flexible tongue between two rigid bars that form an arc on one end produces sound when gentle breathing is combined with plucking the harp's tongue. It's easier said than done. The shape of the mouth produces different tones.

Its origin is ancient, and it has been played in many cultures world-wide. The instrument was mentioned as early as 1595 in England, and its earliest spelling is thought to be jewes trump. Nothing in its history connects it with Judaism or Jewish people, and its name likely came from some other word. To youthful ears, it sounded like "juice harp," which is appropriate because playing the harp produces lots of saliva if you are a novice.

According to information I have found, it was called gewgaw in England, Maultrommel (mouth drum) in Germany, munnharpe in Norway, and genggong in Bali. These are only four of more than forty names. The harp is made, depending on its location, of metal, bamboo or wood. The instrument seems to be well traveled.

Jim Trantham of Canton, who builds dulcimers and continually researches folk music and instruments, said, "I know next to nothing about them. I attempted to play one with little success. Its sound is mouth-resonated as the tongue is plucked." He has heard them called "jaws harps."

"They used to use them in old western movies and on back porches when people got together to make music. They would play fiddles and Jew's harps and stomp their feet. A bass fiddle was made from a wash tub and a broom handle," said Hoyt Mason, country musician, from Cruso.

Use of this obscure instrument has dwindled in the Appalachians, apparently, but not in Europe. In 2002, the Fourth International J-harp Festival was held in Norway. J-harp players and investigators from all over the world came together to play and study.

Old documents report that Jew's harps were used to barter with Native Peoples by Spanish explorers in America during the late 1500's, even as partial payment for land. A company from Massachusetts was producing them as early as 1650, according to an inventory.

The harps were used to induce trances and heal the sick in Siberia and Mongolia, say Jew's harp aficionados who have done extensive research.

Amazing what a little research can reveal. I am dumbfounded that what I thought was a musical instrument indigenous to the Southern Appalachians has such a long and distinguished history.

FOLKMOOT USA, NORTH CAROLINA'S INTERNATIONAL FOLK FESTIVAL

Folkmoot, an Amazing International Event

A unique cultural exchange happened in Waynesville in July of 1984, when dancers and musicians from eight countries were gathered together. This "meeting of the people" was and is called Folkmoot, and it endures thirty-one years later.

The international folk festival, in a sense, takes audiences on brief visits to these countries, allowing them to experience the diversities of cultures other than ours. The performers, in turn, are immersed in our culture for two weeks. Language is no barrier as the visitors mingle with spectators and with each other, forming lasting friendships.

Amazed while watching the interchanges, we have learned that people around the world are essentially the same. The groups are not professional performers, although they appear so. They are ordinary folk with jobs or professions who, like our square dance teams, united for the pleasure of music and dance and the desire to preserve and demonstrate their respective cultures.

The winking toes of Irish dancers, the swirl of voluminous skirts on talented dancers from Mexico's University of Colima, stilt dancers from France, and the first group from Russia (accompanied by KGB officers) as well as the varied offerings of the first Israelis at Folkmoot were tantalizing events.

The cooperation of the Haywood County Board of Education made the undertaking possible. Tuscola High School teachers emptied their classrooms, and the school became a hostel to house and feed the troupes. School buses transported dancers and musicians to performance sites. Folkmoot now has its own building, a former elementary school.

Each country is assigned a guide, who lives with them throughout the event. Some come with interpreters and some do not; communication is essential.

In retrospect, it seems unreal that a group of volunteers in an organization with limited funds and no real experience in directing such a massive undertaking were able to stage a successful festival.

Volunteers continue to be the mainstay behind Folkmoot. Men and women addicted to Folkmoot and all that it is have spent more than a quarter of a century dedicated to Folkmoot, now officially designated by the state as North Carolina's International Folk Festival.

Policies set by the initial board of directors are bypassed only in extreme circumstances. Ethnic groups in the USA are not included; performers come from their native countries. No team appears twice, except by special invitation.

Travel to festivals overseas for screening possible participants, obtaining VISAs, transportation from port of entry, gathering food and making menus to meet special requirements, finding host families for those who arrive early and stay late, gathering enough beds and linens for 300 to 400 people, advertising, and cleaning are among the pre-festival preparations, both large and small.

Always a major concern, money has been provided by individual and corporate donations, grants, allocations from federal, state and local governments, and other entities. Some income is generated by the festival but, as with most art-related functions, it is not enough to cover expenses.

Recognized nationally and beyond after thirty-one successful years, the Festival has benefited from the state's official designation and has earned recognition in the top twenty events in the southeast by the Southeast Tourism Society (STS). The STS and others know that Folkmoot means quality presentations of cultural heritage programs from around the world.

In August 1973, "Red" Ivestor and his square dance team were invited to perform at a festival in Sidmuth, England. Ivestor had recently undergone major surgery and invited his friend and surgeon, the late Dr. Clinton Border of Waynesville, to go along as team doctor. They would return to England in 1975 and travel to Poland in 1976.

Ivestor remarked to Border, according to his sister Ruby Pressley, that he felt Haywood County, with its strong cultural heritage, could support a similar event. Ivestor's health was a barrier to his pursuing the idea, but Border could and did take the idea and run with it. Thus, Folkmoot was born.

At least 200 performers from more than 100 other countries have been a part of Folkmoot USA, North Carolina's International Folk Festival.

Strong Bonds Formed at Folkmoot

Folkmoot has been, among many things over the years, an enjoyable learning process punctuated by hours of hard work donated by many people. Involvement with the festival is also addictive.

My job during the first years was writing press releases, stories for the souvenir program, and profiles of the visiting performers who are intent upon preserving their heritage through music and dance.

We learned why the French walked on stilts. In 1985, Zig Zaghini from Galdo, Italy, produced stirring music that still reverberates in my ears. Promni from Warsaw, Poland, in their historic, colorful costumes, and lively dances, are unforgettable. The flashing swords and shields of Turkey's Bursa Sword and Shield group drew frequent gasps from audiences. Troupes from both Israel and Russia attended in the same year. Females with Hupsakee from Holland each carried two milk pails attached to wooden yokes on their shoulders throughout one routine.

The stories behind the troupes are intriguing as well as living history lessons.

We learned at picnics at Lake Logan, sponsored by Champion Papers, that many were not hampered by feelings of modesty. Swimming in the cold waters of the lake was so enticing that any old bush would serve as a change room.

Shopping trips for jeans, shoes, and electronic devices have always been popular. Ilya, a Russian interpreter, wanted only to buy herbs and spices for his mother.

Strong bonds have developed among early arrivers and those who hosted them in their homes. One Canton couple spent considerable time and money to enable a Romanian dancer to get the college degree she so desperately wanted. A local doctor, Chris Wenzel, who was a guide for Folkmoot in younger days, found his life mate in Georgiana, a performer.

Each year, hugs and kisses and tears prevail as buses load with performers departing for the airport at festival's end. Cultural and political differences are not barriers to friendships at the festival, proving that those who inhabit this earth can get along and become friends.

The late Dr. Clinton Border of Waynesville, Folkmoot USA President, believed this to be the case. He said, "Our purpose is to stimulate international good will and understanding, to help educate ourselves to customs and manners of foreign peoples and to show that in spite of our small cultural differences we are, after all, quite alike in many, many ways."

BITS AND PIECES

Chestnut Trees and Extract Industry Not Blight-resistant

The American Chestnut Foundation Association planted a chestnut tree on the White House lawn recently. If the Foundation has succeeded in developing a truly blight-resistant tree, Western North Carolina would surely herald its return to our woodlands.

The Champion Fibre Company employees who spent their working days producing a high grade of chestnut wood extract (tannin) for the leather industry worldwide, trademarked Bludtan in powder form, would have welcomed the news.

Closed in 1951 because supply of chestnut wood had dwindled to a trace, the extract department had "played an important role not only in the development of Champion but also in the progress of the nation and the world for almost half a century," according to a story in Champion's in-house publication, *The Log*.

When the department ran at full capacity, 300 barrels of liquid extract were produced every 24 hours; Champion was the world's largest producer of chestnut extract.

Briefly, hewn Chestnuts were split into 5-foot sections to be transported from forest to mill by oxen and flumes to narrow-gauge railways. At the rate of twelve cords per hour, split logs were fed by conveyor into five giant revolving chippers, reducing them to small chips poured into thirty-six huge, steam-tight, metallic autoclaves (cauldrons), where boiling water and steam leached tannic acid from the wood. Evaporators dried the extract into powder. It was also sold in liquid form.

In addition to domestic markets, extract, both dry and liquid, was shipped to twelve foreign countries: Cuba, Mexico, the United Kingdom, Australia, New Zealand, Japan, China, Canada, South America, South Africa, and all over continental Europe. The United Kingdom was the largest foreign market.

Extraction began in 1908, when chestnuts were plentiful. After blight began killing the trees, dead trunks were used until the supply was depleted. The dead wood was so difficult to reach and remove that safety became an issue. The department was shut down after forty-three years, and the long building demolished

Mary Sellers' father, Earl W. Price, was department superintendent until his death. She shared an old pamphlet, complete with photos, that outlines the extraction operation. Sellers lives in Canton with husband Howard.

Bob Phillips, former Canton mayor, was working in Champion's lab in 1947 where colleague George Trostel, was responsible for testing the extract to determine its tanning ability (quality control). "Chestnut processing was completely separate from the rest of the wood," he said. "After the extraction of tannin, the small chips were made into pulp, a beautiful pulp. They utilized the entire tree."

John Churchill of Asheville, retired pulp mill manager, wasn't located at the Canton mill then, but he knows of the extraction operation. "It was a significant business at Canton's mill," he said. "There was a lot of publicity when it shut down, underscoring its importance from two aspects: demise of the chestnuts, and Champion's closing a big operation."

Chestnut Blight

An insidious fungus, a terrorist of sorts, smuggled itself into the United States from Asia in the late 1800s. Very prolific, it multiplied and spread from New York southward through the Eastern forest, boarding conveyances such as birds, insects, and animals, even traveling in the air, leaving in its wake a path of destruction.

The American chestnut tree was and still is its victim. A devastating blight parented by the fungus robbed the Eastern forests of a giant tree, one of the most important growths in the forest.

Earl Rayburn of West Asheville, seventy-five, after observing his fiftieth year of involvement with foresting, can speak about chestnut trees with personal knowledge. "Its lumber was the backbone for building log houses and barns, and for splitting into stakes to make rail fences," he said, "because it was rot resistant. It was a wonderful board to work with, soft, easy to nail, and could last 100 years or more because it was nonporous."

While working with the U.S. Forest Service in Forest Management, he measured a chestnut stump that was 8 feet in diameter and was told by another forester of a tree 17 feet in diameter and 90 feet tall.

Calling the infection of chestnuts a calamity, he said the tree was an important source of food for forest animals and people. "Deer and squirrels fed on them. My father would come home from hunting with his pockets stuffed with chestnuts. They were good to eat."

James Powell, retired president of Canton Hardwood, and wife Jean have a chestnut-paneled den. Very few boards show holes routed by worms accompanying the blight, he said.

Before the chestnut blight was discovered in New York City in 1904, foresters regarded the trees as the "most useful tree in the woods," according to The American Chestnut Foundation (TACF). "Native wildlife...depended on the tree's abundant drops of nutritious nuts...As winter came on, attics were often stacked to the rafters with flour bags full of the glossy, dark brown nuts. Springhouses and smokehouses were hung with hams and other products from livestock that had fattened on the harvest gleanings," reads TACF's American chestnut story. Its protein-rich nuts were eaten by humans in a variety of ways. (See above: The American Chestnut Foundation)

It was an important cash crop for many mountain families who shipped nuts to northern cities, where street vendors touted fresh-roasted chestnuts. Money earned could buy essentials they couldn't grow or make.

Growing straight, tall, and often branchless for 50 feet, the tree's light colored, straight-grained, rot-resistant timber made beautiful furniture, even musical instruments. It was also ideal for fences, utility poles, railroad ties, shingles and siding or paneling.

Western North Carolina also lost a forest beauty. The mountains were canopied with creamy-white flowers in early summer.

Even now, wormy chestnut is a prized wood, because of both its beauty and its rarity.

Collecting Chinquapins

Chinquapins! It's time to gather chinquapins, those flavorful little nuts encased in a prickly burr like their larger cousins, the chestnuts.

Fall inches its way into the atmosphere, bringing its nippy night air and initiating a sense of urgency to harvest, to gather in before winter.

Searching out "chinkypins," our youthful pronunciation, was fun for my cousins and me, a yearly ritual to be observed rather than gathering them as an important crop. The search was as much about roaming up the mountain, through the woods, swinging on a sturdy grapevine trailing from a tree, and disturbing squirrels with shouts and laughter as it was about relieving the small trees of their burden.

Long pants protected our legs from briars and brush, and deep pockets provided a place to stuff the nuts. We should have worn gloves. Removing the marble-sized goodies without bloody pricks from sharp needles wasn't easy. We carried empty flour sacks, or maybe old pillowcases, to fill with our bounty.

We learned about chinquapins from our parents and grandparents.

"Oh, law yes. I remember going to get chinquapins. Us kids would climb the mountain next to the barn. When we got to the ridge where the chinquapins were, we would shake the bush and they would fall right off. Sometimes we had to pick them." We picked up chestnuts, too," said 100-year-old Florence Wells.

We took the same routes to find the tangle of shrubby trees, two alternate paths; one from the Stamey Cove side of the mountain, or another that took us through an apple orchard in a place we called the "cold field."

Skeeter Curtis remembers wishing for tweezers to pull the nuts from their prickly cocoon. "We cracked the shells in our mouth then shelled them with our teeth and tongue," he said, "spit out the shell and ate the nut." True, but that took some practice. He liked to use them as ammunition in a "pea shooter."

He and Walter Wells reminded me of boiling the nuts in their shells and stringing them with needle and strong thread before draping them around our necks; a handy way to carry treats.

Jean Trantham Littlejohn lived miles away, across town, in the Thickety community. Her recollection of Sunday afternoons spent with a crowd of girls hiking to the foot of Crabtree Mountain and Little Sam Mountain in search of chinquapins is almost identical, even boiling and stringing the dark brown nuts. "We wore them to school, and had eaten them all before the day was over," she said. "We competed to see who gathered the fullest bag. I always got more chiggers than chinquapins."

Worms often invaded the treats, especially if they lay around a few days. I am certain we all ate some worms, or at least half of one.

Chinquapins represented carefree fun to all of us, but the multi-stemmed bushes were more important before our time. The trees were a source of fuel and are said to have been used for fence posts and railway ties, but I saw none that large. Not only were the nuts sweet and edible, ground as a substitute for coffee, but the roots were also utilized to make an astringent, a tonic, and a treatment for fevers. Birds and other wildlife fed on them as well.

Popping Corn

Popping corn over an open fire was a ritual on cold winter nights when we gathered at my grandparents' house.

While aunts and uncles played cards and Granny crocheted, "Daddypaw" taught the children the finer points of popping corn, with each of us clamoring for our turn.

The art of producing white, rather than burnt black, popcorn required close attention and some dexterity as we strived to shake the popper at the proper distance above the flames.

Over time, there were at least two poppers. The older one was round, and had a lid dotted with holes and a mechanism on the foot-long handle that raised the lid. That handle became very hot, and some wimp, probably me, would occasionally let go and drop it in the fire.

The second was rectangular with a wooden grip at the end of the handle. Its lid was also dotted with holes to let steam escape, and the lid, when pulled by a small metal bar, slid along the handle to reveal the corn. These two poppers sit by my fireplace now as reminders of those good times.

My memory recalls a third long-handled popper, with wire covering the container that allowed better judgment in deciding when the corn was ready.

The trick was to shake the popper continuously above, not in, the flames to keep the kernels moving to prevent blackened kernels of corn from coating the bottom of the popper. One had to listen carefully and remove the popper when the tiny explosions inside ceased.

Once ready to eat, the fluffy white corn was turned into a large container, salted, and eaten while another batch was popping away.

Although some put butter or a bit of lard in the popper, ours was popped dry. Daddypaw always grew his own corn for this winter pastime.

Later, I recall that my mother bought a contraption that sat atop the electric stove. This model involved turning a handle attached to a rotating blade to keep the corn from sticking and burning.

In earlier times, popcorn was an integral part of all sorts of festivities, from quilting bees to barn raisings, and from banjo pickings to ghost story tellings. The fluffy white balls might be used as teeth in a Halloween pumpkin, or strung on thread to decorate a tree at Christmas.

Native Peoples introduced popcorn to early European settlers. Research revealed that maize has been around for at least 6,000 years and was used by Incas, Aztecs, and Mayans in Mexico, Central, and South America—and, curiously, in parts of India, China, and Sumatra before the discovery of the Americas.

Stack Cakes Were the Choice

"Stack cake was always the cake for Christmas," Rachel Pack of Maryville, Tennessee, eighty-three years old, told her daughter Linda Yates of Crabtree. "I can close my eyes and taste it now. My mama was the best cook. We had fruit pies and other cakes for Thanksgiving, but it was always stack cake for Christmas."

Pack, who was five years old when her family was forced to move from Cades Cove in Tennessee (as were many Haywood County families who lived in Cataloochee Valley when the land was bought to form Great Smoky Mountains National Park), ended the search for someone who actually makes old-time stack cakes. Hers are made from memory with a recipe passed down through the family.

Stack cake is a tall, heavy, moist, multilayered cake. Built of thin, plate-sized layers of baked cookie-like dough, each layer is slathered with a sweet, spiced-apple or applesauce filling. Initially, ginger and sorghum molasses heightened the flavor. The layers of dough were cooked one by one, in a black, iron skillet.

Not eaten immediately, it normally sat overnight in a cool place—a porch or a springhouse. Slicing the cake was a feat in itself.

Friends were drawn into the search for an old recipe. Remembering the cakes made by our grandmothers, aunts, and mothers, we searched old family cookbooks, one so worn and fragile that its pages are secured by rubber bands. Each was characterized by inserts of scribbled "receipts" on yellowing scraps of paper with penciled or smeared-ink handwriting; some almost indecipherable. Versions of the recipe varied by name and ingredients, but Yates' mother had the final word.

We learned much in our various searches. Dried apples to cook for the filling were readily available on farms and homesteads. Most cakes were apparently six to eight layers, except those destined to be wedding cakes. An old custom had friends and families each contributing a layer of dough. The bride's popularity might be judged by the height of her cake.

Those of us fortunate to have eaten those unique looking and tasting stack cakes agree, the tedious process of making one was well worth the effort.

Heirloom Apples

Aging, neglected, apple trees can be found in unexpected places: old fields, forests, around abandoned farmhouses or homesteads. Chances are good that these wizened trees represent some of Haywood County's edible heirlooms.

The word heirloom usually evokes images of priceless quilts, hand-made furniture, portraits, and even old tools. These things and more, all inanimate objects, have been passed down through generations, prized possessions to be lovingly cared for and displayed by those who value their past and their descendants.

Certain foods that we eat are also a part of our heritage, particularly apples. European settlers brought with them seeds for this fruit, seeds that grew well, and apples became one of their staples. Some 16,000 to 17,000 apple varieties are said to have been recorded over time, but many of these antique varieties no longer exist, victims of an ever-changing society.

By today's standards, they might be judged ugly, too small, too perishable, too oddly shaped for machine picking, or too delicate for mass production. The unique tastes of the old apples, their wonderful flavors, have been sacrificed to meet demand for a product with flawless appearance, long shelf life, and long-range shipping. The loss is compounded because trees that bore the fruit were once naturally resistant to most pests and diseases. We have lost hundreds of these old mountain apples, with their various flavors, including "fresh bananas," "pear-flavored vanilla ice cream," and "spiciness."

George Cogburn of Hungry Creek knows about heritage apples. His grandfather, Will Cogburn, bought and planted mountainside orchards in the Pisgah Creek area in 1865, and Cogburn has a few older trees. Some of the strains were called "Pound, Sheepnose, Cameck, Spine, Hoovers, White Banana, Bellflower, Cheese, Wolf River, Ben Davis, Gano, Red and Golden Delicious, Horse, Yankee Sweets, and Black Twig," he said.

Cogburn describes the appearance of each, telling which were best for eating, for cooking, and for making jelly, applesauce, or cider. "Sheepnose are dull red and don't have any acid. If you have ulcers, they don't bother your stomach. White Banana, yellow with red blush, is good for cooking and eating," he said.

"We stored our apples in rock apple houses built on the north side so they would stay cool...put loose in bins built above the floor. Dirt floors kept the air moist and moisture prevented apple skins from shriveling," he said.

Old-timers talk of other varieties with interesting names: Stayman Winesap, Winter Jon, Limbertwig, McIntosh, Northern Spy, June, Pippin, Russet, Buff, Early Harvest, Yellow Transparent, Maiden's Blush, Rome Beauty, and Virginia Beauty.

Lists of these nostalgia apples with their individual descriptions, attributes, and origins can be interesting reading. Many originated in North Carolina and one, Buff, is said to have been developed in Haywood County in the 1850s. A couple of references mentioned an apple named Buncombe, referring to our neighboring county. Another listed a Junaluska apple.

Those of us lucky enough to have spent time on a farm sprinkled with apple and other fruit trees know the pleasure of searching among the branches drooping with fruit until you find an apple or two that suit your fancy. An apple fresh-picked from the tree, stem and all, and rubbed on a shirt to add a little shine, somehow tastes better than one from a supermarket bin.

Hasty moves were necessary to catch the tasty liquid before it dribbled down your chin after your teeth punctured the taut skin with an audible popping sound, releasing a spurt of sweet juice.

A shaker of salt, borrowed from Granny's kitchen and tucked into a pocket, was handy for adding a bit of zip to the flavor of certain apples, particularly those with a tartness. Caution was used to avoid the buzzing, stinging critters attracted by fallen, rotting apples. And if impatience led to eating those hard, green apples before they ripened, laden with salt, a painful bellyache usually followed.

Efforts are alive to find and recapture the old apples, to assure their availability on a limited basis. Long Branch Environmental Education Center, in Haywood and Buncombe counties, is one such location.

Cornbread

A triangle of cornbread, baked golden brown on the outside, white and flaky on the inside, topped with melting butter, sets many taste buds a-tingle.

Some call it the bread of the South.

Cornbread, or "pone" as it was called early on, is a legacy of the Native Peoples, who taught the first settlers the importance of corn and its many uses. It might also be called a survival tactic, used when very little other food was available.

Southerners have traditionally been particular about their cornbread, preferably using fresh ground white cornmeal in the mixture. Little else is required; milk or water, an egg, a bit of baking soda, hot grease—and a black cast-iron skillet. There is no flour, and definitely no sugar, in cornbread if one adheres to old-timey recipes.

My first attempt at cooking was under the tutelage of my grandmother, who taught me how to mix the batter and cook cornbread in her wood-fired cook stove. I don't remember how the bread tasted, but I cherish the memory of her taking time to teach me something useful.

No wonder Haywood County had so many gristmills, located in numerous communities. Cornmeal, grits, and flour were staples in everyone's kitchen. Although a skillet was likely preferred, cornbread could be cooked on a hot hearth, in the ashes of a fire, and even on the blade of a hoe propped near the heat.

Through the years, this bread has been called by as many names as there are ways of fixing it; ash cakes, johnnycake, hoe cake, corn dodgers, muffins, and corn sticks. Leftover bread, if there was any, was carefully saved. Supper might consist of nothing more than cornbread and milk, with the bread crumbled into a glass of either sweet or buttermilk. Menfolk in my family seemed to consider the mixture the best method to calm a growling stomach, to obtain the endurance to go back to work.

Good cornbread begins with a hot iron skillet, a skillet that has been properly seasoned to prevent sticking and greased with a fresh coating of oil. Fatback is considered a no-no in today's diets, but my grandmother used a slab of the pork in her skillet to obtain the right amount of oil, a bit of which was poured into the cornbread batter.

When the skillet was judged to be of the right temperature, the mixture was added to the pan and it went immediately into the oven.

She believed, as do many, that the best bread included buttermilk. The egg, more often than not, was fresh from the nest; washed, of course. Milk was added slowly so the batter would be thick, not thin and runny. If she wanted an entire cake for the coming meal, she quickly hid it. The aroma of freshly-baked cornbread alerted heavy traffic through her kitchen. Pilferers were admonished with the snap of a handy dishcloth, which could leave a blister on a hand or arm.

Research tells me that those who live north of the Mason-Dixon Line prefer yellow cornmeal to white, another no-no for southerners.

The addition of ingredients such as jalapeño peppers, sour cream, and whole kernels of corn sometimes enhance cornbread and the result is tasty, but nothing can take the place of cornbread prepared by the time-honored recipe.

Pearl Harbor Anniversary Revives Memories

December is a month for celebration, a month to observe a joyous occasion. December is also a month for remembering some historical events that were not so joyous in nature.

Sixty-three years have passed since Japan made its ill-fated decision to attack America on its own soil and bombed the U.S. naval fleet at Pearl Harbor in Hawaii on December 7, 1941. America had remained neutral while war raged in Europe until that day, a date President Franklin Delano Roosevelt declared "would go down in infamy." An angry giant was unleashed.

On December 16, 1944, with America fully involved in the war, the Battle of the Bulge began along the border with Germany and Belgium. Although the German army took the American troops by surprise, it would be their last hoorah—a desperate attempt to repel Allied forces drawing near Germany. They underestimated American determination and resolve, and a man named (Lieutenant General) George Patton who had a few tricks up his sleeve.

World War II ended in 1945 with the Allies defeating the Axis. America took its revenge and played a tide-turning role in a costly war that ended at least one dictatorship, and introduced the world to the awesome power and threat of atomic weapons.

It was a different kind of war. There were no jets or sophisticated electronic war machines like those of modern armies, only propeller-driven planes with bombs, naval warships, tanks, and troops in the foxholes. There was no instant replay on television of anything; actually, there were no TVs. News was often slow in coming by radio broadcasts, mail, or grainy black-and-white movie reels in theaters. Russia was an American ally.

Life was drastically different for Americans at home, as well.

Time dictates that within twenty or so years, voices who can relate actual experiences will be silenced and only history recorded in print, black-and-white photos and old movie reels can tell a part of the story.

Recollections of WWII veterans, told proudly and with great pain, are recorded. But what about those who remained at home?

A young child's vague memories were infused with confusion, because radio broadcasts continually mentioned two aunts, Berlynn (Berlin, Germany) and Pearl (Pearl Harbor). A blackout siren sounding at night was an eerie sound, and all lights had to be extinguished. Towns were seas of darkness as civilians readied themselves for possible attack.

The heavy drone of military aircraft passing overhead each day was an ominous sound and planes were scrutinized for red orbs on their bellies, the mark of a Japanese plane. Calling someone Tojo, Hirohito, Mussolini, and especially Hitler, seemed the vilest of insults.

America's patriotism was clearly evident in various symbols, including the flag, and in word and deed. Industries changed their assembly lines to produce planes, weapons, and war materials rather than cars or even vacuum cleaners. All available metal was collected in scrap metal drives, including aluminum peeled from chewing gum wrappers, to fuel the factories.

One collection point was a fenced-in parking lot in downtown Canton containing all kinds of metal objects, even pots and pans. The late C. C. Poindexter, Canton High School coach, devised an obstacle course with walls and other barriers for physical education students, to physically prepare future soldiers. U.S. Army groups visited high schools, showing various weapons, flame throwers, gas masks, and other implements of war. A Home Guard was organized among older men, since the National Guard had been "called up."

War bonds were sold to help finance the war. Many consumer goods were rationed, limiting the purchases of vital needs. Among those rationed were gas, meats, coffee, shoes, butter, and sugar. Silk stockings became a luxury or nonexistent, so socks were appropriate attire for ladies.

The Selective Service System administered the draft; every able-bodied male was expected to feel an obligation to defend his country. Every 18-year-old male had five days following his birthday for registering for the draft. The I-A classification meant fit to serve. IV-A meant physically unfit to serve.

Colorful posters declared to potential soldiers "Uncle Sam Needs You," and advised caution, "Loose Lips Sink Ships," because enemy spies did exist. Any home with a family member in service showed a star emblem in a window. If the star was gold, a former occupant had been killed in service.

With so many men gone, women took their positions in the workplace. Champion Paper employees, for the first time, included many females. "Rosie the Riveter" became a symbol of women engaged in manufacturing war materials.

As time passed, harsh realities brought the war in Europe, the Pacific, and Africa closer home. War took on a new meaning when a beloved uncle, a pilot, died in a plane crash in Italy. A newspaper photo showed an aunt and cousin with dazed, bewildered expressions as they accepted their husband and father's Purple Star.

Japanese Americans were confined to camps, primarily on the west coast, because their numbers might include spies. They were prisoners of war, of sorts.

Word of atrocities against those of Jewish descent and infamous concentration camps in Germany began surfacing. The diaries of Anne Frank revealed a bit of what those overseas were experiencing.

Americans everywhere, at home and on foreign soil, were at war in one way or another. Most of all, they were proud. Proud of each and every effort to defend and protect their country.

Approaching Winter

Mother Nature is slowly wiping away the bright golds and reds of autumn, while darkening the greens and browns and adding various swatches of gray.

The mountains are slowly revealing another side of their everlasting beauty. As the tempo of growth slows, plants and trees prepare for winter's sleep, to rest, to gather strength deep into the core; a rejuvenation period.

Meanwhile, icy waters in the mountains continue their bubbling and trickling and rush, tumbling over rocks and boulders, seeping from crevasses, or meandering down the slopes. The evidence of a never ceasing flow of water is reassuring, as are boggy areas where moisture gathers and lingers.

Now is a time to ramble through the forest and observe the natural cycle of the forest as leaves, fallen branches, and uprooted trees begin the continuous process of replenishing the earth, becoming nature's compost. Evergreens contribute dried needles that create an impression of falling snow on a windy day.

It is time for a final picnic atop a mountain in the Hemphill/Jonathan Creek area on a glorious day when the aroma of grilling food competes for attention with a view of layer upon layer of mountain ranges, on which Mount Pisgah and Cold Mountain are clearly visible.

On a calm day, usually accented by an expanse of bright blue sky unmarked by heavy clouds, leaves loosen their hold and leisurely drift to the ground. Puffs of wind hasten their descent, sending them in a whirl, a flurry to the earth. If a falling leaf lands on your head, a head cold is not in your future, old-timers say.

And as the leaves disappear from tree branches, vistas open up to allow a visual exploration of peaks, valleys, vast rock outcroppings, unexpected waterfalls, a distant lake, or even an old log structure hugging a creek bank, all previously hidden by thick foliage of summer.

The forest floor is carpeted with decaying leaves, patches of green moss, lichen-covered rocks, and acorns that crunch underfoot as squirrels chatter and leap among the trees, busily storing their winter food. Disturbing frosted leaves with a gentle search reveals green rattlesnake plantain lying under a leafy blanket.

Naked woods don their winter decoration of bright red holly berries, patches of shiny galax, and clumps of mistletoe clinging to trees. Balsam, hemlock, and pines relieve the starkness with their perennial green shades.

Wind plays a mournful tune as it sighs through barren trees, creating a clattering castanet of dry leaves reluctant to loosen their hold on their lofty perches.

A grove of poplar trees, with their light gray bark, march up a valley in the Pigeon community in a ghostly parade. Stands of dark green balsam are etched on the skyline of the Plott balsams, in bold contrast to a deep blue sky and leafless trees that surround the growth.

Deep thickets of rhododendron are a temperature gauge, leaves curling ever tighter as temperatures drop.

Cold Mountain, the Newfound range, and Mount Pisgah glitter in the cold thin light of early morning when rime ice coats mountaintops and trails down the ridges.

Backpackers snuggle in their down-filled cocoons waiting for some hardy soul to emerge, build a fire or ignite a camper stove and put on the coffee.

In the valleys, smoke curls lazily from chimneys, inspiring visions of a cozy kitchen and a roaring fire.

In the fields, dry, brown corn stalks stagger and droop wearily. Mounds of hay, rolled now rather than baled, sit ready to feed livestock during the approaching winter. Tobacco clumps, classed and wired together, are disappearing from barns and sheds, headed for auction. Dry, speckled apples hang like ornaments in fading colors from harvested trees while their comrades lie on the ground underneath, brown and mushy from decay, but alive with the buzz of insects seeking food.

This season is not a sad time, although the landscape provides little color and a weakened sun fails to warm our bodies. It is a time of gathering inward, of reflection, of planning for the coming year, a time to take stock of our blessings, and to give thanks for the opportunity to live in this beautiful area.

Look to the mountains. They stand in beauty and reassurance as they have for eons, encircling us all in their perpetual hug.

About the Author

Edie Hutchins Burnette is a native of Canton, in the mountains of Western North Carolina. She graduated from Wake Forest University with a degree in English and Journalism. Burnette was first employed by The Asheville Times as Woman's Page Editor and then as a teacher by Haywood County Schools. She retired after 33 years of teaching at both her alma mater, Canton High School, and the consolidated Pisgah High School.

She has maintained ties with *The Asheville Citizen-Times* through the years as a county correspondent, feature writer and then as a columnist, continuing to contribute columns occasionally.

Her many interests have included hiking and backpacking, writing, reading, painting, golf and travel. She has volunteered in many capacities, including 33 years with NC International Folk Festival Folkmoot USA. As a child, she spent a great deal of time at her grandparents' farm in Pigeon River Valley. Her home-away-from-home is on the banks of Lake Chatuge in Hayesville, NC.

She is the widow of Charles R. Burnette and has one daughter, Alison (Ray) Frazier and two grandchildren, Amanda and Dale Rice.

www.ingramcontent.com/pod-product-compliance
Lightning Source LLC
Chambersburg PA
CBHW031230090426
2742CB00007B/133